Ruth

UNDER THE SHADOW
OF HIS WINGS

SPENCER WALTON

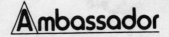

This Edition Published by
AMBASSADOR PRODUCTIONS LTD
Providence House
16 Hillview Avenue
Belfast BT5 6JR
Northern Ireland

First Published 1895
© 1988 Ambassador Productions Ltd.

ISBN 0 907927 27 0

To my beloved Friend,

THE REV. ANDREW MURRAY,

of Wellington, South Africa,

(Author of "Abide in Christ," &c.,)

IN MEMORY OF HOURS OF LOVING FELLOWSHIP AND SERVICE
AND AS A SMALL TOKEN OF LOVE AND
GRATITUDE FOR MUCH HELPFUL COUNSEL AND ADVICE,

I dedicate this little book.

Contents.

RUTH:

OR

UNDER THE SHADOW OF HIS WINGS.

"The Lord God of Israel, under Whose wings thou art come to trust." *Ruth ii. 12.*

"Hide me under the Shadow of Thy wings." *Ps. xvii. 8.* 1708

"In the Shadow of Thy wings will I make my refuge." *Ps. lvii. 1.*

"The children of men put their trust under the shadow of Thy wings." *Ps. xxxvi. 7.* 34U7

BENEATH THY WINGS.

THOU who hast trod the path of mortal life,
  And felt its keenest woe, its fiercest strife,
From all the evil that the way may bring,
  Hide me beneath the shadow of Thy wing.

When error steals with subtle step around,
  Tuning her voice to soft persuasive sound,
O! from her breath so cold and withering,
  Hide me beneath the shadow of Thy wing.

Hide, not from sorrow, but from bitterness,
  From rebel thoughts in moments of distress,
From sullen silence, faithless murmuring,
  Hide me beneath the shadow of Thy wing.

Hide 'neath the love that led Thee once to seek
  The wand'rer on the mountains bare and bleak,
And brought him safely to the pastures fair,
  That for Thy chosen flock Thou dost prepare.

Hide 'neath the might Thou hast so oft revealed
  Thy tried and tempted ones from harm to shield;
The wisdom that can guide their steps aright,
  E'en when the path seems lost in gloomiest night.

Hide 'neath the faithfulness that ne'er forsakes
  The soul that in Thy name her refuge makes—
Beneath the truth that never can deceive.
  The mercy ever ready to relieve.

Hide 'neath Thy glory, lest my roving eyes
  The fleeting things of earth too highly prize;
O let the shadow of Thy brightness be
  A cloudy pillar of defence to me!

Thus safe and blest, may I pursue the road
  That leadeth upward to that bright abode
Where they who once found shelter 'neath Thy wing
  Through all eternity Thy praises sing.

S. G. STOCK.

CHAPTER I.

INTRODUCTION.

TO the Bible student, the depths of spiritual teaching in the book of Ruth, are wonderful. Some would pass it by with the book of Esther, as being merely a peep into Eastern life and custom, or as representing simply a few historical facts, but to those whose eyes have been opened to behold "wondrous things out of His law," both books present lessons, taught of God, which not only bring out His heart of tender love, but also the joy of living up to all that that love has provided in Christ Jesus. "In all things ye are enriched by Him."

To consider the position of this book will be helpful, taking the preceding books, from Genesis to Judges, as steps which lead us to its precious truths.

GENESIS—*The book of ruin*—It begins in Eden and ends in Egypt. It begins in fellowship with God and ends in bondage. The apostle Paul, in his Epistle to the Romans, (chapters 1 and 2) before he dwells upon God's love revealed, seeks to show us our depraved condition. Having been taught ourselves, we see in amazement that *we*, His enemies, utterly lost and corrupt, are the objects of His grace, delight, and special care. But before we can know all this, *we must know ourselves*. So if we would understand the teaching of the books that follow Genesis and lead on to the sweet experiences of Ruth, we must first see ourselves as God sees us—in bondage, sold under sin, literally fallen, His enemies by nature—then learn that *He* seeks *us*, and in the school of divine love would fain teach us as Ruth was taught to know the Shepherd's heart, the Shepherd's care and the Shepherd's desire.

EXODUS—Reveals to us God's wonderful redemption and deliverance from bondage and death. Israel learnt their own utter inability to deliver themselves, but found God to be "the God of their salvation." His light and love, which are inseparable, go together all through it.

LEVITICUS—Presents Sacrifice and Priesthood, tells us we are worshippers and shows us how to worship, and the ground of our worship in type. The shadow is in Leviticus—the substance in the Epistle to the Hebrews.

NUMBERS—God's purposes hindered by man's unbelief. He never intended Israel to come out of Egypt into the wilderness—Ex. iii. 8. In the 13th and 14th chapters of this book we see an awful picture of unbelief, and only two faithful men. For this unbelief Israel was to spend forty years wandering in the wilderness, and at last, their blanched bones were to be the sad lessons and memorials to their children. How often we hinder the free action of God's loving purposes by our unbelief. Let us always say *" God can ! "* but never *" can God ? "*

DEUTERONOMY—The book of practical consecration or pre-paration for Canaan. It is worth noticing how constantly we meet with these words " observe to do." If we turn to the 8th chapter, we get the key note—" All the commandments which I command thee this day shall *ye observe to do*, that ye may live, and multiply, and go in and possess the land which the Lord sware unto your fathers."

Our consecration must be complete—*all*.

Our   „   „   „   now—this day.

Our   „   „   „   practical—observe to do, not to argue—not to admire, but *observe to do* ; practical obedience. *Now* faith can go in and possess. This leads on to Joshua.

JOSHUA—The book of rest and victory, of plenty and joy, of purity and power, grand types of all we get in OUR *blessed Joshua*.

"More than all in Thee I find."

Here we find no defensive war as in the wilderness, but aggression. Forward is the word, and forward God's children go—on, on, on, from strength to strength, and vic-tory to victory. " One man of you shall chase a thousand ; for the Lord your God, He it is that fighteth for you, as He

hath promised you."—Josh. xxiii. 10.   Only before Ai were
they defeated, but when Achan was judged, defeat was a
thing of the past.   They lusted not for Egypt's fleshpots, for
they now had the old corn of the land—a land flowing with
milk and honey—a land of promise.   Shadows and types of
" good things to come," good things which we are called
to enjoy.   Let us take up the words of the Apostle and say
" Blessed be the God and Father of our Lord Jesus Christ,
who *hath* blessed us with all spiritual blessings in heavenly
places in Christ Jesus."   What a present portion for us to
enjoy !

God the Blesser :—

    Character of blessing—Spiritual.
    Fulness   ,,   ,,   —All.
    Sphere   ,,   ,,   —Heavenly Places.
    Measure and } ,,   —Christ.
      Security }

  This is the blessing, dear reader, God has called—
chosen—us to enter into.   It is ours.   We need not ask
for it, but " go in and possess."   A friend, well-known
in China, was seeking this blessed life most earnestly.
He had been in prayer for some time, but still all seemed
dark and so very uncertain.   Rising from his knees, and
turning over the leaves of his Bible, his eyes fell upon
this blessed text.   " Hath—hath—hath "—he said.   " Why
I have been asking for what He has given me ! It *is* mine."
His prayers were changed to praises as he entered into this
glorious Canaan.   Let us look back and ask ourselves
where are we—Is it unbelief ?   Is our consecration incom-
plete ? Or have we never realized God's *hath* as ours?
From this standpoint we are able to see mountain upon
mountain of God's purposes and blessings, while He says

to us "All that I have *is* thine."

> I rise to walk in Heaven's own light,
>   Above the power of sin,
> With heart made pure and garments white,
>   And Christ enthroned within.

Oh! for active appropriation, then there will be continual enjoyment.

It is sad to notice the contrast between the Book of Joshua and the Book of Judges. Victory, joy, and communion are changed to defeat, sorrow, and backsliding. Gilgal is changed for Bochim, and He who had promised and blessed, now mourns over His erring people, with all their dead profession and evil. He who wept over doomed Jerusalem has chosen this place of weeping, while He tells them: "I made you to go up out of Egypt, and have brought you unto the land which I sware unto your fathers, and I said I will never break My covenant with you. And ye shall make no league with the inhabitants of this land; ye shall throw down their altars; but ye have not obeyed My voice; Why have ye done this? Wherefore I also said, I will not drive them out from before you; but they shall be as thorns in your sides, and their gods shall be a snare unto you." Judges ᴎ, 1, 2, 3.

It seems to me that in Joshua we get a very blessed picture of the early church in all her freshness and the enjoyment of her privileges, realizing the smile of her Lord, and living, not only in the sunshine of that smile, but on His exceeding great and precious promises. No lusting for Egypt's flesh-pots and no semblance of Egypt's habits left, but truly satisfied with her Lord, she had no craving for the world and the things of the world. It was a feast of tabernacles to her then, for "she sat down under His shadow with great delight, and His fruit was sweet to her taste." Church defence was unknown, but Church aggression felt. It was a constant song of victory, even on the lips of martyrs, and her Lord loved to gaze upon her in her purity, for her garments were not stained with worldliness, and her heart was an undivided one, fixed upon Him who was her Bridegroom, He who could bless her, and did. His great heart loved to pour its gifts upon His Bride. His desire was towards her, for "as the bridegroom rejoiceth over the bride so shall thy God rejoice over thee."

In the last chapter of Joshua we read of three burials : " And it came to pass after these things that Joshua the son of Nun, the servant of the Lord, died, being an hundred and ten years old, and *they buried him* in the border of his inheritance," 29, 30 v.   " And the bones of Joseph, which the children of Israel brought up out of Egypt, *buried they* in Shechem," 32 v.   " And Eleazar the son of Aaron died, and *they buried him* in a hill," 33 v. So these three men whom Israel looked up to, passed away from the scene—Joseph the leader, Joshua the saviour, and Eleazar the Priest.   Yet had Israel any excuse for backsliding now that these three were no longer with them ? No !   Israel's God was left.   The God of Abraham, Isaac, and Jacob, the Lord of Hosts, He who had said, " Surely I will be with thee," had not failed !   Much less is there any excuse for us, for our Leader and Saviour was dead and is alive again for evermore, and is now our blessed High Priest at the right hand of God, ever presenting our prayers and praises, with the fragrance of His incense, and ever bearing our names on the breast-plate of love, and on His shoulder of might.   Take our eyes off Christ and where are we ?   Other lords will have dominion over us.   The old lords of self and sin will be taking the heart's throne again, and all the disasters resulting from this dominion will soon be experienced. The rest, the victory, the joy, the power will all cease, and His glory in us will wane, as it says in the closing verse of this book; "In those days there was no king in Israel; every man did that which was right in his own eyes."

> Oh fix our earnest gaze
> So wholly, Lord, on Thee,
> That with Thy beauty occupied
> We elsewhere none may see.

To return to our former remark—The Book of Joshua is undoubtedly a blessed picture of the Early Church, but as we gaze upon the state of the *professing* Church now, how much in every way it corresponds with Israel in the times of the judges. Alas! Alas! faithful men may well weep at the worldliness seen on all sides :—the sons of God mingling with the daughters of men (Genesis vi.) and taking all *they* choose ; and many so-called leaders in the religious world, men looked up to as spiritual fathers, not only mingling with the world, but organizing worldliness, preaching its so-called virtues from the pulpit, and so making the door which Christ has called narrow, wide enough to admit the world with its two companions, the flesh and the devil.   I will not dwell upon the "down grade" errors which that faithful champion of the truth, the late Rev. C. H. Spurgeon, so nobly attacked—those which touch the very Person and work of our ever adorable Lord, and so sap the power of the Church, and grieve away the Holy Ghost. But do we not see on all sides the *world spirit possessing* certain sections of the professing Church, and creeping in under the pretext of attracting the young members. Penny readings, monthly concerts, amateur theatricals, fancy dress bazaars, lotteries to raise money for furthering Church work or building—all these speak for themselves. If one of the beloved Apostles could walk through our cities, towns, or even villages, how amazed he would be at the many coloured notices on the walls announcing all these varied entertainments in connection with God's work! "The Church has mistaken her calling," he would say, "and has taken up catering for the world's amusements." He too would find his way to Bochim, and there mingle his tears with his Lord's. Has the Cross—the story of Calvary—lost its power? If He is *faithfully* lifted up, would He fail to draw? Does this age of advancement want something more than Christ and His work? All these are vital questions which we must answer as before God, *and which will drive us* also to Bochim. All around us the thorns in the side are felt. Unrest takes the place of rest. The gods are a snare, and in many temples we see "the god of fashion," "the god of pleasure," and "the god of this world" worshipped, while the God of all grace is only tolerated in order to keep up the form of religion. "A name to live but dead. A form of godliness without the power."

Stand on the pedestal of God's Word, and the sight is appalling. Come down into the midst of it, be a worldly, half-hearted Christian; and the low level on which you stand will prevent your seeing the ruin which surrounds you.

JUDGES. In chapter i we see disobedience; constantly the words ' Did not,' ' neither did,' occur.

PROMISE.

"All that thou commandest we will do."—Joshua i. 16.

"God forbid that we should forsake the Lord to serve other gods."—Joshua xxiv. 16.

DISOBEYED.

Did not,
Neither did. } Judges i. 21, 28.

"And the children of Israel did evil in the sight of the Lord, and served Baalim."—Judges ii. 11. "And they forsook the Lord."—13th verse.

Their promises "All that Thou commandest us we will do" (Joshua i. 16), forgotten, in Judges ii we see the result. Power to exterminate their enemies is gone, so they put them under tribute.

Still, in the midst of surrounding darkness, we have to rejoice over the devotedness of some who walked with God and were living witnesses. These men seemed to be raised up, like many in the Church's history, to be instruments in the work of revival, gathering Israel's forces, and inspiring them once again to seek the Lord with all their heart. Wonderful were the results, and the old days of blessing were enjoyed for a season. "The land had rest forty years"—(Ch. v. 31). But these revivals, while they produced blessed effects were only followed by worse periods of declension. Has it not been so in the Church's history? *Our* Luther, Whitfield, Wesleys, and men of their stamp, men of mark, godly men, were raised up to do a work of revival. Coming out as they did in the darkest hours of the Church's history, they left behind them, like Joshua, "Elders who had outlived them, who had seen all the works of the Lord."—Judges ii. 7. But are their followers keeping now to these old paths? On the contrary are they not opposing or neglecting the counsel of these leaders who were taught of the Spirit and raised of God?

We see Protestantism eaten away by the canker of
Ritualism, rites advocated, transubstantiation taught,
the confessional upheld, the Virgin Mary worshipped, and
all sorts of Popish authority admitted. The very principles,
for which the blood of our martyrs was shed, are now
openly condemned, and the Reformation looked upon by
some as a *curse!* On the other hand the "larger hope,"
and other broad Church views, setting aside the work of
the atonement, are preached from many pulpits; and
worldliness is advocated as necessary, and allowed in
connection with Church work. Thank God, we have
a few who are clean, not having defiled their
robes, who still preach the old, old story, and believe the
power of the cross of Christ a sufficient attraction without
drawing in the world's assistance. But in what a scene of
ruin these lighthouses stand! True to their Lord and
Master, willing to bear His reproach, they are the Gideons,
the Baraks, the Samsons, and the Jephthas of the present
day (Heb. xi.); the true witnesses for whom the
Lord looks. This necessity for faithful witnessing is, I
believe, the one great lesson the Book of Judges teaches,
and so leads on to the sweet story in the Book of Ruth, the
story of individual witnessing and devotedness even on the
part of a Gentile girl. Let us not forget that Ruth lived
in the days of the judges (Ruth i. 1), otherwise we shall
miss what this book is meant to teach us.

I would not close this chapter without a word of
warning. Even the witnesses in Judges *failed*. Let us
be always found *abiding*, and say, with a consciousness
of weakness:

"I can do all things through Christ which strengtheneth me."

Grievous wolves have entered the fold, some clothed in sheep's clothing. How can we oppose them unless "strengthened with all might by His Spirit in the inner man."

Seducing spirits wax worse and worse, and how can we discern them, unless His Spirit, "the spirit of revelation and wisdom," unreservedly fills us. We are living in perilous times, and our only safeguard against this peril is the safety we get in Him and His Word.

May we be found true; true to our Master, true to his word. Unreality abounds. Oh! for reality in every detail of our life and walk, that it may be said of us—"Among whom ye shine as lights holding forth the word of life."—Phil. ii.

> "Living in us His own pure life,
> Giving us rest from inward strife,
> From strength to strength, from life to life—
> Halleluia."

"Now it came to pass, in the days when the judges ruled, that there was a famine in the land. And a certain man of Bethlehem-judah went to sojourn in the country of Moab, he, and his wife, and his two sons. "   *Ruth i. 1.*

"And the name of the man was Elimelech, and the name of His wife Naomi, and the name of his two sons, Mahlon and Chilion, Ephrathites of Bethlehem-Judah. And they came into the country of Moab, and continued there."   *Chap. 1, ver. 2.*

. "It is not His will that we should do anything without Him, and therefore, whatsoever we do without Him we do against His will."—GEORGE BOWEN.

"Two several loves built two several cities. The love of God buildeth Jerusalem. The love of the world buildeth a Babylon. Let every man inquire of himself what he loveth, and he shall resolve himself of whence he is a citizen."—ST. AUGUSTINE.

MY Saviour—I will never doubt
    His tender, loving will,
      That heart of love would ne'er conceive
  To do His children ill.

When clouds are dark, there shines a bow,
  With many a coloured hue,
And as I gaze I love to know
  That God is looking too.

I cannot always trace His ways
  Through cloud, through storm, through calm,
But this I *know* ; if he should wound,
  I *always* have His balm.

And through the darkness of the night
  My pillow is His breast ;
My bed—His everlasting arms ;—
  Oh this is perfect rest !

He tells me of his changeless love,
  A love that knows no ill ;
What can I do but acquiesce
  In His most sacred will ?

So on I go—soon, soon to see,
  With loved ones gone before,
Jesus, my Saviour and my all,
  On yonder glory shore.

CHAPTER II.

ON THE DOWN GRADE.

HOW acceptable on a dark night a light is, however small it may be! The storm-tossed mariner cheerily cries out "Light on the lee bow," when the long-looked-for lighthouse rays are seen dancing on the troubled waters. It tells him of a safe haven of rest from the winter blast. Yes, the storm may rage but he is soon anchored within the harbour. The weary labourer as he trudges home through wind and rain, hails with joy the glimmer of the candle in his cottage window; it gives him fresh energy, and he already seems to feel the glow of his fireside, and rejoices to think of the loving welcome and the good meal that await him. Sometimes the lights are weak and flickering, like stars that peep through rifts in the flying scud, and at other times steady and clear, like the bright flash that shoots from the Eddystone lighthouse: but what is so sweet as light in the darkness on a stormy night? So in the midst of ruin the clear ray of the "Light of the world" and the feeble flicker of a weak witness, reflecting but feebly His Light, are welcome : they come as a beam of hope across the troubled wave, and bring cheer and comfort to many a storm-tossed, weary heart. "The heart seems lighter and the face grows brighter" when the light is seen, and how often new courage is infused into a weary soul, and the very reflected light draws that one to find that the Light of the world is the Saviour of the world, and the Christian can exclaim as he realizes this, "He faileth not."

The book of Ruth seems to be just such a bright gleam, and standing as it does between the ruin of Judges and 1 Samuel, the story of the Kingdom, we might call it "the book of individual witnessing."

We have been dwelling on a darkness which has driven us to Bochim (weeping). Let us not abide there but step out into Bethlehem (House of Bread) — Judah (praise of the Lord); we may find a famine to test our faith but remember a tested faith should be like a ship driven by a fair gale, blowing us into the harbour of plenty. We meet with some of God's children who always stay at Bochim, and seem to fancy that this is the place God would have them abide in, until the summons to glory comes. They are constantly crying "Oh that my head were waters, and mine eyes a fountain of tears, that I might weep day and night;" and one word seems to be in their mouth, "Ruin, ruin, ruin!" their harps have long ago been hung upon the willows, and they persuade themselves they are in a strange land and cannot sing.

It is good, dear reader, to weep over such a wreck as the

professing Church, where the walls of separation are broken down and the heathen trample over the sacred city, but in our weeping let us be like faithful Nehemiah, who "sat down and wept and mourned certain days and fasted," then let us go on and pray before the "God of Heaven." (Neh. i. 4, 11.) We can mourn over facts and humbly confess them, but let us claim promises as he did (9), and while we may gaze around and see the ruin (ii. 13, 15), let us "strengthen our hands for this good work (18), for the God of Heaven He will prosper us: therefore we His servants will arise and build," so that it may be said of us "the people had a mind to work" (iv. 6), and then our very enemies may see, and the heathen perceive, that this work was wrought of our God (vi. 16). This is true witnessing.

God looks for this, practically in every way, in separation, in active service, in true devotion, in personal consecration, which means holy living. It is not for us to patch up the ruin, nor to spend our time mourning over it, or waste our time in seeking its improvements or defence, but, as lights in the power of the Holy Ghost, we should seek to bring out of it precious souls, ever finding our unfailing resources in the One "in whom it has pleased the Father that all fullness should dwell."

His Kingdom will come one day, and the blaze of millennial glory dispel all darkness, and the harmony of millennial music hush all discord: blessed day for this world! There will be darker days first, when all His witnesses will be caught away to meet their Lord in glory, but as it is darkest just before dawn, so then the gloom will only herald that day "when the kingdoms of this world have become the kingdoms of our Lord and His

Christ, and He shall reign for ever and ever. " (Rev. xi. 15.)

How true it is that " God hath chosen the foolish things of the world to confound the wise : and God hath chosen the weak things of the world to confound the things which are mighty ; and base things of the world, and things which are despised, hath God chosen, yea, and things which are not, to bring to nought things that are ; that no flesh should glory in His presence. " (1 Cor. i, 27-29.) We have an instance of this in the history of Ruth.

A weak Moabitish damsel, she became a bright witness by her decision and devotion (Chap. i. 16, 18). Hidden away in heathendom, she came forth to trust and find shelter under the wings of the God of Israel (Chap. ii. 12), and displayed in her life spiritual lessons which have been handed down from generation to generation. From being an obscure Gentile, she became the mother of kings, and so, on to a direct genealogical line with our Lord, (Matt. i.)

But a sad lesson is to be learned in the first chapter, and it opens with a remarkable example of Israel's condition. A famine was in the land, and among the unbelieving Israelites was a man of position and learning, of the lofty name of Elimelech (My God is King): his family seemed to share his privileges, for all their names had a very significant meaning. His wife, Naomi (sweetness), and his sons, Mahlon (song) and Chilion (completeness.) These words seem to express a beautiful family chain, each one linked together and revealing some sweet grace. Would to God he had always carried out his name in his life. *Sweetness* then would never have been bitter, the *song* then would not have been hushed, and the last link of *completeness* would not have been broken. It was a fatal step indeed when he went to sojourn in the land of Moab, ending in disaster and death.

We see the same result in the case of Lot: he chose, and following his choice, he soon became a citizen of Sodom: when he left it, it was only to experience destitution in an awful sense.

We shall have these famines in our Christian experience, to deepen our spiritual life, and to call into exercise our trust.

But faith unlocks the door of God's storehouse. A well-known Christian freed slave, who lives in the very presence of the Lord, one day met, in New York, a dear friend in the deepest distress: it was a famine indeed with her. Wringing her hands she said "Oh! Amanda, what shall I do, what shall I do? The trial is too great." "Bless de Lord, Honey, now is de time to trust Him." She knew a famine oftentimes, but rested in an unfailing God. Dear reader, when the famine comes let those words come home to us, "now is the time to trust Him." "Many are the afflictions of the righteous, but the Lord delivereth him out of them all." (Psalm xxxiv. 19.) Thomas Adams, the Puritan, says of this: "Be our troubles many in number, strange in nature, heavy in measure, yet God's mercies are more numerous, His wisdom more wondrous, His power more miraculous. He will deliver us out of all."

Some commentators suppose the famine, during which Gideon was raised up to save his country, was the same as that which induced Elimelech to go down to Moab. This would bring them into immediate contrast. Faithless Elimelech goes to Moab for food, he could not trust

the God of Abraham, of Isaac, and of Jacob, and, consequently his days are shortened. Faithful Gideon is found
" threshing wheat by the wine press," (Judges vi. 11.)
God having provided, although the " Midianites eft no
sustenance for Israel" (ver. 4) ; and his path goes on
from strength to strength and glory to glory. " The
Lord is with thee, thou mighty man of valour ; " (ver. 12).
" Go in this thy might," (ver. 14), and He honours His
servant's faith when He promises " Surely I will be with
thee " (ver. 16). Lack of faith is invariably accompanied
by disobedience. In spite of the Lord's commands
concerning Israel and Moab (Joshua xxiii. 7), Elimelech
journeys thither. He might have applied to his richer
brethren, or moved to another district, and still kept
in God's land, but no—Moab was his destination. No
doubt he only meant to sojourn there until the famine was
over, but we find he continues there. His soul out of
communion, he cares not for the Father's bread and the
Father's bounty. He loses his taste for the food of the
King's banqueting house, and acquires a taste for Moab's
food. Once he tasted and saw that the Lord was good
in those blessed days when " he sat down under His
shadow with great delight and His fruit was sweet to his
taste," (Cant. ii. 3.) His spiritual health then gave him
a spiritual appetite for Bethlehem's bread, but now, " his
life abhoreth bread and his *soul* dainty meat." (Job.
xxxiii. 20.)

His old appetite has revived and he seeks Moab's husks,
but the life and soul find these things distasteful. Alas !
how true this is of the wanderer ! Many seek to create a
desire for the things of God, before they return, but are

disappointed. Only an ungrieved Spirit creates a spiritual appetite, and obedience means restoration, and restoration, communion.

These people of Moab not only had a shameful beginning (Gen. xix. 31-37), but were, in the days of the Judges, known idolators. Baal-peor was their God, and although Israel had an awful warning in the days of wilderness wandering, (Num. xxv.) this Israelite seeks an asylum amongst these God-dishonouring people, and in this God-dishonouring land! No divine oracle had been consulted, and when we seek to Self as an oracle, we are indeed trusting to a poor fallible thing. How such conduct must grieve our God and hinder His cause. "One sinner destroyeth much good," said Solomon (Ec. ix. 18), and we read that those who looked up to Elimelech were led into this land by the one, who above all, should have pointed them to Jehovah-jireh, and bidden their fainting hearts take courage. As we have already seen in the history of Lot, Sodom, that wicked city, was his destination, and those dear to him were led on by him to evil. His daughters were married to the men of Sodom, and their union only led them to commit a deeper act of sin; while his poor wife's end was sad indeed. What a lesson to us to avoid first steps out of the path of obedience!

May I ask you, my reader, are your eyes upon the world and your heart leaning towards it? If so, I pray you take this story as a warning from God. Do you desire for the sake of position and money to match your children to its sons and daughters? Is a title, a rent roll, a position, your only aim. For the sake of God, for the sake of your children, stop! 'ere you take the fatal step.

These things are transient, and you may aim at them only to blast a young life and break a young heart. "How can two walk together except they be agreed?" Perhaps, you say so-and-so is a Christian, but certainly a Christian in Moab—the world. Then are you going to marry your child to trouble! For our righteous God will certainly lay His hand upon the backslider to bring him back again. Alas, alas, this sinful Moabitish match-making is so rife in the professing Church of God, and consequently children, whose parents were looked upon as godly, are not following in their steps.

Consecrated money and position are real blessings, but if unconsecrated, become as thorns in the Christian's side, and curses to them and their children. I do not write this with a hard feeling, far from it, but during several years of work for the Master, which has brought me into contact with all grades of society, I have seen, in so many cases, these awful sins freely indulged in, viz: unholy matches made for the sake of rank, or wealth. Such alliances blast bright hopes, blight the sweet fruit of Christianity, and make shipwreck of many lives. Oh! mothers, oh! fathers, have a loftier aim, and seek first God's glory before the passing glory of position, and God's gold, before the gold that perisheth, and " your children will rise up and call you blessed." God grant you may take this solemn warning, and remember that although you may be an Elimelech, you may nevertheless be in Moab, and committing Moab's sins.

IN tenderness He sought me,
　　Weary and sick with sin,
And on His shoulder brought me
　　Back to the fold again,
While angels in His presence sang,
Until the courts of heaven rang.

He wash'd the bleeding sin-wounds,
　　And poured in oil and wine,
He whispered to assure me,
　　" I've found thee, thou art mine; "
I never heard a sweeter voice,
It made my aching heart rejoice !

He pointed to the nail-prints,
　　For me His blood was shed,
A mocking crown so thorny,
　　Was placed upon His head.
I wondered what He saw in me,
To suffer such deep agony.

I'm sitting in His presence,
　　The sunshine of His face,
While with adoring wonder
　　His blessings I retrace.
It seems as if eternal days
Are far too short to sound His praise.

So, while the hours are passing,
　　All now is perfect rest ;
I'm waiting for the morning,
　　The brightest and the best.
When He will call us to His side,
To be with Him His spotless bride ;

"And Elimelech, Naomi's husband, died; and she was left, and her two sons. *Chap. 1, ver. 3.*

"And Mahlon and Chilion died also, both of them." *Ver. 5.*

"Orpah kissed her Mother-in-law, but Ruth clave unto her." *Ver. 14.*

"I went out full, and the Lord hath brought me home again empty." *Ver. 21.*

"* * * and they came to Beth-lehem at the beginning of barley harvest." *Ver. 22.*

"A sense of forgiveness does not proceed from marks seen in yourself, but from a discovery of the beauty, work and freeness of Christ." McCHEYNE.

CHAPTER III.

THE RETURN.

THE storm bursts at last, Elimelech dies. It *was* a
storm for weeping Naomi, but surely it was only to
clear the atmosphere of her worldly life, and to
bring her into God's sunshine once more. What a scene
of grief! The open grave, the desolate widow, and no
true, divine comforter.

To a soul in communion, grief is often a sweet
messenger, it brings out the deep tones of divine tenderness from the human heart of the One who wept at the
grave. Words are heard in sorrow, words of love and
sweetness, only heard in the night, like the nightingale's
song that fills our English country lanes. It is hushed
in the day of prosperity, but in the night of sorrow is
heard the sweetest, clearest music. Only crushed grapes
produce the wine of joy. The broken alabastar box sheds
the spikenard abroad. The cut diamond sparkles

with new lustre.   But this applies to a soul in communion, who knows the One

> " Who in each sorrow bears a part
> That none can bear below,"

and not to the soul out of communion.   Naomi had hard thoughts of God (ch. i. 20-21 v.) This hurricane of sorrow did not drive her to the haven of God's love, to an unchanged heart of true sympathy, but only drove her more and more out upon the sea of wordliness.   Sometimes this is the case, but it will increase divine discipline, for God *must* have His child back.

The two sons now seek wives in Moab, and unholy marriages take place ; the result, no fruit, although ten years of wedded life was theirs (4 verse.) This is truly the case with backsliders.   They cannot bring forth fruit unto God (John xv. 5.) A grieved Spirit yields no *sweet* fruits.   Oh ! how darkly the clouds had gathered, and yet another storm bursts.   Death again visits that home, and with his cold touch lays low these young men.

> Leaves have their time to fall,
>   And flowers to wither at the north wind's breath,
> But thou, all seasons—all ;
>   Thou hast all seasons for thine own, Oh ! death.
> We know when moons shall wane,
>   When summer birds from far shall cross the sea,
> When Autumn hues shall tinge the golden grain ;
>   But who shall teach us when to look for thee ? HEMANS.

Three widows stand weeping around open graves, but Naomi's sorrow was deepest, husband and sons had gone and she *was* bereft ; she " went out full," but she is now desolate, broken, empty ! " Then she arose with her daughters-in-law that she might return from the country of Moab ; for she had heard in the country of Moab how that the Lord had visited His people in giving them bread, wherefore she went forth out of the place where she was."

A very decided step, for she not only arose that she might return, *but she went forth*. We must notice that it was for the Lord's bread, and not for the Lord, so she had no influence over one daughter-in-law. When a point in the road was reached, her entreaties were listened to by Orpah but set aside by Ruth. Naomi's was an influence for evil—"Go, return," she said. How could she recommend the Lord she had forsaken? Her conduct had estranged her from Him. He changed not, as we shall see, and yet she sought to make out that He would be found in Moab, the land of idols. Oh, the subtlety of a backsliding heart! "The Lord deal kindly with you," she said, and later on (15 v.) she speaks of Orpah as having gone back to her people and her gods, thus contradicting her own words. How this brings out the awful hindrance a backslider becomes, and shows us that such conduct is the great cause of infidelity, and a stumbling-block to thousands.

The people of Sodom listened not to the voice of Lot. "But he seemed as one that mocked unto his sons-in-law." (Gen. xix. 14.) How could he seem anything else? His life was inconsistent, and thus his preaching was a mockery.

The stedfast-mindedness of Ruth silenced her mother-in-law and she pursued her journey homewards in bitterness of spirit. But although her thoughts of God were hard, yet she found an unchanging Jehovah. The last clause of the last verse is very sweet, and expresses the fact that in the Father's house there is enough and to spare. "And they came to Bethlehem at the beginning of barley harvest (22 v.), a true type of plenty. The very ones that met her were a testimony against her. They had remained, and the Lord had provided for them through the famine, and now although Naomi had found plenty in Moab, she returns empty, bereft. " I went out full and the Lord hath brought me home again empty " (21 v.) but He had brought her home again, and truly to find a barley harvest of plenty. Oh, what a heart our Father's heart is ! " If we believe not (are unfaithful) yet He abideth faithful. He cannot deny himself." (2 Tim. ii. 13.)

"Orpah kissed her mother-in-law, but Ruth clave unto her."—*Ver. 14.*

Worldliness is —" Dropping buckets into empty wells, and growing old in drawing nothing up." COWPER.

She has chosen the world
    And the paltry crowd ;
She has chosen the world
    And an endless shroud ;
She has chosen the world,
    With its misnamed pleasures :
She has chosen the world
    Before Heaven's own treasures.

"CHOOSE YE TO-DAY."

HIS word it came in tend'rest love
  And whispered in her ear,
   "I gave my life for thee, my child,
I paid a price so dear.

On Calvary's Cross I hung and died
  With broken heart and groan.
And now I long for thy heart's love,
  To make thee all My own.

The crown of thorns the cruel stripes,
  The mocking and the sneer,
The wretched traitor's false embrace,
  The priest's derisive jeer.

These, these, I felt, but not so much
  As, when God turned His face;
While there alone I drank the cup
  And took the sinner's place.

Oh! canst thou choose to walk with those
  Who still My love neglect,
And find thy pleasure in a world
  Whose Lord they still reject?

They never did what I have done,
  They never bled and died,
And oh! my child, I long to press,
  And draw thee to My side!"

CHAPTER IV.

ORPAH'S FATAL CHOICE.

FAR away in the West of Ireland, one lovely May day, I stood admiring the beauties of my surroundings. The sea was like the Bay of Naples, and hushed into a calm. A spring of water made music as it sprang from rock to rock. The lark was warbling forth its praises and the earth seemed like a lovely carpet of sweet flowers, while the gorse was one mass of golden splendour. A merry band of children from the Irish Church Mission Orphanage at Spiddal were adding enjoyment to it all, with their well-trained singing, merry laughter, and bright faces. But in the midst of it there stood a gloomy monument of the past. A mound of sand was on my left, and out of it peeped human skulls and bones of all descriptions. No coffin, no decent burial, but a sad reminiscence of the awful famine. *It was a famine burying place*, and those

bones and skulls seemed to send forth a warning note
in the midst of such a scene of joy and beauty.   Never shall
I forget the solemn lessons it conveyed as I stooped down
and took in my hand the blanched skull of some woman,
and pictured to myself the awful craving which ended in
a lingering death.   Oh ! could that skull have spoken, how
it would have told of the failure of the bread which
perisheth, of disappointment after disappointment, until,
weak and sorrowful, the young life ended and the poor body
was laid to rest.   The famine is described as follows :—

" Sorrow and dismay seized upon the vitals of the people.
The potato was their life and stay.   Their hopes of harvest
were blasted.   Starvation and death stared them in the
face.   The poor people sat in their cabins, or leaned over
their fences, looking with stolid indifference and silent
horror on the wastes of destruction.   Laughter and the
natural merriment of the Irish nature were seen no more.
Despair was stamped on every face.   Even the very dogs
ceased to bark, and there was a loud wail from man and
animal for food throughout the land.   It was not an
uncommon sight to see a rough wooden cart drawn by an
ass, and led by the husband who was taking his wife and
children to burial.   And often it happened that, too weak
to dig the grave, he would leave them barely covered with
earth, and the dogs the next day would be found making
a horrid meal of their carcases.

" There are beautiful though sad stories told of parents
suffering the agonies of starvation and of slow death in
order to keep their children alive.   But there is also
another story of a mother who ate the limbs of her child
to support her own life.   Nor was disease, which always
follows in the wake of famine, absent from the sorrow-

stricken land. It seized young and old, rich and poor, and helped the famine to finish the work of desolation and of death. There was scarcely a house where there was not one dead. The workhouses were converted into national hospitals, and around their walls lay the people dying and dead, their features emaciated and sodden, their tongues shrunken, and their furred teeth showing between their poor dried lips, a ghastly sight indeed!

" People dropped down dead in the streets. Mothers and wives, nursing their children and husbands, died while they were administering the medicines. Thousands had no graves. The dead were taken to the burial-ground in a hinged-bottomed coffin. The body was dropped through the bottom, and the coffin taken back for another corpse. Famine and the plague, and their ever busy agent, death, were triumphant everywhere."

I turned from the sickening sight to hear the sweet voices of my young friends, surrounding a dear lady whose heart and life were spent for them at Spiddal and Kingstown, as they sang—

> " I've found a friend in Jesus, He's *everything* to me.
> He's the fairest of ten thousand to my soul."

Marvellous contrast! On my left a solemn, silent sermon, with its text—famine and death; on my right, sweet voices raised to sing of One who was everything to some young hearts there (for God had saved many during *that Mission*), the satisfying portion, the bread which if any man eat he shall never die. A song that told of victory over famine and death. Some years have passed by, but that scene comes vividly before me.

A choice has to be made by some who read this.   The
famine and death on the left, or the Friend who is *everything*
on the right.   This book of Ruth for beauty is like that
May day scene, but it is not without its mounds of warning, for we have in the preceding chapter spoken of three
graves, and now we see how Orpah goes back to the land
of death, to her people and her gods.   Naomi had at last
started for home, and with her walked her two daughters-in-
law, Orpah and Ruth.   (It is remarkable to notice how wonderfully the meaning of their names is carried out in their
lives.   Orpah means a skull, or nakedness, Ruth means
satisfied, filled.   This we see as we proceed.)   That little
company of three widows *was* a sad one.   Their hearts were
still tender, for we read they wept much.   The centre one
was using her weakened influence to persuade them not to
come to God's land, but to go back to their land of idols.
It is an epoch in the life of the younger.   Idols and death,
or God and life.   Orpah seems to have shown the most
outward demonstration, for twice she kissed her mother-
in-law, even saying " Surely we will return with thee unto
thy people," (10 v.) but it was all lip expression and not
heart determination.   The test came again (12-13 v.), and
she yielded to her heart's craving and returned—a fatal
choice !   What an awful fact Naomi expressed to Ruth,
"thy sister-in-law has gone back unto her people and unto
her gods."(15 v.)   We hear nothing more of Orpah ; her
name seems to be a *finale* to that fatal choice, and in spite
of all her profession, empty and dead, she is back again in
the land of soul famine and death.   Naomi spoke of rest
(9 v.), but how could there be rest where the God of rest
was not found ?   The tears, the expressions of devotion, were
false.   Would to God they had never been shed and never

been made! Years have rolled by, but that scene stands like a finger post pointing to the many Orpahs who now walk in her steps.

The broken vows, the dead religion, the empty profession of the present day are the curse of Christendom. Church membership does not imply conversion to God. There are numbers of Church members who are quite unsaved.

Bishop Ryle says—" Coming to Church is not coming to Christ, for thousands do that from Sunday to Sunday, who are none the better for it. Nor is it merely coming to the minister, for whilst thousands come to their ministers and hear them, and are taught by them, they never come to Christ. A man may use every ordinance of the Church, aye, and attend regularly at the Lord's Supper, and yet never come any nearer to Christ. How, then, are they to come to Christ? They must put aside their negligence, wake up to see their sinful state, and come to Him for forgiveness, pardon, and peace. This is all that is required of them. How simple it all seems! yet how hard it is to get men to see, to realise, and accept all the blessings offered by Christ!"

It is a painful fact that, at the present day, many take the Holy Communion who are known worldlings, thus eating and drinking condemnation to their souls! The confirmation vow is forgotten and disregarded; the world, with its pomps and vanities, is not forsaken, and instead of fighting manfully under the banner of Jesus Christ, His blessed name is denied. The head may be bowed at the name of Jesus, but it is mockery if the heart is not yielded. Sweet hymns may be sung, but there is no music unless there is singing and making melody in the heart *to the Lord.* Like Orpah's, it is the kiss of profession on Sunday, and the rest of the week "her people and her gods."

"God does not look at the outward appearance but at the heart."—1 Sam. xvi. 7.

It would not be so unutterably sad if these dead professors would take their right place and own they are not Christians, but, like counterfeit coin, they seek to pass as coins of God's realm, with His likeness and superscription stamped on them. These are the true manufacturers of infidelity. Their inconsistencies are damning men and women, hindering true seekers, and increasing scepticism. *My reader, are you an Orpah?* If so, what will all this profession do for you when you come to die? A broken vow will haunt you, a wasted life will rise in judgment against you, and your dead profession will seem as if you sought to make God a convenience only to find the unreality of it all at the end. I once stood by the bedside of a dying lady of position and wealth. She was an Orpah. Church was visited on Sunday, and all the rest of the week given up to pleasure. And now that young life was closing. Rapid consumption had set in. "Look at me," she said, holding up her wasted hand, "who would have thought it? I was running wild a year ago." I told her of a Saviour's love and His willingness to save, even now. "What is the good?" she replied. "I know it all in my head, but it has never touched my heart." I offered to pray with her, but she declined, and a few days after, shrieking in agony of soul, she passed into a Christless grave. Dear reader, do calmly consider all this. Are you a real Christian? Are you one who has decided for Christ?

If not, let this solemn word be a warning, and make not a fatal choice.

> Away then—Oh fly
>   From the joys of earth !
> Her smile is a lie,
>   There's a sting in her mirth.
> Come, leave the dreams
>   Of this transient night ;
> And bask in the beams
>   Of an endless light.

McCheyne.

"Whither thou goest I will go." *Chap. i, 16.*

"The Lord do so to me, and more also." *Chap. i, 17.*

"Ruth clave unto her ... Thy God, my God ... She was steadfastly minded to go. *Chap. i, 14. 16. 18.*

"We do not want the glory of the world ; we have caught a sight of Thy glory, blessed Jesus, and everything pales before that. "Oh! bless us with Thyself, only with Thyself."—

W. PENNEFATHER.

"May our life be such that it cannot be understood apart from Jesus : take Him away and our whole character would become an inexplicable mystery."

"There is a point in grace, as much above the ordinary Christian, as the ordinary Christian is above the worldling. Their place is with the eagle in his eyrie, high aloft. They are rejoicing Christians, holy and devout men, doing service all over the world, and everywhere conquerors, through Him that loved them."—

C. H. SPURGEON.

JESUS HIMSELF.

I've seen the face of Jesus,
    He smiled in love on me ;
It filled my heart with rapture,
    My soul with ecstacy.
The scars of deepest anguish
    Were lost in glory bright ;
I've seen the face of Jesus,
    It was a wondrous sight !

And since I've seen His beauty,
    All else I count but loss :
The world, its fame and pleasure,
    Is now to me but dross.
His light dispelled my darkness,
    His smile was oh ! so sweet ;—
I've seen the face of Jesus,
    I can but kiss His feet !

I've heard the voice of Jesus ;
    He told me of His love,
And called me His own treasure,
    His undefiled, His dove !
It came like softest breezes
    Across an ocean calm,
And seemed to play so gently
    Some wondrous holy psalm !

I've felt the touch of Jesus :—
    My brow it throbbed with care,
He touched it oh ! so softly,
    And whispered " Do not fear ,"
Like clouds before the sunshine
    My cares have rolled away,
I'm sitting in His presence :
    It is a cloudless day.

I know He's coming shortly
    To take us all above,
To sing redemption's story,
    The story of His love.
We'll hear His voice of music,
    We'll feel His hand of care ;—
He'll never rest, He says so,
    Until He has us there !

W. S. W.

CHAPTER V.

UNFALTERING FAITH.

WE have now come to the decision of this Moabitish damsel, which took her out of Moab's land of idols and soul-famine, and brought her eventually under the wings of Israel's God. At every step the path now grows brighter.

Let us divide this book into four heads, descriptive of the progressive steps in the Christian life :—

| I *chap*. Deciding. | III *chap*. Confiding. |
| II *c.* Abiding. | IV *c.* Delighting. |

Indefiniteness is a great hindrance to spiritual progress.

An indefinite sinner will *never* find a Saviour, and an indefinite Christian will *never* enjoy the promises and blessings of God. Abraham was *definite* from first to last in his obedience, faith, and progress, and he received *definite* blessing. "God blessed Abraham in *all* things."

The same lesson is taught in the story of the Queen of Sheba. Her every step was a *definite* one, and she returned home blessed beyond her expectations, because she was *definite* (1 Kings x. 13).

Definiteness characterised the conduct of many who came to the Lord when here upon earth; and He always recognised and owned it !

A *definite*, weak, dying woman, pressed her way through the crowd, touched His garment, and was made whole.

A blind beggar, *definite* in his desire for the restoration of his sight, made the ruins of Jericho echo with his cries for mercy to the Christ of God, and he received his sight.

The *definite* step of the prodigal son brought him into the father's house of plenty, into the father's arms of love.

Oh ! friends, we must be *definite* in our start and in our course.

In these days of commercial competition the merchant who succeeds is one who is *definite* in all his transactions. Men can trust him, for they know him to be a man of his word, and his word is his bond, and so he rises to the position of a merchant prince. He looks back upon years of toil, and as his son "steps into his shoes" he says, "Be *definite*, and you will succeed."

Oh ! that Christians would take this advice to heart. Their start must be *definite*. "I will arise and go," was the resolve of the prodigal, and "he arose and came." Their purpose must be *definite*. "For to me to live is Christ," Their service must be *definite*. "As for me and my house, we will serve the Lord." Their warfare must be *definite*. "Nay, in all these things we are more than conquerors through Him that loved us." Their trust must be *definite*, " I will trust and not be afraid." Their hope must be *definite*. " For I am persuaded that neither death, nor life, nor angels, nor principalities, nor powers, nor things present, nor things to come, nor height, nor depth, nor any other creature shall able to separate us from the love of God which is in Christ Jesus our Lord." (Rom. viii., 38-39). Then they will not only have an abundance of peace, an abundance of life, an abundance of power, but an abundant entrance. May we be *definite ?* Ruth was thus *definite all through*, and her steps led her into blessed union with Boaz, the mighty man of wealth.

Naomi's attempts to persuade Ruth to return to Moab were of no avail, and as I have already remarked, were unaccompanied with power. A soul out of communion has no power. Ruth could look back and see that the hopes and joys of this world were unsatisfying and transient, and although Naomi presented them as things to be desired, she could look beyond to an unchanging God. "Thy God (shall be) my God." Father and mother, home and friends, were lost. Only one desire filled her heart. One purpose was before her. She must have Israel's God at all costs. *Are you as much in earnest ?* A decisive step must be taken before you can know anything of the Christian life. Like the Thessalonians, you must "turn to God from idols to serve the living and true God" (1 Thes. i., 9). Then as you walk with Him you will sound out His Word, so that the world will look upon you as His, and His life manifested in you will be a burning, shining light, and a blessing to others.

She had never seen what we see, a once crucified but risen Lord. (Heb. ii., 9.) Her heart had never been touched by the love of an agonizing Saviour, her tears had never fallen at the sight of His awful sufferings, but still Naomi's God was to be her God. This must condemn many who are holding back, who shudder and murmur when they know the cost of decision. Oftentimes I am asked : "But what must I give up ?"—"Give up !" I reply. "Have you ever seen Jesus?" St. Paul had seen Him, and what before was gain he now counted loss ! His ambition was— not earthly pomp and position—but fellowship with His Lord in His sufferings. He looked beyond the narrow limits of time to that which was eternal in the heavens, " A treasure that faileth not." What did he want with a flickering candle now he had the glory? What did he want with the gilded now he had the gold ? What did he want with the world now he had Christ ?

" I count all things but loss for the excellency of the knowledge of Christ Jesus *my* Lord : for whom I have suffered the loss cf all things, and do count them but dung that I may win Christ." (Phil. iii., 8.) Like blind Bartimæus, let Jesus touch your eyes, and you will be drawn by golden chains of love, to follow Him glorifying God. (Luke xviii.)

> "It was the sight of Thy dear Cross
> First drew my heart from earthly things ;
> And taught me to esteem as dross
> The mirth of fools, the pomp of kings."
>
> SPURGEON.

In these days of missionary enterprise we see with admiration young people leaving home, position, and a thousand other things for Christ's sake. They do not talk of giving up, but as one of them said to a well-known missionary, "It is all gain, all gain!" We read: "Ruth was steadfastly minded to go." Let us follow in her steps, and with such a past to muse upon; and such a Saviour to look up to; gladly leave all for Jesus. Hosea seemed to express it fully when he wrote: "What have I to do any more with idols? I have heard Him and observed Him." (Chap. xiv, 8.)

Have you not heard him? Listen to His pleadings. "Behold, and see if there be any sorrow like unto My sorrow, which is done unto Me, wherewith the Lord hath afflicted Me in the day of His fierce anger," (Lam. i, 12); and then as if this will not break the heart now he complains, "Ye will not come to Me that ye might have life." (John v, 40.)

Come and let His beauty win your heart, your heart's devotion. Then, the three texts in the Song of Solomon will just express its fulness.

1. My Beloved is mine, and I am His.—Positive.

2. I am my Beloved's, and my Beloved is mine.—Comparative.

3. I am my Beloved's, and His desire is toward me.—Superlative.

St. Ambrose says, concerning these three sayings, "that they give us a threefold diversity in the manner of the Bride's expressions, which denote the three stages of her progress in the love of God; to wit, her beginning, advance and perfection. First she thinks most of possessing Christ; next she realises chiefly that He possesses her; and at last she rejoices in the unspeakable knowledge that His desires

are toward her, and that she is necessary to His joy."
This latest apprehension is the fulfilment of Paul's prayer
for the Ephesian Christians in 1st chapter 17 & 18.

> " Only one look, dear Lord,
>   One look from Thee ;
> Heaven wlll not miss it,
>   But it's heaven to me."

"Lord do so to me, and more also." *Ruth i, 17.*

Sanctified Knowledge saith: "There is an infinite fulness in Christ, the fulness of an ocean." Faith saith: "This is all for me, for He is my Bridegroom." Then prayer saith: "If all this is thine, I will go and fetch it for thee." And thankfulness saith: "I will return praise to God for it (and that's better than the receiving of mercies)."—MATTHEW LAWRENCE, 1657 A.D.

As the hart panteth after the water brooks,
So panteth my soul after Thee, O God.

---

1 cannot breath enough of Thee,
  Oh gentle breeze of love:
More fragrant than the myrtle tree
The Rose of Sharon is to me—
  The balm of Heaven above !

I cannot gaze enough on Thee,
  Thou fairest of the fair ;
My heart is filled with ecstasy,
As in Thy face of radiancy,
  I see such beauty there.

I cannot work enough for Thee,
  My Saviour, Master, Friend ;
I do not wish to go out free,
But ever, always, willingly,
  To serve Thee to the end.

I cannot sing enough of Thee,
  The sweetest name on earth,
A note so full of melody
Comes from my heart so joyously,
  And fills my soul with mirth.

I cannot speak enough to Thee :
  I have so much to tell,
Thy heart it beats so tenderly,
As Thou dost draw me close to Thee
  And whisper, ''All is well !

CHAPTER VI.

MORE TO FOLLOW.

ON our way to the Keswick Convention, my companion, a well-known Scotch evangelist, told me the following incident which recently came under his notice.

It was washing day in one of the small Scotch villages, and many of the women were to be found on the banks of the river. Suddenly a cry of distress was heard; one of their number, a poor widow, had fallen into a deep pool, and they seemed powerless to help her. A Highlander, attracted by the cries, plunged in, and with a great effort succeeded in bringing her to the shore, although in an unconscious state. A crowd had assembled, and while restoratives were applied they good-naturedly made a collection for the poor rescued one. She was sitting up in a half-dazed condition, when they emptied the hatful of coins into her lap. "Na, na," she said, shaking her head, "I dinna want the money, let me see the mon." I remember the

depths my blessed Saviour went into ere he brought me on to
Salvation's shore.   " I found him whom my soul loveth ;
I held Him, and I would not let Him go."   Beautifully
indeed is this brought out in Ruth's decision.   Boaz knew
right well the momentous step she had taken when he
heard she had left her father and her mother and come to
trust under the shadow of the God of Israel.

From the moment she decided, new joys and new
blessings became hers ; no passing dream, but deep heartfelt
realities.   Cannot we, who have decided thus for the Lord,
say, as we look back upon a path of obedience and communion which commenced when we made Him our choice,
" the half has not been told ? " And those who have scaled
the loftier heights can echo back, " 'Tis better on before."

Decision for Christ brings with it joys the world knows
nothing of ; new joys " for old things pass away and all
things become new."   The very expressions Ruth made use
of in speaking to Naomi, bring to our minds realities and
privileges which are the part and portion of every true child
of God.   I do not say *she* meant it in her utterances, but still
those utterances convey to *us* what He would have all His
loved ones enjoy.   Of course one has to spiritualize these
expressions to bring them to bear on the subject of the
Christian life, and it is helpful to notice how seven distinct
experiences are represented.   These we will call

(1)   " COMPANIONSHIP "—It has a sweet keynote—" I
will never leave thee," (chap. i, v. 16) and seems to be the
prelude of a melody that brings holy boldness to a droop-
ing soul.   In this night of sorrow, it is as sweet as nightingale's trill, in the dawning day of joy, it pours forth its
music like the birds in early spring.   Angels' music can-

not be compared to it, 'tis a note that comes from a heart once broken, through lips that uttered the bitterest cry earth ever heard, bringing hope to the hopeless, joy to the sorrowing, nay, more, bringing the Christ of God down to our side, yea, right within our hearts! When He says " I will never leave thee nor forsake thee," true companionship is indeed enjoyed by faith. "The Lord is my Helper, and I will not fear what man can do unto me." Are you, like many, afraid to decide because of failing on the morrow? Remember, *the Shepherd keeps the sheep.* "I'm afraid to decide," said a poor broken hearted girl to me once in Dundee, "the girls in my factory are so wicked I can never keep Jesus." Does the Shepherd ask the sheep to keep Him? Never. The one Who bled, the Good Shepherd *Who died,* is the great Shepherd *Who keeps.* The good Shepherd had a lonely path but the great Shepherd has many companions, " When He putteth forth His own sheep He goeth before them," "and the sheep follow Him, for they know His voice;" the breathings of a heart of love. "Thou art all fair, my love, says the Heavenly Bridegroom, there is no spot in thee;" and oh! matchless condescension He asks, "let me see thy countenance, and let me hear thy voice, for sweet is thy voice and thy countenance is comely." May our hearts reply, "My voice shalt thou hear in the morning, O Lord; in the morning will I direct my prayer unto Thee, and will look up." It is a fair day, a day without clouds, when the sunshine of His presence bursts upon our view.

Companionship with Jesus, what can be compared to this? The 23rd Psalm tell sus something about it, and even before He revealed Himself to the two disciples walking to Emmaus, the unknown Companion made their hearts burn within them as He talked with them by the way. Oh! there is no joy like it, and we exclaim with rapture: "The voice of my Beloved, behold He cometh leaping upon the mountains, skipping upon the hills."

> "To walk with Jesus is most blest,
>   It bringeth peace for ever;
> And Oh! what joy His presence gives,—
>   A joy that nought can sever.
>
> Through storm, through calm, whate'er it be,
>   Through sorrow's darkest hour:
> With Him my heart will fear no ill,
>   I'm resting on His power.
>
> Then casting every burden down,
>   His love all fear expelling;
> We tread the path that leads to God,
>   To bliss, all bliss excelling."
>
> MAY BIGGS.

(2) "DISCIPLESHIP."—Three words express this, viz: "Following after Thee." Standing on the deck of a fine East-Indiaman, ploughing her way through the Southern Seas, one evening, I, with others, was lost in admiration at the glories of the setting sun. Never in Northern climes had we seen anything so beautiful. It was what the Captain termed a "musical sunset." The clouds were drawn out in long bars dotted with smaller clouds like notes of music; through these the golden glory of the dying sun shone with resplendent light. There seemed to be music in the hush, for no one dared to break the silence, but while we gazed it was gone. Not so with *His* presence. No setting sun, no passing glory, but Jesus Christ, the same yesterday, and to-day and for ever. "I am the Lord, I change not" (Mal. iii. 6); the "Sun that rises with healing in His wings." Night passed away in

the darkness of Calvary. No hushed music, the melody of His voice is now always present. " His speech is comely," for never did we hear such words as " Follow thou Me.' They were to the disciples of John as a strong magnet; they called the toiling fishermen, who gladly left their nets to follow Him; and now *we* can say, as He puts the golden chain around us, " Draw me, we will run after Thee."

> " O draw me, Saviour after Thee,
>   So will I run and never tire ;
> With gracious words still comfort me,
>   Be Thou my hope, my soul's desire ;
> On thee I roll each weight and fear,
>   Calm in the thought that Thou art near."

(3.) CITIZENSHIP.—We are citizens of no mean city, our hearts are up there with Him, and we say, " Whither thou goest I will go." (Chap. i, 16.) The Apostle Paul knew this when he wrote to the Philippian Church " Our citizenship is in Heaven " (Chap. iii, 20). He had just before told them where his heart was. That one glimpse of the altogether lovely One had made what was once gain ; loss. The heart attached to the risen Christ detaches us from all down here and makes us pilgrims and strangers, while we look for the Saviour, the Lord Jesus Christ, " who shall change our vile body that it may be fashioned like unto His glorious body, according to the working, whereby He is able even to subdue all things unto Himself.—Phil. iii. 21.

> ' Tis the treasure I have found in his love,
>   That has made me a pilgrim below.

(4.) FELLOWSHIP—Ah, but my reader may say, are we not still in the world although not of it ? Granted. His companionship makes the path joyful and light, but still we are passing through an enemy's land ; the world hates

our Master, and if we are true to Him, will hate us. Is
He to lodge alone ?   Far be the thought. " Where thou
lodgest I will lodge," and thus gladly bear the reproach of
Christ and have fellowship with Him in his sufferings.

> " All borne for me, and shall my coward heart
>   Refuse its best to Thee?
> Lord Jesus, take me to Thy fellowship
>   Whate'er the cost may be.
> A fellowship of suffering, but no curse,
>   *That* cup was drained by Thee.
> A fellowship of Resurrection joys,
>   And life of liberty."

Let our hearts echo " That I may know Him and the
Fellowship of His sufferings." This fellowship with him
has its practical results. When truly enjoyed, we learn
the Master's mind and so carry out the Master's desires,
" that we may be one even as He is one," one in Faith,
one in Hope, one in Charity. We know we have passed
from death into life because we love the brethren.
" Thy people shall be my people," (v. 16).   Oh, that every
Christian knew this, how denominationalism would sink
into oblivion and be a word not found in our religious
dictionary. St. John, the aged, so church history tells us,
when too old to take part in his much-loved Master's
service, used to be carried about by his disciples from
assembly to assembly, to give his parting blessing and say
with his feeble voice : " Little children love one another."
This is a fellowship which tells in the world, as set forth
in the words of our blessed Lord : " By this shall all men
know that ye are my disciples, if ye have love one to
another." I think this brotherhood in Christ, so much
overlooked by Christians, can only be fully appreciated
when we realize, as God would have us, our next
word—

(5) RELATIONSHIP—" thy God my God." This is represented to us at the beginning of St. John's Gospel, i. 12, 13 : "But as many as received Him to them gave He power (*margin*, the right) to become the sons of God, even to them that believe on His name, which were born not of blood, nor of the will of the flesh, nor of the will of man *but of God*," and at the close, our blessed Lord, when He arose from the grave and met Mary, sent her to His disciples with the message of their relationship : "Say unto them, I ascend unto my Father and *your* Father, and to my God and *your* God." (John xx. 17.)

The work of reconciliation had been fully accomplished at a tremendous cost, the rays of that rising sun had ushered in the first Easter morn, and now He who had said in the bitterness of Calvary, "My God, My God, why hast Thou forsaken Me?" could send that message of reconciliation ; God was no longer the veiled God ; the veil had been rent in twain, and the barrier of our sin, which had kept us from His presence, had been fully dealt with when He forsook His Son. No one can fully comprehend the cost of this new relationship. God had friends and servants in the old dispensation, but in the new, rebels become His sons, the scattered sheep were to be brought into one fold (John x. 16), and all true believers to realize the Fatherhood of God. Recognition and realization are two different things : numbers of Christians stop at the former, but the latter is enjoyed by some, and its practical expression is fellowship with all God's people.—Oh that the world might see this : how it would silence the scoffer and infidel. They look on and must think we are a very quarrelsome family. "Children of God," they say, "and all recognizing one

Father, but not their brothers and sisters: surely they
do not practice what they preach!"

St. Paul, when writing to the Corinthian Church,
knowing the gross sins into which it had fallen, though
adultery and drunkenness were amongst them, attacks
at the commencement of his epistle, this lack of love and
union. Is Christ divided? he asks. A searching question, for surely they had, by their petty differences and
cramped ideas, begun to split up God's great family into
small sections. God forbid that we should have fellowship
with those who are walking as disorderly children! Let us
not turn our backs upon them, but seek in the spirit of love to
win them and wean them from their errors and sins. But
may I add with greater emphasis, God forbid that we should
shut ourselves up from those who are consistently following their Master. If I am rich, with grace let me consider
my poor brethren; if I am poor, let me with gracious respect
coupled with brotherly love consider my richer brethren,
nor seek to thrust the doctrines of a democrat forward,
for that would be taking a mean advantage of grace. Let
rich and poor alike, in lowliness seek to serve one another
in love. This is divine relationship practically carried out.

" Chosen, through the Holy Spirit, through the sanctifying grace,
Poured upon His precious vessels, meetened for the heavenly place,
Chosen—to show forth His praises, to be holy in His sight,
Chosen—unto grace and glory, chosen unto life and light,'
                                                    F. R. H.

We will now pass on to another expression which
forcibly presents an important phase of God's truth,
viz :

(6.) PARTNERSHIP.—" Where thou diest will I die, and
there will I be buried." We are apt through our weakness

and infirmity oftentimes to take up an unequal balance of God's truth. For instance, some Christians are always dwelling on the blessed fact of their standing in Christ. They seldom speak on any other subject. They seem to forget that standing and state are truths that must run together; in plainer words, justification and sanctification should be inseparable, and so this one-sided preaching does not result in making practical Christians. Then again some are always dwelling on our state, the blessings of an indwelling Christ, His life in us. Our standing in Him is quite lost sight of, and so oftentimes their hearers do not enjoy true solid peace with God. Oh yes, some say, I know as my substitute He died for me, and I am saved; but when the glorious fact of partnership with Him in that death is presented they do not seem to understand what it means. Let us then remember we have a *full* Gospel. I look back upon that Cross and know as my Saviour He died for me. This delivers me from the penalty of sin, namely, condemnation; but it is only as I claim the fact of my partnership with Him in that death that the same blessed Spirit of God makes real to me true deliverance from the power of sin. We often read these texts, and sometimes learn them. Oh, like men of faith, let us put our feet upon this glorious truth and claim our partnership with Him in His death, burial and resurrection, exclaiming " I am crucified with Christ, nevertheless I live, yet not *I* but Christ liveth in me, and the life which I now live in the flesh I live by the faith of the Son of God, who loved me and gave Himself for me." (Gal. ii. 20.) Blessed death, dead to the world, dead to sin. Blessed life, alive to God, living in God, and by-and-bye living WITH God. " If we have been planted together in the likeness of His death, we shall be also in the likeness of His resurrection." "Knowing this, that our old man is crucified with Him, that the body of sin might be destroyed, that henceforth we should not serve sin, for He that is dead is free from sin." (Rom. vi. 5, 6, 7.)

"O hearts that sigh for saintliness as harts pant for water-brooks," have ye counted the cost? Can ye bear the fiery ordeal ? The manufacture of saints is no child's play. The block has to be entirely separated from its mountain bed, ere the Divine chisel can begin on it. The gold must be plunged into the cleansing fires ere it can be fashioned into an ornament of beauty for the King.

"As Abraham was separated from one after another of nature's resources, so must it be with all aspirants for the inner chambers of the palace of God. We must be prepared to the world and its censure or praise ; to the flesh, with its ambitions and schemes ; to the delights of a friendship which is insidiously lowering the temperature of the spirit ; to the self-life, in all its myriad subtle and overt manifestations ; and even to the joys and consolations of religion.

"All this is impossible to us of ourselves. But if we will surrender ourselves to God, willing that he should work in and for us that we cannot do for ourselves, we shall find that He will gradually and effectually, and as tenderly as possible, begin to disentwine the clinging tendrils of the poisoning weed, bringing us into heart-union with Himself.—(F. B. Meyer, "Abraham, the Friend of God.")

"Buried with Christ and raised with Him too;
    What is there left for me to do?
Simply to cease from struggling and strife,
    Simply to walk in newness of life—'Glory be to God.'
Risen with Christ, my glorious Head,
    Holiness now the pathway I tread.
Beautiful thought, while walking therein,
    'He that is dead, is freed from sin.' 'Glory be to God.'"

RYDER.

It is worth while noticing one more word which seems to comprehend all the preceding ones; at the same time giving us a recapitulation of the whole. I mean the word

(7) OWNERSHIP.—"Ye are not your own, for ye are bought with a price." (1 Cor. vi. 19.)

I belong to Jesus, the One who has purchased me, therefore He is my companion.—*Companionship*.

As I belong to Jesus, and he is my Master, I enjoy the privilege of following Him.—*Discipleship*.

The world will not have Him. By-and bye He will set up His Kingdom and reign. And because I belong to Him and He is at the right hand of God. I am a citizen of no mean country, a heavenly country.—*Citizenship*.

Because He is hated down here, and I am His, the world will hate me if true to my Lord, for has He not bought me, therefore I am privileged to suffer.—*Fellowship*.

What a dignity is placed upon me, not merely am I His purchased possession, but the willing bond-slave is made a child of God.—*Relationship*.

He does not leave me in the menial's place, although I am His by purchase, but He makes me His partner. All things are mine, and become mine experimentally through

participation in His death and burial. Blessed precious
ownership! "I love my Master, I will not go out free."

"Ah! this is what I'm wanting, His lovely face to see,
  And—I'm not afraid to say it—I know He's wanting me.
He gave His live a ransom, to make me all His own,
  And He can't forget His promise to me His purchased one."

I must not close this chapter without spiritualizing the
portion of one verse. Let us change it into a prayer, for
if breathed from the heart it is a blessed supplication :
"The Lord do so to me and more also." (17 verse.)

Faith would add, exulting in His fulness, "Now unto
Him that is able to do exceeding abundantly above all
that we ask or think, according to the power that worketh
in us, unto Him be glory in the Church by Christ Jesus
throughout all ages, world without end."—Amen.

I WILL GIVE YOU REST.

Hush my soul thou canst not murmur,
  Thou hast such a gracious Friend,
In His heart of love He planneth
  All thy path from end to end.
Naught but good that heart conceiveth,
  Best of blessings He'll bestow,
Guarding, keeping, guiding, leading,
  All thy journey here below.

Hold His hand 'twas pierced to save thee,
  Let Him draw thee to His side,
Put thy head upon His bosom,—
  Now in Him thy cares confide.
How He loves to hear thee speaking,
  Loves to gaze upon thy face,
Will not lose thy softest whisper
  Meant to catch His ear of grace.

Like a river ever onward,
  Flows into an ocean calm,
Lit up with a golden sunset,
  Echoing with an evening Psalm.
So this rest gets broader, deeper,
  Till it's lost in Heaven above,
Where the glory's ever brighter,
  And the song is always love.

"A mighty man of wealth . . . . his name was Boaz (strength)."
Chap. ii, 1.

"For it pleased the Father that *in Him* should all fulness dwell."
—*Col. i, 19.*

"*In whom* are hid all the treasures of wisdom and knowledge."—
Col. ii, 3.

"For *in Him* dwelleth all the fulness of the Godhead bodily,"—
Col. ii, 9.

"And ye are complete (made full) in Him."—*Col. ii, 10.*

"Yea, He is altogether lovely."

"This is My beloved and this is My friend."—*Song of Sol. v, 16.*

"A christian's growing, depends on Christ's watering."

C. H. Spurgeon.

"God feeds the wild flowers on the lonely mountain side without
the help of man, and they are as fresh and lovely as those that are
daily watched over in our garden. So God can feed His own planted
ones without the help of man, by the sweet falling dew of His
Spirit."   Mc. Cheyne.

FULLY SATISFIED.

Dissatisfied with earthly joy
   O Lord I turn to Thee,
The broken cisterns all have failed
   But now in Thee I see
Deep springs of life, and joy, which flow
   In sweetest purity.

I craved for love, but found it not,
   Except an ebb and flow;
But now in Thee I have a love
   That sets my heart aglow,
A love that's measured at the cross,
   I ne'er can fully know.

My weary heart it longed for rest
   From sin's cruel sway within,
I've found it now, my precious Lord,
   For Thou dost reign as King;
My sins before Thy presence fled,
   And Thou hast made me clean.

My eyes were once so dim, dear Lord,
   No beauty could I see
In Thy sweet face, once marred with pain
   Upon dark Calvary;
But now I gaze without a cloud,
   In deepest ecstacy.

I'm satisfied so fully now
   With thine own boundless love,
My heart's at rest—Thou callest me,
   Thy undefiled, Thy dove;
It is a foretaste deep, divine,
   Of Thy blest heaven above.

CHAPTER VII.

CONSIDER HIM.

COME with me in thought to the summit of a high mountain, and there, in the pure air of dawn, above the region of fogs and mists, let us look towards the East.

The grey light of early morn grows brighter and brighter, until a golden ray shoots out, and the whole range is lit up with the glory of the rising sun. It seems as if we were really standing in the very glory of Immanuel's land! All that was hidden away in the darkness of night is now brought to light, and where the sombreness of death reigned, life in its light is supreme. What a change! Mountain heights can be scanned and admired. And the valley, carpeted with green, and dotted with its many trees, can be looked into, with its rippling streams like silver threads running in and out amongst the rocks and boulders.

This is a picture of the heart yielded up to Christ. His "come" leads me to find in Him a living, loving Saviour. His "come unto Me" gives me perfect rest. His "come and see" leads me into His blessed abode, for "The King hath brought me into His chambers." Then the "come with" takes me up to the mount, and there He is transfigured before me. First the glimmer, then the glory. First the voice, then the Person, and from the mountain lit up with the Glory of His Person we can see everything in a new light. Even the very world itself seems new, for

> Heaven above is softer blue,
>   Earth around is sweeter green,
> Something lives in evey hue
>   Christless eyes have never seen ;
> Birds with gladder songs o'erflow,
>   Flowers with deeper beauties shine,
> Since I know as now I know
>   I am His and He is mine.

Here I find Moab's land, with its fascinations and pleasures, changed for Bethlehem—God's house of bread. Moab, the land of death with its three graves, left for the new life and a new joy.

Ruth's resolve to cleave to Naomi was not merely the outcome of natural affection. While she could see and love her poor backsliding mother-in-law, she had the clear vision of faith, and could discern the Lord God of Israel, under whose wings she had come to trust. (ii. 12.)

The first chapter is full of God's dealings and God's leadings. Now we enter upon the second stage. Boaz, a blessed type of the Lord, revealing his heart and his love to one who has turned her back upon what she counted gain.

Let us first of all look at the man.

Boaz means strength, might.

In Psalm lxxxix. 19 we read " I have laid help upon one that is mighty." Just the help we needed when we came to Him, for we found Him " mighty to save." But this was only the start. When Rebekah decided to become Isaac's wife and commenced her journey, we read " they rode upon the camels and followed the man," Gen. xxiv. 61. A strength other than her own was provided to carry her all the way to her bridegroom, and one to lead her by the right path. So it is with us when we decide to " go with this Man." He gives us unfailing strength and unerring guidance, until that day when our heavenly Isaac comes forth to meet us.

What wonderful strength our Boaz gives us, for " in the Lord Jehovah is everlasting strength," Isa. xxvi. 4. " He has been a strength to the poor and needy," Isa. xxv. 4. " The strength of our life," Psalm xxvii. 1. "A refuge and strength," Psalm xlvi. 1. Can we say "Thou strengthenest me with strength in my soul," and are we going on day by day from strength to strength, learning that apart from Him we can do nothing? It is such a comfort to know that the Blessed One we decide for is all we need after we decide—all we need in this world, where the Prince of this world reigns and opposes—all we need in life's sorrows and cares—all we need in its temptations and trials.

> Our need and thy great fulness meet,
> And we have all in Thee.

Blessed Lord! We *can* do all things through Christ which strengtheneth us.

Let us now look at Him in another aspect : In the Epistle to the Colossians we get a letter to a Christian Church. They knew Christ as their Saviour, but needed help on the matter of holy living, and were in danger of turning to the poison of Ritualism for what they required, letting beggarly elements take the place of Christ. In the first Chapter of this book we have a wonderful estimate of His fulness, in the 19th verse: "For it pleased the Father that in Him should *all* fulness dwell." Then again in Chapter ii. 3. we see God's treasure-house of wisdom and knowledge;" and Christ the treasurer: "In whom are hid all the treasures of wisdom and knowledge." And in verse 9, the store-house of God's fulness and Christ the storekeeper; "For in Him dwelleth all the fulness of the Godhead bodily." Then, we have the glorious fact—"*And ye are made full* (R.V.) *in Him which is the head of all principality and power.*" What can we want more than this? But still people turn from this fulness to the broken cisterns which hold no water. Oh, may we realize that when we come to Christ as our Saviour, He does not merely save us and leave us to struggle along through life the best way we can, but we have in Him an inexhaustible store from which faith can constantly draw. Let us see what this Boaz was, and how beautifully he typifies Christ. He is the—

Lord of the Harvest	ii. 3 —	Psalm xxiii. 1.
Supplier of wants	ii. 13, 14 —	Phil. iv. 19.
Near kinsman	iii. 12 —	{ Rom. viii. 17. 1 John iii. 1, 2.
Redeemer	iv. 9 —	1 Peter i. 18.
Bridegroom	iv. 10 —	Isaiah lxii. 5.

Decision for Christ brings out this manifestation. We never know how wealthy we are until we come to the One who has the keys in His girdle. The starving Egyptians went to Pharaoh, who sent them to Joseph, who could unlock all the storehouses and supply all their need—so in our case every storehouse in heaven and earth is the Lord's, and He has opened them for our full supply.

The names and titles of our dear Lord are very wonderful.

If I am a poor sinner, I find He is *the* Saviour.

When I am saved He will be my Keeper.

Do I need soul health ? He is my life abundant.

Am I in sorrow? As the Man of Sorrows He comforts me.

Am I tempted ? As the One who was tempted, and yet without sin, He can succour me.

Is my place on the Battle-field ? He is the Captain of my Salvation and can never be defeated.

In service He is my Master and teaches me how to serve.

Am I feeling my inability? His grace and wisdom are enough.

I am never to want, for He is my Shepherd.

This is not all, for He will never rest until I am a partaker of His kingly glory by-and-bye.

" Thou broughtest us out into a wealthy place."— Psalm lxvi. 12.

*" Yea, I have loved thee with an everlasting love : therefore
with loving kindness have I drawn thee."*

Jer. xxxi, 3.

He could not love me better,
  (A sinner dark as night);
For me He left the glory,
  That glory fair and bright.
From heights of cloudless sunshine,
  To depths of deepest woe;
Oh! love that passeth knowledge,
  To think He loved me so!

He could not love me better;
  He gave His life for me,
A willing, spotless victim,
  Upon Mount Calvary!
And there alone He suffered;
  He bore the curse, the guilt;
The Just One, for the unjust,
  His precious blood was spilt.

He could not love me better,
  As Victor o'er the tomb;
He took the sting of death away,
  Dispelling all the gloom.
Captive He led captivity,
  And set the prisoner free,
Brought joy, and peace, and gladness,
  In place of misery.

He could not love me better,
  He keeps me all the way,
And when I grasp His pierced hand,
  He never lets me stray.
When empty then He fills me,
  When weak, He makes me strong,
And e'en the wail of sorrow
  He turns into a song.

He could not love me better,
  For me He doth prepare,
Among His many mansions,
  A special place up there;
And I, with many another,
  Am called to be His bride,
His own especial treasure,
  His Church for Whom He died.

"Her hap was to light on a part of the field belonging to Boaz."
Ruth ii, 3.

"Go not to glean in another field, neither go from hence, but abide here fast by my maidens. Let thine eyes be on the field that they do reap, and go thou after them: have I not charged the young men that they shall not touch thee? And when thou art athirst, go unto the vessels and drink of that which the young men have drawn." *Ruth ii, 9.*

"Blessed be the God and Father of our Lord Jesus Christ, who *hath* blessed us with all spiritual blessings in heavenly places in Christ." *Eph. i, 3.*

"To abide in Christ means you are so satisfied with Him, that you do not want anything outside of Him, so you abide there."
ANON.

Marvel not that Christ in glory
   All my inmost heart hath won,
Not a star to cheer my darkness,
   But a light above the sun.

All below lies dark and shadowed,
   Nothing there to claim my heart ;
Save the lonely track of sorrow
   Where of old He walked apart.

I have seen the face of Jesus,
   Tell me not of aught beside :
I have heard the voice of Jesus,
   ALL my heart is satisfied.

In the radiance of the glory
   First I saw His blessed face,
And for ever shall that glory
   Be my home, my dwelling place.

ANON.

CHAPTER VIII.

"THE BLESSED HAP."

I ONCE heard of a sculptor who for seven years worked at a block of marble. At length he finished the face of the Man of Sorrows, and so exquisitely beautiful was the expression that all who gazed upon it were moved to tears. He had by this work of art made himself a name, and was at once asked to carve out the face of some heathen goddess, but refused, remarking, he could never carve another face after the face of Jesus. No money could tempt him, so he abode by the one whose face he had with such wonderful art produced. If cold marble can move hearts, and even win one heart, what must the reality be? We might gaze with the crowd, and with tearful eyes behold that cold face with all its perfection, but it is far, far

short of His face.   No wonder the Apostle Paul counted all
loss when He had seen Jesus.   The eye of sense ever seeks
to rest : it cannot, for "the eye is not satisfied with seeing,"
but the eye of faith, penetrating all the clouds of self and
sin, gazes with inexpressible rapture on His face and exclaims : "Thou *art* beautiful, oh my Love ! "

The look of faith should lead on to the action of faith.
I may be won by His beauty—that one look did it !—but
faith, like the miner, discovers inexhaustible resources
in Him ;—let us remember, only *in Him*—and so the man
of faith finds out how rich He is, and suddenly enters into
a new experience.   In these days of Christian activity
we hear much about what is called "the second blessing,"
or the "blessing," I am not writing to find fault with the
expression, far from it, but if we would be correct
we must not say "it," but *Him*—not a sufficient *blessing*,
but an all-sufficient *Blesser*.   I would pause here, for it is
most important, and I do believe many are kept out of
blessing by aiming at an experience, to be obtained by
their effort, instead of claiming a sufficient Saviour, *and*
the experience, the outcome of what He is, to, for, by,
through, and in them. The former is an act of self-effort—
I try to be what I ought to be, I try to work myself up into
a certain experience, and it only ends in disappointment.
May I simply put it this way—TRY is the expression of
your action.   Take off the last letter and put "UST" at the
end.   This brings you into direct communication with the
person of God's Son.   "In whom it has pleased the Father
that all fulness should dwell," and "who of God is made
unto us wisdom, and righteousness, and sanctification, and
redemption."   A dear young Christian school girl expressed
it so sweetly that I feel constrained to quote from her

letter: "I am so happy, I have been TRYING for more than a year . . . ., but on Friday night I knocked off the Y and put UST at the end and began *trusting*, and now the only wonder to me is how it could have seemed so hard all the time, for it is quite easy. Oh! is not *He* good! I have been through my hymn books to find a hymn with enough praise in it but I can't find one anywhere. Oh! pray for me that that Y may never come again."

This blessed experience is brought out in the history of Ruth. Her steps were steps of faith—from Moab to Bethlehem—from Moab's idols to Bethlehem's God, "under whose wings she had come to trust." Ruth had heard of the rich kinsman, the mighty man of wealth, and with her trustful heart she said: "Let me *now* go to the field and glean ears of corn after him in whose sight I *shall* find grace." The same decision which characterised her first step is brought out here. "Let me NOW go," no indefiniteness at all about her actions, and this was accompanied with the most entire faith: "In whose eyes I *shall* find grace." What an example to many a trembling one who fears to go on, and thus their unbelief keeps them out of this matchless grace. Is not His grace manifested for you in the person of His Son? Does He stop there? Are you simply to see in Him the one who forgives and saves only—great as these first blessings may be? Look up, my beloved reader, however weak your faith may be, doubt not His word: "He that spared not His own Son but delivered Him up for us all, how shall He not *with Him also freely give us all things?*"—Rom. viii. 32. Then again: "And God *is* able to make *all* grace abound toward you; that ye, *always* having *all* sufficiency in *all* things, may abound to *every* good work."—2 Cor. ix, 8. Oh, that you may respond: "And of His fulness have all we received, and grace for grace (grace upon grace, R.V.)." —John i. 16. It is not that the supply is short, but unbelief keeps the Supplier from carrying out His promises as in days of yore. "He could not do many wonderful works because of their unbelief." It is not enough to have faith, but faith must be put into action, and this opens up the unsearchable riches in Christ Jesus for the weakest of God's children. I heard of two men who bought a property in Scotland. They were comfortably off, and thought it a good investment. Coal and iron were found in it, and at once they worked it with remarkable results. Soon they become the recipients of large incomes. If they had never worked it, they never would have realized its value. So with us. We have all we want, aye, more than enough in Christ Jesus, and all at our disposal. Let us no longer be passive but active. It might be asked "Is not faith a gift of God?" We would not set aside this for one moment. One of the fruits of the Spirit is faith. A yielded heart is a heart possessed by God, and a heart possessed by God is the mainspring of Christian life. A tree full of sap has no difficulty in producing fruit—it is the natural result. So with a Christian full of the Holy Ghost, the fruit of the Spirit is a spiritual result.

Disobedience and unbelief go together. How wonderfully we see this all through God's Word, especially in the story of Israel in the wilderness. God calls for a full surrender (Rom. xii. 1.) I respond, and God fills me. Faith is the result, and so I prove " what is that good and acceptable and perfect will of God " (verse 2.) My beloved reader, have you come out of Moab yet? If not, take that *step* and come at once. *Then* faith will be unhindered and exclaim : " Let me NOW go...I *shall* find grace."

I have not now to ask for blessing, for this plants me *in* blessing. Ruth's first step led on to the second, and the result we find : " Her hap was to light on, or *in*, a part of the field belonging to Boaz."

Blessed be the God and Father of our Saviour Jesus Christ,
Who hath blessed us with such blessings all uncounted and
unpriced!
Let our high and holy calling, and our strong Salvation be,
Theme of never-ending praises, God of Sovereign Grace to Thee.
F.R.H.

How many of us have been asking, instead of thanking, all the time He has said, " All things *are* yours," and we have been saying, "Oh ! Lord, give me ? " Our hap is a blessed one. We are in Christ Jesus as regards our standing, and we get all we want in Him as regards our state.

A Bank of England note can pass all over the world, and is eagerly taken—alas, how seldom when offered, is this bank-note on the Bank of Faith accepted. St. Paul knew its value when he said (Phil. iv. 19), " My God shall supply all your need according to His riches in glory by Christ Jesus."

One has quaintly likened it to a bank-note as follows :—
My God—Banker's name.
Shall supply—This corresponds with " I promise to pay."
All your need—The amount is immeasurably more than
£1,000. Temporal as well as spiritual.
According to His riches—Here we have the Capital of
the Bank.
In glory—The address of the Bank, where no thief can
break through and steal.

By Christ Jesus—Here is the Cashier's name, signed at
             the foot, without which no Bank-note
             could go into circulation.

Let a deep heartfelt "thank you!" burst from your lips,
my dear reader.

I was travelling some months ago, and was joined at our
first stoppage by a member of "God's Royal Family."
He was a pauper out of East Grinstead workhouse. After
a passing remark, he asked me, with very many apologies,
if I loved Jesus. Of course I gave a very joyful reply.
"Oh!" said the dear old man, the tears of joy rolling
down his cheeks, "He is so precious to me—He is everything to me." He knew what it was to have found grace
in His sight, and, although a pauper, was enjoying this
blessed "hap."

It is wonderful to notice how link after link fits in
throughout this story. We have dwelt upon entering into
this fulness of blessing ; in our next text we see how it is
to be maintained—"Go not to glean in another field,
neither go from hence, but *abide ye here fast.*" The blessing is unchanged, but a path of absolute separation and
obedience is necessary to constantly enjoy Him in His
fulness. An everlasting "Yea" to *all* His commands—a
"Yea" that comes from a heart only too glad to express it
—Duty displaced by devotion—I Do it because I love Him.

        Not a sense of right or duty,
        But the sight of peerless worth.

"I love my master, I will not go out free." I abide in
that field because it is His. There are many fields around
us to allure us from the fields of Boaz. There is the field
of worldliness with its withering flowers. There is the

field of Ritualism with its scarlet poppies full of the opium of a false religion. There is the field of gain with its worked out mines. There is the field of popularity with its many pitfalls. There is the field of sensuality with its slimy ditches and stagnant pools. But this field has the "old corn of the land" in it. It is hedged about with a God-made hedge, and the Rose of Sharon and Lily of the Valley make it fragrant with their perfume. Sweet music sounds, with no discordant note, for all is real harmony when abiding in Him. Nothing can hurt us. "For they shall not touch thee," and we are as safe as the apple of His eye. We have ever a sweet well of living water to drink out of. "When thou art athirst go unto the vessels and drink." Here the Lord of the Harvest tells us not only to drink, but rivers of blessing shall flow out of us to others. Cannot you hear Him say, for he longs and loves to bless us and have us near to His heart of love: "Go not to glean in another field. *Abide ye here fast?*" Let it be said of us : "They came . . and saw . . and abode with Him." (John i. 39.)

Let me sum this chapter up in three words—words we can all remember.

Position.—perfect and complete—In Christ, "As He is so are we in this world." (John i. 4.) "All spiritual blessings in Christ." What a hap! Surely we can say : "I have *all* and abound."

Protection.—Nothing can touch us here. The pierced hand of our blessed Lord brought us and put us into the Father's strong hand, and when Satan comes to attack me he has to do with the Almighty hand of God. "They shall not touch thee."

Invitation.—When thou art athirst. "Drink, yea, drink abundantly, O beloved." (Song of Sol. **v. 1.**) " . . his place of defence shall be in the munitions of the rocks . . . his waters shall be sure." (Isaiah xxxiii, 16.)

> My God, the Spring of all my joys,
>   The life of my delights,
> The glory of my brightest days,
>   And comfort of my nights.
>
> In darkest shades, if thou appear
>   My dawning has begun,
> Thou art my soul's bright morning star,
>   And thou my rising sun.
>
> The opening heavens around me shine
>   With beams of sacred bliss,
> While Jesus shows His heart is mine,
>   And whispers "I am His."
>
> WESLEY.

"It hath fully been shewn me all that thou hast done."
Chap. ii, 11-12.

"For God is not unrighteous to forget your work and labour of love, which ye have showed towards His name, in that ye ministered to the Saints, and do minister."   *Heb. vi. 10.*

"A soul winner must be a soul lover."   C. H. SPURGEON.

"I feel persuaded that if I could follow the Lord more fully myself my ministry would be used to make a deeper impression than it has yet done."   MC CHEYNE.

"It was that one look, that one call that did it.   Like a chain of gold, that seemed to wind round me, I was drawn by an irresistible power right into the heart of my Lord.   His beauty had thrown everything else into the shade, and by that constraining power, I serve Him.   His heart is mine, and mine is His.   Oh inexpressible privilege, this little while is to be filled up gloriously. Can it be?   Yes, it is so, that same beauty is to be seen, and that same voice heard in my life.   The "yet not I," but the Christ that liveth in me is to be the one attracting object in my service.   I will not draw to myself, but souls will be drawn to Him, who lives in me.   Oh! it is all the Christ of God!"

" And the Lord turned and looked upon Peter."—

Luke xxii. 61.

I SAW His face of Sorrow;—
His eyes of tenderest care,
They gazed in deep compassion
Upon my wanderings here.
I tried to hide but could not,
While as He looked, He said:
"Poor sinful soul, *I love you*,
For you My blood was shed."

It seemed as if He followed
Along my sinful track,
And as He did He told me
" He died to bring me back."
It broke my heart, it won me,
Down at His feet I fell;
His love in all its fulness
I try but cannot tell.

I saw His face of beauty;
My heart was growing cold,
The world had tried to share it,
And had secured a hold.
But, oh! He whispered "follow,"
While as He called I saw
In Him such wondrous beauty,
I want the world no more.

And since I've followed Jesus,
I'm held in His embrace,
I love to rest and listen,
While gazing on His face.
My heart is won completely
·From all the world could give,
And now 'tis Jesus only,
To work, to die, to live!

Once more I'll see His beauty,
'Tis when He comes for me;
The day is not far distant,
Sometimes I think I see
His light, like bursting sunrise
But then it fades away,
And as I wait I whisper,
"He'll come for me one day."

CHAPTER IX.

UNKNOWN AND YET WELL-KNOWN.

WE have seen in the two preceding chapters something of the character of Boaz and of the blessedness of Ruth's hap in lighting upon his field. We have traced too, the spiritual meaning of this rich inheritance for us, but it must ever be borne in mind that these blessings are all centred *in Him*. In the 4th verse of 2nd of Ruth we have the personal introduction of Boaz to Ruth, and in his person she had presented to her the fountain head and source of all the blessings that flow like a stream through this chapter. So it is with us and the person of our blessed Lord. The little word "IN" is alike the keyword of the Epistle to the Colossians and that to the Ephesians. Just as the subject dwelt upon in the two preceding chapters is the old Testament counterpart of the burden of the Epistles to the Colossians and Ephesians, so in the first verse of the 2nd chapter of Ruth we have the same keynote as those sounded so strikingly in the Epistles. Thus in Colossians we have Christ and His glories, the fountain head from which flows the river of the Holy Ghost in blessing to the Church, for all blessings flow from our Risen Head. " All my fresh springs shall be in Thee" (Prayer-book version). Again in verse 8, as Boaz points out to Ruth the only place of safety and blessing—abiding in his field—so we have indicated to us in Ephesians our only place of perfect safety and power—IN Christ—(chap. i. 3.), " Blessed be the God and Father of our Lord Jesus Christ, who hath blessed us with all spiritual blessings IN heavenly places IN Christ." The blessings Boaz heaped upon Ruth humbled her to the very dust (verse 10), and surely His blessings should weigh us down, that at His pierced feet we might recognize that it is *all* of grace, and like her exclaim " Why have I found grace in Thine eyes that Thou shouldst take knowledge of me, seeing I am a stranger ? " This is not only the position of safety but of further blessing.

When David, the man after God's own heart, summoned Mephibosheth into his presence (2 Samuel ix.) and commenced to tell him the kindness he was going to show him and the possessions he was to have, even promising him a seat at the King's table (verse 7), poor Mephibosheth was overwhelmed and could only fall down and say " What is thy servant that thou shouldest look upon such a dead dog as I am ? " (verse 8). From that point David's " I wills " were changed into " haves," " I have given " (verse 9). Not only is this lowly attitude cne of blessing but in it we are in the proper position of soul to hear God's Word and God's secrets. St. John in Patmos found it so—falling at His feet as one dead. In the awe-inspiring presence of Divine majesty and glory he still recognised the voice of the One upon whose bosom he used to lay his head—no longer the Man of Sorrows in His humility but the Man Christ Jesus in His glory—the Conqueror, the Victor who had passed through the up-lifted gates—the Lord mighty in battle. What secrets he heard, giving him an insight into the very purposes of God! It is there, at His feet, my dear reader, that our Lord can speak to us. Let us bow down to that place of self-abnegation, let His very feet be put on us that self may be crushed out by the power of love (for His feet are pierced). Then He can tell us what He sees and knows, and we can bear it. How often, through the assertion of self, we prevent Him speaking. We talk of what *we* have done, and what *we* have said, and what *we* can do, and that word "*we*" keeps Him out or mars the sweet-ness of His voice. I was once driving home late at night through a lovely country lane, and as I neared a little wood the sweet song of the nightingale filled the air. I reined in the pony and listened, when suddenly all was marred by the harsh discordant hoot of an owl which came flying by. That one jarring note hushed the sweet song of the nightingale! So it is with us, when we hoot out self instead of by faith reckoning self dead. Oh! how this self-assertion hinders true communion and fellowship with God. How it drowns the still small voice of His Spirit and prevents us from hearing what He desires to tell us. Let us fall down, right into the very grave, that self may be buried and we may in the power of risen life listen to His voice. We cannot bear it otherwise. Like St. John, we must see before we can hear. We must be as one that is dead before His "fear not" can sound out. Then the breathings of His heart of love will not puff us up, but we shall listen to them with a sanctified ear. "Then she fell on her face and bowed herself to the ground, and said "Why have I found grace in thine eyes that thou shouldst take knowledge of me, seeing I am a stranger?"

Yes, we too, were . . . "strangers from the covenants of promise," (Eph. ii. 12), but that was in the past, and He tells us, "Now, therefore, ye are no more strangers and foreigners, (Moabites) but fellow citizens with the saints, and of the household of God," (19 v.) From what depths He brings us and unto what heights He exalts us! No longer strangers and foreigners, He bids us take our right place and let the world know by living a holy life that we belong to the King's Household.

We will now pass on to a very sweet portion of this Chapter which should cheer, encourage, and stimulate the weakest of God's servants. How many of God's true servants are ofttimes cast down, because they think their service is fruitless! Are we not too apt to make our own plans concerning the work God calls us to, instead of following Him? "If any man serve Me *let him follow Me*, and where I am there shall also My servant be; if any man serve Me, him will My Father honour." (John xii. 26). Service must not be a duty—that is not acceptable to Him at all. I must not say "I suppose I *must* do something." *No, no,* that will never do, but "Here am I, send me." How often we see district and Sunday school work taken up as a religious duty, and while we may say at Church

"Whose service is perfect freedom" inwardly in our hearts we do not feel it to be so. A district visitor I knew well—a half-hearted Christian, decidedly worldly—was going round her district with a sort of must-do-it-routine. "I know what you are doing," I said. "Yes," she replied, with a sigh, "*only* three more houses *and then I have done!*" Her heart was not in her Master's work because her heart was not fully His. Love and devotion *must* be the mainspring of service. How we spring forward with joy to do anything for those we love! We do not think it an effort or burden and long for it to be finished. Oh, no. We are only too glad to do it, and the smile, the "thank you," more than repays us. We read of Jacob; "And Jacob loved Rachel and said, I will serve thee seven years for Rachel . . . And Jacob served seven years for Rachel, and they seemed unto him but a few days for the love he had to her." (Gen. xxix. 18-20.) Blessed service, how love makes time fly! When I hear of people taking up work for God merely as a profession, it seems to take all the "love" out of it, and how burdensome it must be. Let us turn profession into devotion, and what a change we get! "I love my Master, I will not go out free." *Ex. xxi. 5.*

True service then is the outcome of devotion, and this is what our Master values. Not the magnitude of the work, but its object. A devoted servant looks upon suffering as a privilege and self-denial as a joy. Though Ruth had given up much she did not dwell on it like some would, but marvelled that Boaz should take notice of her and that she should find grace in his sight. She did not declare to the servants of Boaz her sacrifice—for it was a sacrifice from one point of view—but simply asked permission to glean in the field. Humility characterized all her actions, but what she hid from the servants was known unto the Lord of the Harvest. " It hath fully been shewed ME all that thou hast done." That which was done in secret was rewarded openly.

How wonderfully this self-renunciation is seen in our Lord Jesus, who is the ideal of a true servant. Never did He seek His own will, never did He seek His own glory. His meat and drink was to do the will of Him who sent Him. " I have glorified Thee, I have finished the work Thou gavest Me to do." " Who pleased not Himself." " For I do always those things that please Him." (John viii. 29.) And again, " He made Himself of no reputation, but took upon Him the form of a servant."

The mountain top, the solitary place, the wilderness were His hiding places. There He could pour out His heart to His Father, there He could hear His Father's voice and get fresh comfort and fresh power for the coming strife. " All men do seek THEE " said His disciples, but the one object of His ministry was to lead them to the Father. If the Father's mansion was magnificent, He was the door. If they looked for Him, He desired that they should see the Father. How He sought to instil this lesson of self-effacement into His disciples' minds. " Ye know that they which think good to rule over the Gentiles, exercise lordship over them, and their *great ones* exercise authority upon them. But so shall it not be among you : but whosoever shall be great among you shall be your minister : and whosoever of you shall be the chiefest, shall be servant of all. For even the Son of Man came not to be ministered unto, but to minister, and to give His life a ransom for many." (Mark x. 42-45.)

"The Lord recompense thy work, and a full reward be given thee of the Lord God of Israel, under whose wings thou art come to trust." *Chap. ii, 12.*

The Master called with words of love,
   It won our hearts, it set us free;
Then came His voice so wondrous sweet
   "Who, who will go and work for Me?"

     Who'll work for Me?
     Who'll work for Me?
       The Saviour calls to you and me.
   We'll gladly go our hearts reply,
  To work, to suffer, or to die.

" Also I heard the voice of the Lord saying, whom shall I send, and who will go for us? Isaiah vi. 8.

To heathen lands, where darkness reigns,
    And thousands have a Christless grave,
Who, who will go? He loudly cries,
    To tell them I am come to save?

Or into haunts of woe and vice,
    To men and women, slaves to sin.
We hear Him call, we hear Him plead,
    Who, who will go those souls to win?

In court, and lane, and crowded street,
    In mansion fair and fever den,
He tells us He has precious souls
    Among the dying sons of men.

The sailor on the troubled sea,
    The soldier on the battle field,
Who'll tell them of My " Peace, be still,"
    My power to keep, My arm to shield?

With aching limbs and fevered brows,
    Poor sick ones pass the sleepless night.
Who'll bear My messages to them
    And make their darkness shining light?

Who'll bring the lambs like those of old,
    That I may bear them in My arms;
A sheltering fold, a perfect rest,
    A safety from all wild alarms?

CHAPTER X.

WHOSE SERVICE IS PERFECT FREEDOM.

CHRIST'S service was true service indeed and a sweet savour to God. The "all power given" unto Him never for one moment caused Him to take an independent path, but every step He took was taken in entire and perfect obedience and dependence on His Father.

It is so blessed and cheering to know that all service with this object and on these lines is acceptable and fruitful. This is sweetly expressed in the story of Ruth. "It hath fully been showed me *all* that thou hast done unto thy mother-in-law since the death of thine husband: and how thou hast left thy father and thy mother and the land of thy nativity and art come unto a people which thou knewest not heretofore. The Lord recompense thy work, and a full reward be given thee of the Lord God of Israel, under whose wings thou art come to trust." (Ver. 11-12). Here we get three points noticed and commended: Devotion—obedience—dependency. This is what Boaz saw—it was fully seen—not one jot left out, " all that thou hast done," and a full reward was Ruth's.

Oh! dear reader, surely with our unfailing Master looking on, however small our service may be, if done to Him, and in obedience and dependence on Him, it is truly acceptable. This should cheer us on ; should lift up our hands which hang down, and should strengthen our feeble knees. In the weariness of watching, in disappointment, in opposition, in much weakness, when chilled by contact with half-hearted Christians, when falsely accused, when misunderstood, remember He is looking on, and with that radiant smile of approbation He is saying : " It hath fully been showed Me." However black the cloud, this will be the bow. However loud the discord, this will be the harmony. However dark the hour, this will be the light. The widow's mite was not overlooked, but glittered in His eyes with a brighter gleam than all the gold of the rich. Sweet was the spikenard from Mary's alabaster box, for He Who knew her heart, saw her object and told them : " She hath wrought a good work *on Me*." (Mark xiv, 6.) This intense personal love and devotion is often seen in those prostrated with physical weakness or crippled with poverty, and reveals the fact that their service is to God, and their strength from God. I know a dear little fellow badly afflicted and hardly able to walk at all. He sat on my knee one day and told me with a smile, that he not only loved Jesus, but worked for Him. " You work for Jesus, Alfie ! " I said. " Yes I do, said he. I buy tea with my pocket money, and whenever I see a beggar I call him up to my little carriage and give him an ounce in a small packet with a little book, and ask him if he loves Him." Oh! the joy that beamed from that sweet young face, as he sat there; and I seemed to hear little Alfie's Master say: "It hath fully been showed Me."

At a large Conference in Kent, where Missionary claims were being pressed home, the question was asked "What can you give for Jesus?" Can you help Him with your substance? Can you, if poor, help the work with your prayers? Or can you, dear parents, who are blessed with Christian children give them up to the Lord for the Heathen? Many were bowed down that night and were asking themselves: What can I give? The next day a letter was received from the wife of a poor Railway porter, who knew and loved the Lord. "What can I give," she wrote, "was the question which kept on rising before me all night—silver and gold I have none, my husband's wages being so low, but I have my Mary, a fine healthy girl of 18, very decided as a Christian and fairly educated, she shall go and carry the water of life to the poor dying heathen." You will understand the greatness of the sacrifice, when I tell you this daughter was her mother's right hand at home, and helped her in all her household duties as well as in looking after seven brothers and sisters. Her strong love for her Saviour enabled this poor mother to part with her daughter, while He, beaming upon her, could say: "It hath fully been showed Me."

Oh! loving eyes of Jesus, how they follow the toiling worker in our slums, often oppressed with the burden of souls around her, and overwhelmed with the sights and sounds of sin and sorrow. Through all the din comes that voice : "It hath fully been showed Me." How they watch the young man holding up his beacon light in some dark business corner, where although jeered at, he still speaks out for his great Master. The sneers and laughter are lost in that sweet voice : " It hath fully been showed Me." How those eyes watch the Christian soldier in the barrack-room or the sailor on the ship's deck. True to his great Captain, he seeks to serve Him against great odds, and often amid the storm he gladly hears that voice : "It hath fully been showed Me." With what a loving gaze those eyes of Jesus rest upon the toiling missionary under a tropical sun, surrounded by heathen, who with his devoted wife, has gladly left home and home comforts to point heathen souls to Christ. The music of the old home with its familiar voices is silenced before that great echo : " It hath fully been showed Me." In the public school the Christian lad fresh from home is cheered by it, while the undergraduate who belongs to the " pious lot " finds that voice the music of his soul. When life's sands are falling and the eyes are getting dim, how it has cheered the aged pilgrim and thrown a halo round his couch. It has been the " lullaby " to the weary sick one and to the martyr the voice of victory. Yes, yes,

> Only a little while—
>   For toiling a few short days,
> And then comes the rest, the quiet rest,
>   Eternity's endless praise.

The Master's " Well done " will more than repay for all the suffering, and His smile and welcome will be the full reward given. A chain of texts in my Daily Light just expresses it.

" She hath done what she could." (Mark xiv, 1.) "This poor widow hath cast in more than they all." (Luke xxi, 3.) " Whosoever shall give you a cup of water to drink in My name, because ye belong to Christ, verily I say unto you, he shall not lose his reward." (Mark ix, 41.) " If there be first a willing mind, it is accepted according to that a man hath, and not according to that he hath not."(2 Cor.xiii,12.) " Let us not love in word, neither in tongue ; but in deed and in truth." (1 John iii, 18.) "When ye shall have done all those things which are commanded you, say : ' We are unprofitable servants : we have done that which was our duty to do.' " (Luke xvii, 10.) " For God is not unrighteous to forget your work and labour of love, which ye have showed toward his name, in that ye have minis-tered to the Saints and do minister." (Heb. v, 10.)

" And Boaz said unto her, at mealtime come thou hither, and eat of the bread, and dip thy morsel in the vinegar. And she *sat* beside the reapers ; and he reached her parched corn, and she did eat, and was sufficed, and left." *Ruth ii, 14.*

" The Lord is my Shepherd, I shall not want." *Psa. xxiii, 1.*

" I have *all*, and abound." *Phil. ix, 18.*

''Most Mighty Redeemer! let Thy compassion not only save me, but so take hold of me, and dwell in me, that compassion may be the very breath and joy of my life. May Thy compassion towards me, be within me a living fountain of compassion toward others.''
ANDREW MURRAY.

He calls me to His side and bids me rest
Beneath His smile, while leaning on His breast.
His hand, once pierced, is full of dainties rare—
"My child" He whispers, "All with me now share."
O! feast of love—I'm satisfied—I rise!
"Others must share it, Lord, and know this prize."
To be, and feast with Thee is heaven indeed;
'Tis heaven to serve, and seek my brother's need!
In for communion, feast of love divine,
Out on His service, carrying bread and wine.

CHAPTER XI.

ABUNDANTLY SATISFIED.

IN the previous Chapter we dwelt much on God's knowledge of our service.   The smallest act done for
His glory is not overlooked, for "It has fully been
showed Him."   Service is the great privilege He has
given us down here.   *We are saved to serve.*   But
there is such a thing as excess of service at the
expense of communion, and then it becomes dry and
unfruitful.   The offices of Priest and Levite were distinct in the Old Testament—they become one in the New.
The Priest a type of communion and the Levite a type of
service, each had their special calling, but now every
believer is called to be a priest (Rev. i. 6. R.V.) "hath

made us to be a kingdom and to be priests unto His God and Father;" and also called to be a Levite: "*that we . . . . might serve Him without fear, in holiness and righteousness before Him, all the days of our life*" (Luke i. 74-75). But both functions must be exercised; *we must go in as well as out to find pasture* (John x. 9.)

So in Matt. iii. 14-15 we read, "And He ordained twelve that they *should be with Him, and that He might send them forth* to preach and *to have power* to heal sicknesses and cast out devils." Martha was cumbered with much serving because she neglected the good part chosen by Mary. The one thing needful made all the difference. At Jesus' feet I take in, to give out; I receive, to impart. Neglect that good part and service is cumbersome.

A man cannot work without food, starve a man, and what sort of service would you get? There must be a meal time when the nourishment partaken of stimulates and strengthens the body for service.

On the other hand to eat and not to work is as bad as to work withot eating.

Some are always taking in, taking in, and taking in, and never giving out. Others have very limited supplies which soon become exhausted, while a few have enough and to spare. I heard a quaint remark once made by that well-known Evangelist, J. McAuliffe. He said :—

" Some Christians are like Hagar. They limit God's supplies and so take a water pot about with them, which soon runs dry."

" Others are like Isaac, who had a well and sat by it. They have their pet preacher and sit by him, they take in but do not give out."

"But a true servant has gone to the great Fountain Head, and He has made a well of water to spring up in him, aye, more than that, 'out of him shall flow rivers of living water.' This is what constitutes a true servant.'

You cannot work if you are thirsty and dry. How can rivers of living water flow out of you? You cannot serve if you are empty and hungry. You have not enough for yourself, and how can you have any to spare? Mr. Moody remarked that many Christians were like force pumps, and may we not add, many who tell of plenty are starving themselves.

The key note of true service is blessedly struck in the verse now before us, and each word seems to bring out the "service lesson" our dear loving Master would teach us.

The key to the whole verse is Boaz.

He spoke. She heard his word.

He invited. She came and sat down.

He gave. She received and was sufficed, and rose up to glean.

In the ninth verse we had the "go thou" of service, now in the 14th verse it is the "come thou hither" of communion. It was after Jesus had sent His disciples forth and they had returned that He said: "Come ye yourselves apart unto a desert place and rest awhile." It was no desert place where He was, but an oasis of sweetness, or the most refreshing Elim, where they could lie down and rest. We go out from His presence refreshed to win more souls, gain new victories, and even unconsciously let the world take knowledge of us that we have been with Jesus.

He speaks : " Come thou hither." A blessed calling to Himself. Notice when: "at mealtime," you can get spiritual nourishment only from Him. " I am the bread of Life, he that cometh to Me shall never hunger, and he that believeth on Me shall never thirst." (John vi, 3.) Do remember it matters not where you are ; whatever your circumstances may be, you have Jesus. You may be in some distant heathen land, cut off from all privileges ; you still have Him. You may be under a dead ministry, and Sunday after Sunday receive no food from the pulpit ; you have Him. You may be on the trackless ocean with its rolling, sparkling waves ; He who walked on the sea is there. You may be in some godless family where the name of Jesus has no place ; He is still there. How often we forget this and complain of our circumstances. Is it the cry of a poor hungry soul ? Listen ! *He says* : " At mealtime come thou hither."

I once heard of one of our devoted London City Missionaries who in his rounds found in a most dilapidated house, a poor old woman dying, without a soul near her. By her side was a dry crust and a broken glass with water in it. Her hands were clasped, and as he leant over her, he heard her breathe out, " I've got Christ, what want I more ?" Rich indeed ! "Poor, yet possessing all things." Oh ! what we need in these days of excitement, with so much to engage our thoughts, and so many religious privileges, *is more of Christ*. To turn from it all to Himself. We get so dependent upon the ministry of others, and the religious literature which has something to say on every creed, doctrine, or sect, that we neglect Him, and at meal time we sit down to but a scanty portion. Whenever I hear Christians complaining of their position and how they are cut off from this and that, I feel sure they do not know the joy of secret communion with Himself. To turn from all else and make Him my portion seats me at His banqueting table, and as one yielded to the Holy Spirit, He feasts me indeed. This is the blessed office of the Holy Ghost.

" He will guide you into all the truth." (John xvi. 13).

" Whatsoever He shall hear that shall He speak." (John xvi. 13).

" He will show you things to come." (John xvi. 13).

" He shall glorify Me." (John xvi. 14).

" He shall receive of Mine and show it unto you." (John xvi. 14).

This suffices, this strengthens, and I can then go forward in His power "with portions for them for whom nothing is prepared."

Many do not know this, and so they run here and there. Why so restless ? We read " *she sat* "—blessed text.

He spoke. Can you say—I heard ?

He invited. Can you say—I came and sat down ?

He gave. Can you say—I did eat ? for "he that cometh to Me shall never hunger ! "

Obedience always brings a blessing. We read " she sat down . . . and he reached her parched corn, and she did eat and was sufficed, and left." " If ye be willing and obedient ye shall eat the good of the land." (Isa. i, 19.) Dear hungry worker, I would echo to you my Master's call: " Come thou hither and eat." Do you not hear it ? It is a glorious invitation to the choicest of feasts, for he gives you nothing short of Himself !

We must also note that this place of cummunion is the place of fellowship one with another, for we read " she sat beside the reapers," and it is alone in this place of fellowship that we learn the true unity, and the little petty differences concerning sects and schisms are lost sight of, while we love to sit in fellowship with others, lost in wonder, love and praise. The absence of this Communion is the cause of so much denominationalism. Oh! to be occupied with Himself as the one absorbing object of our lives. Union is strength, and an awful defeat would follow if each regiment refused to fight unitedly against the enemy. English pluck is of no use without it, and England's greatness wonld soon become a thing of the past unless her regiments went forward shoulder to shoulder. Reader, have you been sitting beside the reapers, or do you isolate yourself because they do not reap exactly as you do ? Perhaps they say too much or make too much noise, or they have not the orthodox swing of the sickle, or perhaps you desire to have a field all to yourself, and while it is white with harvest, for others to help gather in the corn would be poaching ! These differences are all lost sight of when we sit down in His presence and eat, and from that presence go forth to gather or glean. It is His field, and we long for the Harvest Home when

> " We shall come rejoicing,
> Bringing in the sheaves ! "

Every sheaf gathered hastens that day, anl if we cry from our hearts " come, Lord Jesus," how gladly we shall work shoulder to shoulder to gather in the ripe corn.

I remember holding a very fruitful mission once in the West of England, in connection with the Church of England. The Vicar was a very holy man of God and had a burning love for souls. I looked round one evening on the workers—one was a Baptist, another a Methodist, one or two belonged to the Plymouth Brethren, then a Congregationalist was working away, while a good staff from his own Church were hard at it. Union was power, and mightily God worked. Souls were smitten down and cried aloud for mercy, and numbers were "born again." We all met at the close of the mission at a united communion, and the reapers sat beside each other. "God has indeed been with us," remarked His servant, "and while all denominations have been represented we have worked in loving union."

The Master becomes the servant—"He reached her parched corn"—the tender hand that was pierced must hand the food. When on earth He made the hungry multitude sit down, the bread they did eat and which filled them was broken by His hand.

It was parched corn—burned by fire ; and while corn speaks of resurrection—life giving—it takes us back to the the time when the scorching fire of God's wrath fell upon the "bruised bread corn." (Isaiah xxviii. 28.) What a feast, and what a blessed place to abide in and go out from to tell the dying world of a living Saviour, who passed through all this that we might have the "Bread of life."

She did eat—Eat, O friends.—(Song of Sol. v. 12). and was sufficed—I sat down under His shadow with great delight, and His fruit was sweet to my taste. (Song of Sol. ii. 3.) and left.　　—Come, my beloved, let us go forth.— (Song of Sol. vii. 11.)

We never can want, for we have all, and abound.

" And when she was risen up to glean, Boaz commanded his young men, saying: " Let her glean even among the sheaves, and reproach her not. And let fall also some of the handfuls of purpose for her, and leave them, that she may glean them, and rebuke her not. So she gleaned in the field until even, and beat out that she had gleaned; and it was about an ephah of barley. And she took it up, and went into the city; and her mother-in-law saw what she had gleaned: and she brought forth, and gave to her after she was sufficed."—*Ruth ii, 15, 16, 17, 18.*

"Evil can only be evercome by the contact of a most personal self-devotion, never by a love that stands at a distance. " Ye are the salt of the earth," Jesus said: "*Ye yourselves* just as you are, in the midst of society; in every place and every moment a sanctifying power must flow out from your presence. Christ *Himself* is the life and the light. In all that He does, or says, or suffers, it is always *Himself*; whoever separates ought from Himself no longer preserves it, it vanishes in his hands."—M. Diemer.

" Yield yourselves unto the Lord." 2 *Chron.* xxx. 8.

CHRIST possessed; Oh glorious thought!
   Jesus dwells within my heart,
   Every member in His care,
Jesus living everywhere.

Christ possessed; He reigns within,
   Blessed cleansing from all sin,
"I" dethroned, He takes my place,
   Fills me with His own pure grace.

Christ possessed; my Lord is mine
   Sweetest fellowship divine,
Days of heaven on earth begun,
   Never now a setting sun.

Christ possessed; 'tis joy untold,
   All my care on Him is rolled,
Tender Shepherd, Thou wilt keep
   Perfectly, Thy yielded sheep.

W. S. W.

CHAPTER XII.

RICH PROVISION.

AS children and servants of God we are not all called to do the same service. The gifts our ascended Lord gave to His Church were diverse. (Eph. iv, 8 11-12 :) —" Wherefore He saith, when He ascended up on high, He led captivity captive and gave gifts to men. And He gave some, apostles ; and some, prophets ; and some, evangelists ; and some, pastors and teachers ; for the perfecting of the saints, for the work of the ministry, for the edifying of the body of Christ."

Although different, they all serve the *same* Master, they all need the *same* power, and all work to further one grand end. If satisfied *with* Christ as well as satisfied *by* Christ, I am joyfully willing to fill just the post He wants me to fill, and

> " If I cannot speak like angels,
> If I cannot preach like Paul,
> I can tell the love of Jesus,
> I can say He died for all."

In our last Chapter we dwelt upon the necessity of having rest and satisfaction ourselves before we can go out to the world in service, and while I may sit beside the reapers, and gaze upon my Boaz, satisfied with the portion He may hand me, inward satisfaction *with* Him is seen by outward satisfaction with His will, and by my readiness to be and do what He desires.

> "So I ask Thee for the daily strength,
>   To none that ask denied,
> And a mind to blend with *outward* life,
>   While keeping at Thy side;
> *Content* to fill a little space,
>   If Thou art glorified."

Our blessed Lord never made barriers in the great harvest field. "I am of Paul, and I am of Appollos, and I am of Cephas," was man's invention. He meant gleaners and reapers to work together. "Let her glean even among the sheaves, and reproach her not." In these days of sectarianism how often this is set aside, and how some of God's servants, who are reapers, watch with suspicious eyes the approach of the gleaner. Man's permission must be asked quite regardless of God's commands, and any new comer is often looked upon as an intruder, and although there may be plenty to do, quite unnecessary. "Let her glean and reproach her not" stands true to-day, and let us ever remember in the words of the Apostle : "But *now* hath God set the members *every one* of them in the body *as it hath pleased Him ;* and if they were all one member where were the body ? But now are they many members, yet but one body. And the eye cannot say unto the hand, *I have no need of thee :* nor again the head to the feet, *I have no need of you.* Nay, much more these members of the body, which seem to be more feeble, *are necessary.*" (1 Cor. xii, 18-22.)

Remember, to our own Master we stand or fall, and to rebuke gleaners because they may not be reapers is to set aside a member of the body of Christ.

I think the reaper represents a wider sphere of service than the gleaner, although they are both precious to Christ, but if we keep in mind that the greater the service the greater the blessing, and the greater the blessing the greater the responsibility, we shall let fall handsful for those who may not be equally blessed. "There is that scattereth and yet increaseth, and there is that witholdeth more than is meet, but it tendeth to poverty" (Prov. xi, 24.)

Gentle gleaner, you may not be able to go forth to the great harvest field as a reaper, but in the quiet corner you fill, your service is not despised by the Lord of the harvest, but as done to Him, is very precious.

Do not weep, poor suffering saint; do not complain, because you cannot be out in the great field, but have to remain on a bed of pain. Your quiet prayers, your loving letters, your patient spirit are all used to glean some fallen ears of corn, and they are precious to your Lord. Dear mother, with your large family to care for, do you long to go forth and reap? Those little ones around you are waiting to be gleaned, and your motherly service is as blessed as if you tended the Babe of Bethlehem. Business-man, in these days of competition, when you feel all your time and energy are needed for your commercial life, do not forget the corn ears waiting to be gathered up. Your servants, your surroundings need bringing in. Reapers in the great harvest field, rebuke not the gleaners. They may not have the same sphere as you, they may not have the same privileges, but remember they are doing God's work, and are as necessary to Him as you are.

Then again we learn another sweet lesson, apart from that of service. "Handfuls on purpose" are often dropped when our dear Lord knows we are needing them. How many of us can look back and bless the Lord for these precious "handfuls."

"Oh! sir," said a dying man to me, "the Vicar's two daughters come in here every day and sing to me about my blessed Jesus; it does so revive my poor soul." Precious handfuls dropped by two reapers.

"Her visits are like sunbeams, and I always get a feast," said another, as he lay upon his bed near smoky Manchester —*blessed handfuls.*

"Girls, remember you have a glorious keeper in Jesus, and One whose love passeth knowledge," remarked a bright teacher to a band of Christian factory girls. How their faces brightened as they picked up the handful.

"Poor broken-hearted weeping one, Jesus knows your sorrow, and as the man of syrrows can bear your grief." It was a soothing handful dropped at the feet of a young widow.

From the Master— the Lord of the Harvest—from His inexhaustible supply gather these golden ears of corn, and as you gather drop them at the feet of the needy, that they may pick them up, and bless your Master.

In concluding this chapter, let me remark the Lord's portion is a satisfying portion. Yea, more than that, it is enough and to spare.

Glean until the evening comes, and you will find enough to carry you through a night of sorrow.

Beat it out, and you can carry it into the busy city— " and one took it up and went into the city."

Let your dear ones see what you have, and how sufficed you are, then you can give to them a feast as well. "And her mother-in-law saw what she had gleaned, and she brought forth and gave unto her *after* she was sufficed." This is proving gloriously that " God is able to make all grace abound toward you: that ye always having all sufficiency in all things may abound to every good work." (2. Cor. ix. 8.)

"Shall I not seek rest for thee, that it may be well with thee?"—Ruth iii. 1.

THE SECRET OF REST.—O Lord, I am like a little child, knowing neither the beginning nor ending of my ways, but Thou being a wonderful Counsellor, I think it my only Wisdom to be advised and ruled by Thee. O! show me then always, Thy ways in all things even in the least, that I may never miss to do Thy work in due season and due order. Make me such a faithful steward as not to go an inch from Thy will, but on all occasions to act and suffer according to Thy good pleasure."

BOGATSKY.

HAST thou heard Him, seen Him, known Him?
    Is not thine a captured heart?
Chief among ten thousand own Him,
    Joyful choose the better part.

Idols once they won thee, charmed thee,
    Lovely things of time and sense;
Gilded thus does sin disarm thee,
    Honeyed lest thou turn thee thence.

What has stript the seeming beauty
    From the idols of the earth?
Not a sense of right or duty,
    But the sight of peerless worth.

Not the crushing of those idols,
    With its bitter void and smart;
But the beaming of His beauty,
    The unveiling of His heart!

Who extinguishes their taper
    Till they hail the rising sun?
Who discards the garb of winter,
    Till the summer has begun?

'Tis that look that melted Peter,
    'Tis that face that Stephen saw,
'Tis that heart that wept with Mary.
    Can alone from idols draw.

Draw and win and fill completely
    Till the cup o'erflow the brim;
What have we to do with idols
    Who have companied with Him?

ANON

CHAPTER XIV.

"REST."

"THAT I may know Him" was a wonderful expression to fall from the lips of one who could say "I know whom I have trusted." One leads to the other. It was a trustful path which Ruth took when she said "Let me now go to the field and glean ears of corn after him in whose sight I shall find grace" (ii. 2), and this path led her into the rich pastures of grace Boaz manifested in his care for her. "Whose damsel is this?" (verse 5) was a true picture of grace seeking. Then his request "go not to glean in another field" (verse 8) was grace caring. "They shall not touch thee" (verse 9) was grace protecting. "It hath fully been showed me" (verse 10) was grace taking knowledge. "At meal-time come thou hither and eat " (verse 14) reveals grace providing, and well might Naomi say " Blessed be he of the Lord, who hath not left off his kindness " (verse 20). Yes, " surely goodness and mercy shall follow me all the days of my life " ; but I want more : I want Himself, and to dwell in His presence for ever.

> Alas ! Thy gifts cannot suffice
> Unless Thyself be given ;
> Thy presence makes my paradise,
> And where Thou art 'tis heaven.

" She did eat and was sufficed " we read, but she now longed for him more than his gifts. This is a blessed illustration of Christian progress. Let us briefly look at the steps.

Decision is brought out in Chapter i., the first step in the Christian life. My decision for Christ leads me to a manifestation of His love and care, typified in the care of Boaz for Ruth (Chap. ii.). But this, precious as it is, does not bring true rest.

SHE LONGED FOR HIM.

So in the divine life : the grace revealed meets all my needs, but the source of it all is the One in whom I can alone rest. The Psalmist does not say " Rest in blessings " but " Rest in the Lord." So Chap. iii. opens with " Shall I not find rest for thee ? " and is a Chapter full of the giver and not his gifts.

The word " rest " in this chapter has three very important meanings :—

1. A sharer of all.
2. A caretaker.
3. A comforter.

These take you far beyond the gifts, right into the heart of the giver! "All things are yours, and ye are Christ's." What would the former be without the latter?

I once saw a very touching picture in the Royal Academy; it was called "Gone." A young mother sat beside an empty cradle with a little shoe in her hand; tears were on her cheeks, and although around her she had all she could desire, it was nought to her without her child. Where two loving hearts are united in marriage, the wife is the home. It may be full of comforts, well furnished, and all that money can supply may be found within its walls, but let the hand of death take the wife away —then the light and life of the home is gone. It is home no longer. The good things are there, but the heart yearns for the rest those good things can never give—a rest broken by ruthless death.

Weary soul, you may have enjoyed His gifts, but still you say—

"My restless spirit yearns for THEE."

Let us take up this question uttered over 3,000 years ago. "Shall I not find rest for thee, that it may be well with thee?" Does your heart crave for the Lord? Then be sure that His heart craves for thee. For "the man will not be in rest until he have finished the thing this day" (verse 18). But the realization of this rest is conditional. Let us first trace the threefold meaning of the rest here mentioned, and in our next chapter we will open up the conditions under which it may be ours.

The Apostle John seemed to know more of the person of his Lord than any of his fellow-disciples. Peter saw those loving eyes which broke his heart. Mary could sit at His feet and hear His words. Stephen could gaze into an open heaven and behold His glory while the stones hailed on him, and angels waited to carry his soul to join the glorious Army of Martyrs ; but John leaned his head on his Master's bosom, and learnt the love of that heart which was his pillow. In his writings he seems to present Him in greater fulness than the others, bringing to a point all their expressions and representations, and focussing them in his gospel and epistles of love. The description of himself as " the disciple whom Jesus loved " has a depth of meaning few can fathom. He who knew Jesus thus intimately writes, " And truly our fellowship is with the Father and with His Son Jesus Christ " (1 John i. 3.). The word fellowship means " participation in," *i.e.*, an equal partnership, the right of every wife who shares all her husband has. Here we have the first meaning of rest, *i.e.*—a share of all. It was that conscious union with Him which took John to the Father's heart and showed him the Father's fulness.

Eleazar, Abraham's servant, when seeking a bride for Isaac, told of his master's riches, but added " and unto him (Isaac) hath he given all that he hath " (Gen. xxiv. 36). When Rebekah decided to go to Isaac and became united to him, all this was hers. So " Truly " all is ours as those united to our blessed Lord. " For in Him dwelleth all the fulness of the Godhead bodily, and ye are complete (made full, R.V.) in Him " (Col. ii. 9, 10.).

> " With Jesus my heart is delighted,
>   To Jesus my soul is united,
>   I and my Jesus are one."

Just as the step of faith brings me from the far country to my Boaz, so the link of faith unites me to Him as my very own. This is a wonderful mystery but a glorious reality—and I know Him as the blessed sharer of all.

A caretaker.—Love joyfully commits herself to the object loved, for trust is the blessed outcome of love. Does the bride fear to trust herself to him she loves? No, on the contrary she knows her husband will take care of her. Now Jesus has expressed His love to me in a wonderful way, for every gift is a love token; an expression of His great love to me. Thus my heart is won, and it is a joyful privilege to trust Him with all. " I know whom I have trusted (marg.), and am persuaded He is able to keep that which I have committed unto Him against that day" (2 Tim. i. 12.).

I know whom I have trusted,   Past.

and am persuaded He is able to ⎫
keep that which I have com- ⎬ Present.
mitted unto Him   ⎭

against that day.   Future.

What a blessed caretaker ! " He will not suffer thy foot to be moved. He that keepeth thee will not slumber" (Psalm cxxi. 3), for we are " kept by the power of God " (1 Peter i. 5.).

A comforter—" Who comforteth us in all our tribulation (2 Cor. i. 4). He who was moved with compassion can comfort as no one else can. The Man of Sorrows can enter into our sorrow with a depth of tenderness that only those who trust Him know. " To bind up the broken in heart," to heal their wounds, and to wipe the tear-drop away is a work of love He does perfectly. Not a formal word of sympathy, but the God-man as sympathiser. He who has stood where we stand, and is now seated in Heaven's glory can comfort you, poor weeping one, in all your tribulation. He is still the Man

> "Who in each sorrow bears a part,
> That none can bear below."

Let me close this Chapter by again saying it is Himself you need and alone can rest in. Heaven's riches are yours, but He shares them with you. Take Him away and you would be poor indeed. "Kept by His power"—a wonderful keeping, but it is the Keeper whose tender care makes joy in the heart of the kept. Sweet comfort! It is the sweetness of the Comforter, whose presence dispels all the gloom of sorrow. Jesus Himself—my Jesus—my Bridegroom—my all. To Rest in Thee is Rest indeed.

"Get thee down . . . lay thee down and he will tell thee what thou shalt do."—*Chap. iii. 3, 4.*

"The Lord is my Shepherd.—Oh, to be led, drawn, and sent by him continually! and made to lie down too! None but Christ Himself can so fill our souls with the sweetness of His green pastures, as to make us lie down therein; yet how can there be growth unless we *chew the cud* there? The world is rapidly hasting on its course—drawing near its terrible end; but we are sheep, and our heavenly blessing is to be led and fed by the Lamb. What fulness there is in Jesus! He is the Lamb of God and the Son of God; yea, *all* fulness dwells in Him!" ANON.

"Oh! draw me to those feet—those wounded feet
That trod on this poor earth for me
A path so full of thorns, which only led—to Calvary.
And while I'm resting there—Oh! rest complete—
Enrapture heart and eye and fix them on Thyself;
Calmly beholding, from my lowly seat,
Thy face, intensely sweet—
I can rest there, such perfect rest,
And see in Thee, Thou fairest of the fair,
All, all I want, brightness of glory,
Yea! the brightest spot up there.
Lord, this is what Thou lovest,
To tell Thine own, while seated low,
All that is stored within Thy heart of love,
And gently lead them up to the Great Source above—
Thyself to know.
'Tis there we learn, what service cannot tell,
Secrets untold, except to those who choose this 'better part,'
To Mary known so well."

W. S. W.

Let me see Thy face.

SHOW me Thy face—one transient gleam
    Of loveliness divine,
And I shall never think or dream
    Of other love save Thine :
All lesser light will darken quite,
    All lower glories wane,
The beautiful of earth will scarce
    Seem beautiful again.

Show me Thy face—my faith and love
    Shall henceforth fixèd be,
And nothing here have power to move
    My soul's serenity.
My life shall seem a trance, a dream,
    And all I feel and see,
Illusive, visionary,—Thou,
    The one reality !

Show me Thy face—I shall forget
    The weary days of yore,
The fretting ghosts of vain regret
    Shall haunt my soul no more.
All doubts and fears for future years,
    In quiet trust subside,
And nought but blest content and calm,
    Within my breast abide.

Show me Thy face—the heaviest cross
    Will then seem light to bear ;
There will be gain in every loss,
    And peace with every care.
With such light feet the years will fleet,
    Life seem as brief as blest,
Till I have laid my burden down,
    And entered into rest.

ANON.

CHAPTER XV.

"HIS COMMANDS ARE NOT GRIEVOUS."

IN the preceding chapter we dwelt upon the fact of what
Christ is willing to be to us. It brings us into the closest tie of relationship, with all its privileges—the place
next to His heart, the place of the Bride to the Bridegroom.
It means a present realized union, with all its deep-felt
joys. It is nearness to Him—nearer and dearer I cannot
be, blessedly real to faith: to the worldly Christian a
mystery, to the sanctified soul a fathomless enjoyment.
Mine—all mine if I will only comply with the conditions
so sweetly set forth in this chapter. Ruth had learnt by
his acts that the heart of Boaz yearned for her. His gifts
and care had revealed this. She had accepted them.
Now she was reaching out for that which far exceeded the
tokens of love—the lover himself. In him she was to find

rest: to rest in all he was and had, to rest in his tender care, to rest in his heartfelt comfort. It was for her, within her grasp, and whatever was needed the prize must be gained, gained at all costs, for, apart from him, no earthly rest was hers. How fully this is brought out in the Song of Solomon! A mere love song, a worldling would say, but to one who knows the heart of Christ, to one who has consecrated his all, it is a book expressive of that intensity of love, the love of hearts united. "I can never see much in the Song of Solomon," a fashionably-dressed lady once said at a large gathering. A divided heart can never know what a wholly surrendered heart enjoys. Yet all this love is within the grasp of every child of God, nay, more it is, his purchased possession! Why not enjoyed? you ask. Because it is conditional, and how many turn away when the conditions are stated!

Let us now learn the conditions, and as we see them one by one, let everything go that would hinder, and at all costs claim Him as ours altogether. We have them in Verse 3 . . . "get thee down." Again in Verse 4 . . . "lay thee down."

There is a platform so many Christians will stand upon—it has four planks: self-seeking, self-sufficiency, self-assertion and self-defence, all resting upon a very big "self." From this he has to come down, down to the level of denying self in every sense, even with the words of a Christ-denying Peter—I know not the man!

Denying must lead on to crucifying, and on to the Cross self must be nailed and put to death, as truly as Christ was. We must die with Christ. Look carefully at

Gal. ii. 20. What Christ has done for me, and where faith claims it, is made real to me by the Holy Ghost. This is one aspect of His blessed office. Sweep away the foundation and the platform must come down. A dead self has nothing to seek for. As dead it is insufficient. It has no rights to assert, and certainly none to defend. Claim this—dear honest soul, you have struggled against this wretched haunting self—claim that it is crucified and dead, and the Holy Ghost will make it blessedly real, and you will rise to walk in the power of an endless life— "Christ, who is our life." A friend who travelled on the Continent told me he once saw over a church door a big I with a cross right through it. How significant!

"Get thee down". is followed by "lay thee down." This attitude maintains the former act—it is a blessed summary of abiding. Abiding seems to me to imply a deep satisfaction, so nought else is wanted, and there I stop. A "resting in," so to speak, as I lay down on the bed of His will. The way out is by the door of disobedience, but a restful soul is an obedient soul, and rest is maintained by instant obedience. Do not ask "why," but obey.

> "Thou sweet beloved will of God,
>   My anchor-ground, my fortress-hill;
> My spirit's silent, fair abode,
>   In Thee I hide me, and am still.
>
> Upon God's will I lay me down,
>   As child upon its mother's breast;
> No silken couch, nor softest bed,
>   Could ever give me such deep rest."

Child of God, joint heir with Jesus Christ, why should you dread that sweet will?

> "The will that willeth good alone."

Would He give you one unnecessary pain? Would He do one thing to torment His child? Get *into* His love—

its constraining power will make your will, a willing captive. "Why and wherefore" will be drowned in the ocean of love, and the soft whisper of a surrendered heart will be " Oh joy! Oh rest! His will is sweetness itself, it is a silken couch, I can rest there ! "

Verse 4 . . . "and he will tell thee what thou shalt do."—Blessedly true ! Not to be argued out, nor to be realized except by those who have laid down their all at His feet, in true submission to His sweet will. Notice particularly " Learn of Me " comes after " Take My yoke upon you " ; then it is so easy to follow, for we hear His voice and follow Him. Thus we have an ungrieved Spirit who takes of the things of Jesus and shows them unto us. As one has remarked, " Christ says ' Abide in Me,' to show us His beauty, and ' I in you,' to make us beautiful for Himself." It is the office of the Holy Ghost to do this. He never comes to us to reveal Himself, but to reveal Christ and form Christ in us.

Oh! its unfathomable depth, its immeasurable length and breadth, its incomprehensible height ! For "Eye hath not seen, nor ear heard, neither have entered into the heart of man, the things which God has prepared for them that love Him. But God hath revealed them unto us by His Spirit ; for the Spirit searcheth all things, yea the deep things of God" (I. Cor. ii. 9, 10). It is here I learn His secrets, His purposes, " His power to usward who believe," and what outside would seem an impossibility I find inside, to be a glorious possibility.

" My child," said a loving mother to her little one, " let me have your doll." " Oh! mother," said the wee one,

"I love dolly so I never could give it up." "Do you love me, my child?" replied the mother. The little eyes brimmed, the little feet bounded, and dolly was willingly laid on mother's lap.

OH! THE STRONGER LOVE

did it, and it was all so easy. The little will surrendered, and the treasure was joyfully yielded. The careful mother turned the doll over and pulled out a big drugget pin which little Olive had used to pin the clothes together. Then carefully sewing the torn parts, and mending dolly's clothes like a mother can, she put it back into her wee one's arms with a kiss. "Oh! mother darling," said the child, "you are good; it was that nasty pin that kept pricking me!"

Dear reader, this is just what he will do; He will take out all the pricks that keep pricking you, and "instead of the thorn shall come up the fir tree, and instead of the brier shall come up the myrtle tree: and it shall be to the Lord for a name, for an everlasting sign that shall not be cut off."—Isa. lv. 13.

He will tell thee. Oh! that sweet, sweet voice!

The voice of my Beloved! I was wandering far away,
When it sounded o'er the desert at the breaking of the day:
"Come, come poor wandering lost one, for you my blood was shed,
For you the crown so thorny was placed upon My head.

The voice of my Beloved! it ravishes my ear,
I hear him speak in accents sweet, to comfort or to cheer;
He tells me how He loves me, and He bids me there abide,
For He's never, never restful unless I'm by His side.

(w.s.w.)

"All that Thou sayest unto me, I will do."   Chap. iii. 5.

  "It is to those who obey Him, God gives the Holy Spirit, through
"whom the blessed Will of God becomes the light that shines ever
"more brightly on our path.   If any man will do His Will, he
"shall know.   Blessed Will of God !   Blessed obedience to God's
"Will !   Oh that we knew to count and keep those as our most
"precious treasures."

ANDREW MURRAY.—("*Like Christ.*")

" ALLELUIA ! "

Cleansed in our Saviour's precious blood,
   Filled with the fulness of our God,
Walking by faith the path He trod ;
                    Alleluia !

Leaning our heads on Jesus' breast,
   Knowing the joy of that sweet rest,
Finding in Him, the chief, the best !
                    Alleluia !

Kept by His power from day to day,
   Held by His hand we cannot stray,
Glory to glory all the way.
                    Alleluia !

Living in us His own pure life,
   Giving us rest from inward strife,
From strength to strength, from death to life ;
                    Alleluia !

Oh, what a Saviour we have found ;
   Well may we make the world resound,
With one continual joyous sound ;
                    Alleluia !

W. S. W.

CHAPTER XVI.

"PERFECT OBEDIENCE."

OBEDIENCE is the door which lets the obedient Christian into the secrets and blessings of His Lord. It takes him out of poverty into wealth, from weakness to strength, from defeat to victory, from sorrow to joy, and, as our story tells us, from widowhood into wedlock. A real living union with the Bridegroom of my heart's affection. In the preceding chapter we had presented to us the conditions of blessing, here we have the joy of obedience. What glorious results are the outcome of that one testimony concerning Abraham given in (Heb. xi. 8) : "By faith Abraham, when he was called to go out into a place which he should afterward receive for an inheritence, OBEYED." For one moment skip over his life

and read the closing summary : "And the Lord *had*
blessed Abraham in *all things* (Gen. xxiv. 1). We can
never over-estimate the fulness of this blessing, and while
his life was, with but few exceptions, a pathway of
obedience, each step revealed what his loving Lord had
ready to bestow upon His obedient child, which culminated
in those words " All things."

It is worth noticing, as we pass on, a few biographies
culled from God's Word where this grand and important
truth is illustrated :—

Command.	Blessing.
Noah.—" Come thou and all thy house into the Ark."-Gen.vii. 1.	" To the saving of his house."—Heb. xi. 7.
Abram.—" Get thee out of thy country."—Gen. xii. 1.	" I will show thee . . I will make of thee . . I will bless thee."—Gen. xii. 23.
Abraham offering up Isaac.—Gen. xxii.	"In blessing I will bless thee," &c.—Gen. xxii. 17-18.
Jacob.—" Arise, go up to Bethel." Gen. xxxv. 1.	" And God . . . blessed him." —Gen. xxxv. 9.
Gideon.—Judges vi.	" Victory."—Judges vii.
Jeremiah.—" Called to be a Prophet."—Jer. i. 4-19.	" His word was in my heart as a burning fire."—Jer. xx. 9.
Peter—" Let down your nets."—Luke v. 4.	"They enclosed a great multitude of fishes."—Luke v. 6.
Disciples.—" We ought to obey God."—Acts v. 29.	" Joy."— Acts v. 41.

We could quote many more, but refrain, while we
summarise the results of obedience as follows :—" Home
blessing " ; a revelation of God's mind ; a blessing to
others ; the blessing of God ; victory ; " a tongue of fire" ;
" a successful venture " ; and joy. As a grand total let
us take the words of our Divine Master : " If a man love
Me, he will keep my words (obedience), and my Father will

love him, and we will come unto him and make our abode with him."—John xiv. 23.

While obedience opens the entrance into the blessings of God and we float on its ocean fulness, it opens the heart of the believer, and he becomes a temple in which the triune God resides.

Again : "If ye be willing and obedient ye shall eat of the good of the land."—Isaiah i. 19. A feast is spread in His banqueting-house (Cant. ii. 4), where the obedient one is brought and where his soul is satisfied with marrow and fatness and his lips are full of joyful praise (Psalm lxiii. 5).

> Then He spread a feast of redeeming love,
> And He made me His own happy guest ;
> In my joy I thought that the saints above
> Could be hardly more favoured or blest.

While on the other hand : "If any man hear My voice and open the door I will come in to him, and will sup with him and he with Me" (Rev. iii. 20).

It is almost beyond our conception, but it is blessedly true, that the Master can feast on the affection and obedience of a loyal heart. While such possibilities are within the grasp of all God's children, how few, comparatively speaking, are realising this abiding in its double aspect : "Abide in Me and I in you."

Let me add, disobedience in even a small matter can and will shut the soul out of a rich blessing. I was once visiting a large spinning mill in Yorkshire, owned by a Christian friend, and although it was early in the day the whole of the machinery in that vast building was stopped. I was taken to the engine-room, steam was up, and there was no lack of it, what could it be ? Grit had by some means found its way into the machinery—a very small quantity,

but it had stopped the whole mill. Just so little acts of
of disobedience will stop the whole machinery of our
Christian life. The power of God is at our disposal,
but, alas! how often there is this "stand still" in our
life.

Let us notice again the heading of this chapter.
That one word "all" Chap. 3. 5., is the key which
obedience turns in the lock, and the door to the store-house
opens, and I can share the love, affection, life, wealth and
power of my Boaz : "Perfect love casteth out fear."—1
John iv. 18. Ruth's heart had been fully won. Her
only desire now was to realise all that union
with him implied. In our 15th Chapter, Naomi
presented to her the prospect of that union,
asking her : "Shall I find rest for thee that it may
be well with thee ?"—Ruth iii. 1. She did not ask Ruth
if she should seek to win the love of Boaz for her, that was
already hers, by his acts he had shown it. She knew he
loved her. Only to look back upon his dealings in the
harvest-field proved it. She wanted more than his gifts—
they had won her heart ; she wanted the giver. She had
no fear, his love had cast it out, so she could restfully
obey, and obey at all costs. "*All* that thou sayest unto me
I will do" was her trustful reply. If any of our Lord's
children dread to obey all He may say, they never can have
known the fulness of His love, the tenderness of His heart,
and His one deep desire to give them Himself. They
might have had glimpses of it and a "sunshine and
cloud" experience, but that is all. Could they have read
such texts as "Herein is love," "God so loved the world"

"But God commendeth His love towards us," and been drawn to the Cross of Christ, the measure of that love, and still had but passing visions? Oh! dear reader, if this is your experience it is no wonder that you fear to trust your all to Him and obey. What must He think of half-trustful Christians? How they must pain His heart? "What, have I not done all for them and fully revealed My love, and still they fear to thrust out from the shores of distrust, set their sails to catch the breeze of love and sail over the the ocean of divine grace." Let this love cast out all fear, and the result will be instant, trustful and joyful obedience.

What does obedience cost? A man whose hands are full of coppers and who is offered gold does not consider it a sacrifice to cast the coppers away? He does not say: "All this gold cost me as much copper." He rejoices over the wealth he now holds, and looks upon the coppers as poverty discarded. "What things were gain to me those I counted lost for Christ."

Rather let us ask what does disobedience cost? It costs us a life of victory, joy unspeakable, a living union with the living Lord in glory, a sweet consciousness of His smile, and the melody of His voice, heaven below, and a thousand more blessings. This is God's gold which many throw away for copper. Dear reader, look up into His face, hear His voice: "Rise up, my love, my fair one, and come away." Can you still hold back, or will you respond: "All that Thou sayest unto me *I will* do"?

" . . . Spread therefore thy skirt over thine handmaid, for thou art one that hath a right to redeem," (Marg.)—Ruth iii. 9.

"I spread my skirt over thee . . . and entered into a covenant with thee, saith the Lord God, and thou becamest mine."—Ezekiel xvi. 8.

"I declare to you that I had rather be one hour with God than a thousand with the sweetest society on earth or in heaven."

Mc.Cheyne.

"AT HIS FEET."

At His feet, at His feet !
Resting place divinely sweet,
Heaven on earth to there abide,
Pardoned, cleansed and sanctified ;
Well content those feet to kiss,
But He lifts to greater bliss.

In His arms, in His arms !
Rest sublime ! And are there charms
Earth can vaunt to break this peace,
Or can cause His love to cease ?
No ! for changeless is that will,
And He draws me closer still.

On His breast, on His breast !
On His very heart to rest !
Looking upward in His face,
Bending low with radiant grace,
Clasped so closely to His side,
There abiding—satisfied.

K.M.W. 1890.

CHAPTER XVII.

" HIS."

WE are progressing in the experiences presented and the truth brought out in this book. And while the blessings are greater and the possibilities are higher, we must still run on the road of obedience—it will take us through the valley of humiliation on to the rapturous mount of transfiguration.

A man of detail is a practical man, and a Christian whose obedience is one of detail, knows very practically what a living union with his Lord means; while those whose obedience is a theory and not a fact, shut themselves out of, and cut themselves off from, all His great purposes concerning them. To follow this pathway of obedience will take us into the very presence of the Bridegroom of our heart's affections.

"And she went down unto the floor and did according to all her mother-in-law bade her (verse 6) . . . and uncovered his feet and laid her down " (verse 7). " I will make the place of my feet glorious."—Isaiah lx. 13.

First to his pierced feet, the expression of perfect submission. Our love and devotion draw us there and expel all fear, and we trustingly rest.

> Oh ! to lie for ever here,
>   Doubt and care and self resign,
>   While He whispers in mine ear,
>   I am His and He is mine.

What Mary heard when she chose the "good part " we know not, but when first we wept our way there we found it was but one step toward deeper realities.

The blessing received at those feet is sevenfold, for it is
The place of forgiveness.—Luke vii. 38, 48, 50.

",,   ,,   deliverance.—Luke viii. 35.

",,   ,,   learning.—Luke x. 39.

",,   ,,   comfort.—John xi. 32.

",,   ,,   intercession.—Mark vii. 25.

",,   ,,   worship.—John xii. 3.

",,   ,,   power.—Rev. i. 17.

It begins with a sinful heart which He alone can forgive then the very deliverance from the awful power of the devil draws me to my Deliverer. Love sets me in His school and I learn fresh lessons from His heart. So now love is my servant and has ushered me into the presence of the Man of Sorrows, who binds up my broken heart. I know what He is, and can ask at His feet His blessing for another. The costly alabaster box with precious spikenard must be broken there. He loves our worship. The tenderness of His heart of love has drawn me to those feet.

Now His majesty overpowers me and I fall as dead. Blessed attitude—the attitude where His power can be displayed. The stretched-out right hand has imparted resurrection life and I enter into His triumphs. All these " riches of grace and glory " I get at His feet.

But as I have said, we have still a deeper experience to enjoy and a covenant of present union to enter into, "that we should bring forth fruit unto God."—Rom. vii. 42.

There was a nearer kinsman who could claim Ruth (chap. iii. verse 12.) whose claims Boaz could and did meet. It was the work of Boaz alone, and he fully accomplished it. The heart of Ruth had in it no place for the nearer kinsman ; she had seen and heard Boaz and he had won her heart. Now she began to prove his love. To make her his bride he must meet the claims of the law, and he did so when he sat at the gate (chap. iv. verses 1—6).

How the spiritual mind can feast on this picture, setting forth as it does Him who outside the gate suffered (Heb. xiii. 12). Hanging on the Cross, He became a curse, to redeem us who were under the curse of the law (Gal. iii. 13).

The nearer kinsman, the broken law which had a right to claim us, could not—" For what the law could not do in that it was weak through the flesh, God sending His own Son in the likeness of sinful flesh and for sin, condemned sin in the flesh, that the righteousness of the law might be fulfilled in us, who walk not after the flesh but after the Spirit."—Rom viii. 3, 4.

The curse was thus borne and sin condemned.

" Now both the sinner and surety are free."

Every hindrance has been swept away, every claim met,

and He can enter into a covenant of truest union with His redeemed ones.

But we must go back to notice the work in which Boaz was engaged.

"Behold he winnoweth barley" (verse 2). First ripe and first gathered it becomes a true type of the resurrection—the first fruits. The corn of wheat at Calvary had fallen into the ground and died, the much fruit brought forth at His resurrection was to fill the garner of God, but the winnowing begun at Pentecost, was to separate the chaff from the wheat, and a blessed lesson these four words teach. To touch upon them only, is all that we can do, but a quiet and prayerful consideration of them, will more than repay.

Reader, have you yet humbled yourself to those feet? Have you trod the path of obedience with the footsteps of trust? If not you have no part in the covenant, but are shutting yourself out of the blessing of a present union with the Son of God. A fully consecrated soul can have power with Him and prevail. We can claim His right and ask Him to spread His skirt over us without fear of being refused. He has yearned for our love ere this, but we have kept Him from His place over us, and would not take our rightful place; but that love—His love—that mighty drawing power

> "Brought me lower while I whispered,
> 'None of self and all of Thee,'"

and now He exclaims: "I spread my skirt over thee . . . . and entered into a covenant with thee, and thou becamest mine."—Ezekiel xvi. 8.

We have dwelt upon the manward aspect of consecration up to now. The steps taken and the attitude maintained by Ruth told out the covenant of love *she* had entered into—*she was to be his*. But the texts which head this chapter take us to God's side, and we are told what He will do, nay more, what He has already done.

We are too apt to dwell much upon our lying at His feet —our attitude toward him.

In our next chapter we will dwell upon the blessedness of this covenant of our Lord.

"And now, my daughter, fear not; I will do to thee all that thou requirest."—Ruth iii. 11.

"Now unto Him, that is able to do exceeding abundantly above all that we ask or think, according to the power that worketh in us, unto Him be the glory in the Church by Christ Jesus, throughout all ages, world without end. Amen."—Eph. iii. 20, 21.

Love is like wings to the bird, like sail to the ship. It carries a Christian full sail to heaven. When love cools, obedience slackens and drives heavily, because it wants the oil on the wheel that love used to drop.
                                                                Anon.

FEAR NOT! *Rev. i. 7.*

My God, I do not fear
  To yield myself to Thee,
However strange Thy will appear
  It must be good for me.
Oh Father, kind and wise and
    strong,
  Thy will can do no creature
    wrong.

The little babe at rest
  Becomes my minister,
It lies upon its mother's breast,
  And leaves itself to her.
Ah! foolish babe, if it should
    dread
The heart that throbs beneath
    its head.

I do not fear to trust
  My little all to Thee.
Thy every motion must be just
  To all the world and me.
Will as Thou wilt, my joy be still
To kiss thy sweet and sacred will.
    The late Wade Robinson.

CHAPTER XVIII.

"EXCEEDING ABUNDANTLY."

WE closed our last chapter with this blessed promise
"I spread my skirt over thee . . . and entered
into a covenant with thee, and thou becamest
mine" (Ezek. xvi. 8.), linking it with the request of Ruth,
"Spread therefore thy skirt over thy handmaid, for thou
art one that hath a right to redeem." (Ruth iii. 9). The
obedience of faith is a path that leads to the reward of
faith. Along this pathway Ruth had been patiently walking, and now at His feet she was to learn from him, who
had a right to redeem, what his heart of love was willing
to bestow. How true it is—"perfect love casteth out
fear"—expressed by the voice of love which says, "fear
not."

Abram heard it when he had refused Sodom's wealth, for his Lord's sake, and it was no unusual thing to the "father of the faithful." Consecrated Joshua, too, was often cheered by his Lord's "fear not," while Isaiah echoes it in his prophecies from the lips of Him who was revealing His heart's secrets through His servant. The minor prophets take up the refrain, thus expressing the grace of God for His rebellious children the Jews. Bethlehem's plain never heard sweeter music than the Angels' message to the shepherds with its heavenly chorus, "Gloria in excelsis Deo"; while the same "fear not" made Paul bold with a holy boldness even unto death, and sounded over the rocky Isle of Patmos in the ears of him whose head had rested on his Lord's bosom. If like Abram I refuse the world's riches for my Lord's sake, His "fear not" tells me of a better reward. If I face the inhabitants of Canaan with "forward" as my watchword, His "fear not" means certain victory. While from Bethlehem's plains to Heaven's throne of glory, the Lamb—the Son—the Christ of God—shows me, tells me, wins me, and quiets my heart's beating with His "*fear not.*" Surely we can exclaim, " I will fear no evil, for Thou art with me." " *The Lord* is my light and my salvation, what shall I fear ? "

Let us now turn to our covenant-keeping God, and seek to find out the fulness of that covenant He made with us when we became His.

It is a restful fact that His covenants are not made to break. I look at some lofty mountains, majestic, grand, with their snow-capped peaks and rugged sides ; they have stood the storms of centuries. The wild wintry wind has howled and shrieked through their passes and down their slopes, carrying death to many a storm-tossed mariner and desolation to many a quiet home. The vivid flash and rolling thunder have lit up or shaken them; but the storm rolls by, and there they stand unmoved under the blue of heaven. Grand and firm as they look, God tells me they will be removed some day, but His word will stand for ever. (Isa. xl. 8).

"I entered into a covenant with thee. As if He said, "I know thy heart, I have seen thy devotion to Me, the way thou hast followed Me out from all that would tempt or allure. I know thy heart beats true and loyal, and thou hast at My feet yielded thyself up to Me—*thou hast become Mine.* Now my covenant shall be made with thee, an eternal covenant, a covenant of love, and thou shalt see how I can glorify Myself in Thee," Oh! it is so blessed to know while the carrying out of this covenant is for my blessing, my blessing is for His glory.

Psalm xci. 14, seems to express this meaning very clearly. God speaks to those whose hearts are yielded and fixed on Himself, and says: "Because he hath set His love upon Me —THEREFORE—" and then follows a seven-fold blessing—

I will deliver him—Deliverance.

I will set him on high—Power.

I will answer him—Prevailing prayer.

I will be with him in trouble—Comfort and sympathy.

I will honour him—Used in blessing to others.

I will satisfy him—Satisfaction.

And show him My salvation—Present and final.

Let us now turn to our text in Exek. xvi. 8, and see how practically this covenant is expressed—not what He will do but what He *has* done.

Let us pause a moment—it is worth a pause—and ask ourselves the question : How do I stand with my Lord ? Is my attitude one of obedience and submission ? Have I yielded my all as I lay at His feet ? Has His "fear not" comforted and cheered my soul, and am I resting in the promise of my Boaz : " I will do to thee *all* that thou requirest ? " If so, let us claim by faith His promise and hear His " I will " turned into " I *have*."

The *present* blessings expressed in Exek. xvi. are many. We can only touch on *some*. Verse 9 : " THEN washed I thee with water, yea, I throughly washed away . . " —complete cleansing. The consciousness of inward corruption need not be your experience. The depth of His cleansing is unlimited. Do not limit it. Some one has said : " Homer makes his gods mere men, and how often Christians make the saving power of Jehovah weaker than the power of their inbred sin." Your unbelief will hinder Him from performing His covenant, and turn you back into an unholy experience and a life of failure. Ruth's path was a beautiful instance of walking in the light, and led her to the one who performed all he promised. The Highway of Holiness is following Jesus. He says : " I am the Light of the world. He that followeth me shall not walk in darkness but shall have the light of life " (John viii. 12). Let us now link this with 1 John i. 7 : " But if we walk] in the light, as He is in the light, we have fellowship one with another, and the blood of Jesus Christ

His Son cleanseth us from all sin." A present blessed experience. Faith can rest in His word and praise Him for a radical work of inward cleansing.

" And I anointed thee with oil." Special anointing with the oil of the Holy Ghost for service follows, and my work for Jesus becomes fruitful.

In verse 9 we get the cleansing of the "inner life," which is always expressed outwardly by a life which pleases God. Let the inner life be right and it will be outwardly expressed by a holy life. Verse 10 brings this out very beautifully—*that which the world sees*—" I clothed thee with broidered work "—Psalm xlv. 13 : "The King's daughter is all glorious *within,* her clothing is of wrought gold." What more lovely than broidered work of a holy life or the wrought gold of Divine righteousness! I think we can call this the restful expression of one possessed by Christ—no hurry—no flurry—no care— because He controls and lives in the heart. What a garment for the world to look upon! This is the passive side of the life of faith, the next has to do with the walk— the active side. "I shod thee with badgers' skin." One writer says : " Badgers' skins typify the absolute holiness of Jesus." This is what is wanted, and can be ours if we know the former blessing. That Holiness which will be seen— not only in a quiet restful life ; but in the busy mart where every transaction, every commercial contract, every bargain, our dealings with our employées, our servants, our associations, our conversation in company and conduct in the houses of friends or strangers, will bear that one mark "Holiness in the Lord." It seems as if our text is " Then washed I thee," and our life sermon " I clothed thee with broidered work and shod thee with badgers' skin."

Walter Scott, in his helpful book called " The Bible Handbook," says badgers' skins typify " Defence against the various forms of evil without " (page 215). This brings out another glorious truth—the One who cleanses keeps, it takes us to the keeping Psalm cxxi., and we can rejoice that He is a perfect keeper. Let us conclude this chapter with the closing points in this verse, and then in our next text we will see more of this covenant and how wides-spreading it is. " I girded thee with fine linen "=" for the fine linen is the righteousness of the saints."—Rev. xix. 8. To be girded means to be prepared and ready for service, and the preceding verses have led us up to this. Inward holiness is expressed outwardly by holy living and righteousness on the one hand, and by an active life of holy service on the other. It was only when Isaiah experienced this (Isa. vi. 7) that he was ready to go, and girded with fine linen he exclaimed in response to " Who will go for us ?"— " Here am I, send me."

The remarkable increase in service for God, and the numbers of those who of late years have offered them-selves for foreign Mission work, are the outcome undoubted-ly of the Holiness movement. During a recent Keswick Convention " cleansing and filling " was the keynote all through and the result was seen by the numbers who " were girded with fine linen." Several of our own missionaries who are with us now, were blessed and called at that Convention.

" And I covered thee with silk "=" And Pharaoh . .

arrayed him (Joseph) in vestures of fine *silk* (marg.)."—
Gen. xli. 42. He had been brought from prison and made
to sit with princes as a prince of the Royal blood (1 Sam.
ii. 8), and now his vesture of silk was a sign of royalty.
So it is with us. Once enemies we are now sons (John i.
12), and as His sons He puts these kindly marks upon us,
and shod with badgers' skins we can walk in this world as
members of Heaven's Royal family. His covenant is true
—He has entered into it with us. Now let us enjoy all
these covenant blessings.

"Also he said, 'Bring the vail that thou hast upon thee and hold it.' And when she held it, he measured six measures of barley and laid it on her."—Chap. iii. 15.

"Sit still . . . for the man will not be in rest until he have finished the thing this day."—Verse 18.

"So Boaz took Ruth, and she was his wife "—Chap. iv. 13.

"That in *everything* ye are enriched by Him."—1 Cor. i. 5.

"I will come again and receive you unto Myself, that where I am ye may be also."—John xiv. 3.

"Yes, I am happy and satisfied at my very heart; my soul is united to him whom I longed after, in an everlasting covenant of life and peace."—*Isaac Pennington*.

"Tell me that again, it just fills my heart with a holy rapture!
"Tell me He is coming, it thrills me through and through when I "hear it."

THE LATE EARL OF CAVAN.

HE IS COMING.

Oh ! they tell me He is coming,
　And I want to see His face,
To touch those blessèd wound prints,
　Which speak such love and grace.
Oh ! they tell me He is coming,
　Can that joyful news be true ?
For I long, I long to see Him,
　And I know He's longing too.

Oh ! they tell me He is coming,
　It just thrills my heart with bliss,
For then I shall see His beauty,
　And His precious feet I'll kiss.
I will bask in holy rapture,
　In the sunshine of His face,
While all the path He led me,
　With such joy I will retrace.

Oh ! they tell me He is coming,
　He will then make all things plain,
What we thought were bitterest sorrows
　We shall find were greatest gain.
Oh ! they tell me He is coming,
　Then the mists will all be gone,
For we'll dwell in endless glory,
　And enjoy an endless morn.

Oh ! they tell me He is coming,
　Then He'll call me to His side,
I know I am not worthy,
　Tho' He's made me His own bride.
Even now He calls me, " loved one,"
　" His undefiled, His dove,"
He's cleansed me, made me spotless,
　And He wants me there above.

Oh ! they tell me He is coming,
　And my heart it echoes, come,
Come quickly, blessèd Jesus,
　For I long to rest at home.
But until that day of rapture,
　When I'll see Thee face to face,
Keep me watching, working, waiting,
　Ever telling of Thy grace.

CHAPTER XIX.

"AND thou becamest mine." The covenant of blessing dwelt upon by us in our last helped to bring out the glorious fact "That in everything ye are enriched by Him." We are unable in these chapters to dwell more upon the covenant "I wills" in Ezekiel xvi. Those we looked into gave us some idea of this wonderful enriching. But what is it all for? many would ask. To satisfy the longings of my heart alone is but the selfish side. He does love to satisfy the hungry soul, and His promise, "they shall be filled" is a blessed experience in the lives of many of God's children. But we get on a much higher platform. "And thy renown went forth among the heathen for thy beauty (the beauty of holiness); for it *was perfect through my comeliness*, which I had put upon thee, saith the Lord God."—Exekiel xvi. 14. Our beauty is but the perfection of His comeliness, and the outcome of His divine nature *in us* expressed in the lovely garments of a holy life. If we glance back over our preceding chapters we see it is all Himself :

The decision made was for *Himself*.

The place to abide in was *Himself*.

The Person whose feet we laid at took us to His heart.

And now the six measures of blessing he gives is one short of the perfect number, the perfection of that eternal bliss when—

> "He and I in that bright glory,
>   One deep joy shall share,
>   Mine to be for ever with Him,
>   His that I am there."

Living union down here is the ecstacy of our heavenly betrothal. One step more and the Bridegroom's heart will be satisfied with her for whom He bled, and she will be sharing His *one* deep joy.

And so as yielded ones at His feet, the covenant made and enjoyed, while He first told ¦His servants to drop " handfuls on purpose " (Chap. iii. 16) He now tells us to hold our vails (Ruth iii. 15) for handfuls are to be turned into measures, which He will lay upon us ; not " burdens grievous to be borne," but measures of love, and love is a light burden however much the measure may be.

Let us look at these six love measures, which all come from Him, for He is the fountain—the deep sweet well of love.

(1) " I give unto them eternal life."— John x. 28.—*Life*.

(2) " My peace I give unto you."—John xiv. 27.—*Peace*.

(3) " These things have I spoken unto you, that My joy might remain in you and that your joy might be full."—John xv. 11.—*Joy*.

(4) " I have given them Thy Word."—John xvii. 14.—*His Word*.

(5) " Lo I am with you alway."—Matt. xxvii. 20.—*His presence*.

(6) " And the glory which Thou gavest Me I have given them, that they may be one even as We are one."—John xvii. 22.—*Glory*.

His life, which is eternal.

His peace, which passeth " all understanding."

His joy, which is unspeakable.

His Word, which " abideth for ever."

His presence, "alway" to be with us.

His glory—the glory of oneness with Himself.

Pause, dear reader. Did you ever realize this portion is yours in all its fulness? " Bring the vail that thou hast upon thee and hold it." Let His hand measure out a blessed portion, until the moment when He will come and not another.

"The man will not be at rest."—Oh! that restless Heart—the Heart that will not rest until His Bride is by His side in glory, "until He have finished the thing.' One by one from far and near are being gathered, from heathen lands, from centres of civilization and culture, from slums of sin and vice, from young and old alike. Every living stone added will only hasten the day when the top stone will come with joy. Every soul gathered in hastens the day when the number of His elect will be completed.   Then the heart of the Bridegroom will rest, and while the eyes of the Bride will gaze upon His face, all those sweet acts of love will be seen in the unhindered light of Heaven's glory. The love which sought and found, the love which cared for, the love which covenanted, the love which blessed, and then the love of the Bridegroom and Bride.

"Alleluia ! for the Lord God omnipotent reigneth. Let us be glad and rejoice and give honour to Him : for the marriage of the Lamb is come, and His wife hath made herself ready."—Rev. xix. 6, 7.

Ten thousand times ten thousand !
    And thousands, thousands more !
With voices never tiring,
    Are singing o'er and o'er
One blessed never-ceasing strain :
    " Worthy the Lamb that once was slain. "

Their sorrows all are over,
    Their tears are wiped away,
No night, with all its darkness,
    But cloudless, endless day :
The former things are passed and gone,
    They stand in heaven's eternal morn.

List ! list ! what are they singing—
    Those multitudes up there ?
The marriage song of Heaven
    Is ravishing the air !
The Church, for whom the Saviour died,
    Is now with Him, His spotless Bride.

On earth He wooed and won her
    With words of love divine,
He cleansed her from all sin-stains,
    And whispered, " Thou art Mine " ;
Now, clothed in bridal garments fair,
    She dwells with Him for ever there.

His bitter pain and sorrow
    Are things of other days ;
The heart which bled on Calvary
    Is healed and full of praise ;
Rejoiced to have His Bride up there,
    And all His glory bid her share.

Strike, strike the harps of heaven !
    Roll out, ye seraph throng,
In one grand voice of triumph,
    The Bridegroom's nuptial song !
He greets at last His blood-bought Bride.
    He rests in her—*is satisfied.*

THE END.

The
Shoe Princess's
Guide to the
Galaxy

The Shoe Princess's Guide to the Galaxy

Life, love and shoes.
But mostly shoes.

EMMA BOWD

BLOOMSBURY
LONDON · BERLIN · NEW YORK

First published in Great Britain 2009

Copyright © 2009 by Emma Bowd
Illustrations © 2009 by Venetia Sarll

The moral right of the author has been asserted

Bloomsbury Publishing Plc, 36 Soho Square, London W1D 3QY

A CIP catalogue record for this book is available from the British Library

ISBN 978 0 7475 9404 8
10 9 8 7 6 5 4 3 2

Typeset by Hewer Text UK Ltd, Edinburgh
Printed by Clays Ltd, St Ives plc

www.bloomsbury.com/emmabowd

The paper this book is printed on is certified by the © 1996 Forest Stewardship
Council A.C. (FSC). It is ancient-forest friendly. The printer holds
FSC chain of custody SGS-COC-2061

For Darcey and Max
The lights of my life

1. Shoe Love

SHOES, I am afraid to say, really do mean a lot to me.
You know how men seem completely incapable of going
down a street without eyeing every woman in a fox-like flash?
Well, that's me – but with shoes. I simply cannot help it. It's
reflexive. Addictive. Compulsive. Trainspottingly, planespot-
tingly mad.

Why the shoe bug bit me harder than most girls, I can't say.
Does anyone *really* know what makes people the way they are?
Is it nature 60 per cent, nurture 40 per cent? Or maybe the other
way around?

Admittedly, Mum does confess to buying me an array of
exquisitely pretty shoes, from the moment I could walk. But I
suspect this had more to do with dispelling her own ghosts.
After all, a woman denied the pleasure of new shoes an entire
childhood is bound to ensure that her daughter never squirms in
someone else's ill-fitting, worn-out soles. Not a chance.

And as if to prove the 'naturists' right, both my big sister Kate
and I were treated equally, and one can quite categorically
conclude that she does not care an ounce about shoes. In fact, in

shoe styles as well as lifestyles, no two girls could be more different.

From an early age, Kate learnt to tolerate me. In an affectionate way, I think. The sound-sleeping yin to her lying-awake-formulating-fire-exit-plans yang. And typically, in her uber PC fashion, she thinks that my shoe mountain is a tragic example of the modern woman's sell-out to frivolous Western consumer excess.

You see, Kate owns precisely two pairs of shoes. When either pair wears out, she replaces it with an exact replica. Always wool for winter, and cotton for summer ('Animals don't need to die for your feet, Jane'); flat ('High heels objectify women'); and from somewhere that also sells tofu and wind chimes. And she is supremely proud of this.

Our dad is of the I-walked-ten-miles-barefoot-through-snowdrifts-to-school-when-I-was-a-lad persuasion and, like Kate, is genuinely mortified by anyone owning more than one pair of black lace-ups. I don't think Mum's ever forgiven him for helping Kate with her first-year university Women's Studies project: a rough globe shape, suspended from an apron string, made by supergluing twelve pairs of Mum's shoes together and covering them in papier mâché (using the *Financial Times*). A 'symbolic reminder' that the typical world citizen is female, illiterate and performing unpaid domestic duties.

Family shoe battles aside, Mum and Dad still live in relative harmony in our childhood home – a lovingly tended cottage in Oxfordshire. Not that Mum can be found there very often. She's always off to one of her many groups or courses. While Dad is happiest spending his retirement within the comfort zone of his study, garden shed and cable TV sports channels. It's not unusual to find him in awestruck reverence of the quasi-mystical genius of some footballer's boots. 'Just how *does* he do it?' The 'it' being the split-second calculation of the optimal trajectory of the ball during free kicks. Dad was a maths and physics lecturer for forty years.

Our suppertimes as children often involved Dad and Kate scurrying to the blackboard to draw convoluted diagrams of how a television worked, or an aeroplane stayed in the sky. To them, life is just one endless theorem or solvable equation.

Mum and I, on the other hand, seem to delight more in the chaos of the universe. Like Oxford Street on the first day of the post-Christmas shoe sales. I can still feel the snowballing excitement as the bus inched closer to Marble Arch. This was also my sacred 'alone time' with Mum, and always an adventure.

In fact, it's probably true to say that all the most memorable events in my life can be linked with shoes in some way.

First Love

Definitely the canary-yellow patent-leather Mary Janes adorned with white appliquéd daisies and secured by chunky plastic daisy-shaped buckles, that I wore to Sarah Nelson's fourth birthday party. They were like giant jelly beans – a constant source of temptation. I wore those shoes until my toes crumpled up so hard against the front that it was an art to walk without wincing. (A useful skill for my later stiletto-wearing life!)

First Great Feat

When I achieved the coveted life goal of learning to tie – without any adult coaxing, coaching, supervision or manhandling – my very own shoelaces. Scoff, you may. But to a five-year-old in the pre-Velcro era, this was the Holy Grail. My ascent into the world of grown-ups was deemed complete and fully accredited – in my eyes at least. And boy, was I hooked. No set of laces too difficult, no buckle too fiddly, no platform too high.

First Illicit Tryst

Secretly spending what seemed like hours hiding in the forbidden womb of Mum's shoe cupboard, with my next-door neighbour and co-conspirator, Will – aged six. We took it in turns to try on four-inch red platform wedge sandals and fabulous black French faux patent-leather sock boots of 1960s vintage. Several years later, they made it into our dressing-up box; and we spent many happy hours dancing and miming the words to ABBA songs in them. And no, Will is not today a transvestite cabaret dancer at Madame Jojo's. He is in fact a librarian.

Royal Aspirations

It has to be said that I've always fostered an uneasy truce with life. Not in a sad way. More in an is-this-it-can't-we-jazz-things-up-a-bit sort of way. And so it was that for my eighth year on this earth I chose to write letters to myself, Princess Sapphire of Shoelandia, and post them to Shoe Lane, in the City of London. I often wonder where those letters ended up, but more importantly, what a podgy, gap-toothed girl could have found so profoundly interesting to write about *four* times a week.

Shoe Hobbies

Irish dancing (I *loved* those laces), jazz ballet, classical ballet and tap-dancing. I was devastated when demoted to the free-dance class due to my motor coordination skills resembling those of a dyspraxic octopus.

Best Advice

'Good grooming and good shoes hide a multitude of sins.' Mrs Kitty Trigby, expert on all that is sparkly and gorgeous in the world, *circa* 1980. Kitty is a widowed, childless aunt of Mum's who we *always* visited on our trips to London. Now in her late eighties (I think, though I would *never* dare ask) and in a nursing home, she is my shoe co-mentor with Mum. I vividly remember spending many happy hours perched on the edge of her chaise-longue, engulfed in an indulgent fog of Chanel No. 5, playing shoe shops with her sizeable shoe collection. But it was her shoe stories that captivated me most – of journeys to Harrods to get her 'little Amalfis' and 'little Ferragamos' or down to Chelsea to get her 'little Manolos' (decades before Carrie made them famous). I've certainly made a few more 'little' friends of this kind since then, like: Gina, Jimmy, Sergio, Anya, Christian, Robert, Chloé, Jesus, Patrick, Lulu, Kert and Jil.

First School Disco

Flat gold-lamé pumps at least one size too small. The only pair left in the shop; they were to-die-for. And I was not leaving without them, having saved three months' pocket money for the pleasure of their company. I still have the pesky, tiny red mark from the ensuing blister permanently tattooed on my right little toe.

First Kiss (and I mean real kiss, not a fleeting peck behind the sports shed)

White Essex-girl court shoes, or 'tart's trotters', as Dad used to call them. I really did think that I was rather foxy and grown-up. Perhaps it was the way they detracted from my definite lack of décolletage and screamed, 'Look down here at me, I'm beautiful.' Or then again, maybe not!

Pauper Period

I perfected the Cyndi-Lauper-meets-Bananarama-occasionally-mutated-by-Madonna's-latest-incarnation-but-always-involving-a-pair-of-Doc-Martens-and-ill-matching-fluorescent-rolled-up-socks look. Incredibly ugly, actually. But at that age, any negative comments were nothing short of the highest accolade and a sure sign that you were on the right side of cool. Amazing really, what a lack of money and an excess of spare time can lead to. Law students had the lowest number of contact hours of any degree on campus; I may as well have studied via correspondence.

First Broken Heart (mine, not his)

Mr two-toned brogue, caddish rogue. I should have known not to trust such a show pony. Never made *that* mistake again. Point to note: a similar theory applies to men wearing bright-red, yellow or purple shoes. Like a luminescent rainforest snake advertising his lethal venom, stay away from this predator.

First Big Job-promotion

Magenta Joan and David court shoes with two-inch stacked leather heel, dainty strap across the instep and square toe. These were later promoted to the esteemed status of lucky shoes, and have been resoled twice in an effort to eke yet more magic from them.

THE One

When I agreed, without a moment's hesitation, to go on a romantic, post-dinner stroll along slushy, snow-covered streets in my kitten-heeled candy-pink suede slingbacks, I knew Tim was THE one. Shortly thereafter we moved in together – minus one pair of candy-pink suede slingbacks.

Wedding

Sometimes I despair that I'm the *only* person in the whole wedding-industry-world that understands the true importance of the wedding shoes. Quite simply, they dictate *everything*.

Like the style of dress for instance – hemline, cut, train, fabric and neckline. I could not possibly have been expected to decide on my dress without having first chosen the shoes. Have you ever heard of a skyscraper being built before the foundations are laid? I think not. And need I mention the impact of the shoes on the tiara (or lack of), the earrings, the table settings, the music, the candles, the church, the reception venue, the invitations, the cars, the cake, the dance, the whole damn shebang.

Hence the parade of wedding-shoe rejects and my final choice:

❤ Emma Hope Elizabethan brocade slippers. Tim was mortified by my suggestion of velvet pantaloons, trumpeters and a Gothic reception hall, grumbling that I wanted to turn the whole event into a ghastly costume drama.

❤ White kid-leather Vivienne Westwood platforms, studded with chrome spiked hearts. Start as you mean to continue, I always say. Tragically, the junior bridesmaids would have looked a tad vulgar in their bustiers and matching three-inch platforms. Far too risqué for Dad and any attempt at dancing would have been suicidal, à la Naomi Campbell.

❤ Vintage cream Chanel flapper shoes. The corresponding vintage gown gave me the allure of a flat-chested flabby-armed cross-dressing biker chick. Such a pity – as I had visions of booking us into some funky charleston classes for the bridal dance too.

❤ Oyster-shell pink high-heeled satin mules. Big mistake. I couldn't walk two steps without at least one of them slipping off, let alone attempting the forty vertiginous steps to the church door. Stunning as they were, I didn't dare risk turning my hour of glory into a horrific Cinderella moment.

❤   Classic white court shoes, adorned with a celestial spray of powder-puff marabou feathers, cinched in the middle by butterfly-shaped diamanté clasps. Pure confection. With each step, the feathers wafted in surreal slow motion. They obviously had a similarly hypnotic effect on Pierre, my parents' dog, who duly mauled them. The shoes being one-offs (at more than considerable expense), the gown getting no further than the drawing board and Pierre quite frankly lucky to be alive.

❤   I finally settled upon a pair of crimsony cerisey raspberry toned Ottoman-silk Manolo Blahnik court shoes, with exquisite skyscraper stiletto heels, lined in gold leaf with a delicate ribbon-tie across the instep. In turn, parting with more than a sizeable chunk of my last pay cheque as a single girl. They peeked out from underneath the hem of my full-length, silk organza Grace Kelly-inspired gown like the cheeky little courtesans that they were – a sure clue to Tim of adventures ahead.

Honeymoon

Rather a disappointment. Thanks to the hiking boots from hell – my wedding gift from Tim. I was so sure that he was going to whisk me away to a sophisticated pamper-palace in the Seychelles, I had taken it upon myself to buy a full suitcase of coordinated resort wear and shoes. (The last-big-splurge-as-a-single-girl thing again.) Goodness knows, I had left enough brochures of *Six Star Resorts of the World* around the flat for him – with dog-eared pages and little yellow sticky notes with flight numbers and sample itineraries on them. Instead, we went hiking. In Scotland. NO ONE goes to Scotland for their honeymoon. Not even the Scots. It rained for ten days straight. I buried the boots in a muddy grave at the end. And didn't speak to him for days.

Pink Period

Current count: fifty-five pairs of pink shoes – but this *does* also include multiply coloured shoes and some rather gorgeous jewelly slippers.

Pregnancy and Childbirth

How could I forget Clotilde! She was in my antenatal class, and defiantly wore clicky, swingy, sexy high-heeled shoes through-out her *entire* pregnancy. Not to mention effortlessly chic black Lycra tube dresses and G-string knickers (when we were all in granny maxi-supports) – to the jubilation of the dads each week. You really have to give it to the French – they know how to tie a scarf and not let little things like a gravity-defying watermelon stuck to your stomach get in the way of appear-ances. An inspiration to us all.

On the flip side, I discovered the hitherto unknown benefits of flat mules – at Tim's insistence. He was so worried I'd take a tumble and squish 'our' baby in my usual spikes that he dragged me into town to trade them in. I'll for ever remember the miles I walked in my red-and-white polka-dot flats during the early hours of Millie's labour. Not to mention the succession of nameless bad-arse midwives in appallingly dire shoes (white cloggy things with impatient little snub toes).

Motherhood

By rights, I should today be sitting in the front room of my five-storey Primrose Hill town house. Kicking off my sassy yet sensible work pumps and unwinding from a hard day at the London offices of the United Nations, where I head a team of lawyers unravelling the intricacies of international human rights in war zones. The peaceful karma of the house interrupted only by the rhythmical drone of the breast pump, and the contented gurgling of Millie and her adoringly attentive nanny in the nearby nursery. While the housekeeper cooks a scrumptious meal (and a snack for the night nanny) for me to share with Tim when he returns home from a day's hectic auctioneering at Sotheby's.

That's what we *Cosmo* career-girls do, don't we – have it all?

Funny how things pan out, isn't it?

In the REAL world.

2. Head over Heels

'I'M SORRY we're a little late, love. I got caught up with Betty Malthouse at our sewing class,' says Mum as she trots down the hall to put the kettle on. Dad strategically slips into the front room and settles himself on the sofa with the remote control, until I sit beside him to breast-feed Millie and he hastily skulks behind the first opaque object he can lay his hands on – a *Hello!* magazine (my ever-faithful font of anti-knowledge).

Dad's valiantly clinging to his old-school-out-of-sight breast-feeding model and, like the rest of us, is rather shaken by my earth-mother transformation. I'm ashamed to admit that pre-Millie I had been known to tut rather loudly at the sight of mammary flesh daring to suckle a baby outside a darkened room.

Quite bizarrely, it feels like aeons – and not the mere ten weeks it has been – since Millie's birth and this seismic changing of my sensibilities.

I truly shudder to think what I would have done without Mum's help during those very early days (and nights) of elation, exhaustion and unmitigated cluelessness. Though I am fairly certain that Heathrow Airport had fewer security screens and disinfectant sprays than our tiny Kilburn (sort of like Primrose Hill, but without the Hill, or Jude Law) garden flat under her careful watch.

Mum comes in to join us, with a cup of tea in each hand. She gives Dad his Earl Grey and settles herself on the edge of a chair opposite me – tinkering with her teaspoon and not so subtly eyeballing Millie and me, and the general state of the flat. To see how we're holding up, no doubt – which I have to say is middling to OK at best. For in true lioness fashion, she pulled right back on the day-to-day help some time ago – handing the mantle of motherhood firmly over to me.

Tim lollops into the room, gently reminding me that we're late, while trying to tuck in his shirt and do up the buttons on his cuffs at the same time.

'Ah, my favourite son-in-law,' Mum beams. (This is meta-phorical, of course – Kate's so fussy about men she's on roller skates to spinsterhood.) Tim's immediately engulfed by her cardigan-clad arms.

Mum and Tim have always had this mutual-love-fest thing: the-son-she-never-had meets the-mum-he-never-had. Not that Tim's mum is awful or anything. He just doesn't know her particularly well – the old conceived-in-between-cocktails-and-boarding-school-at-seven scenario. As a result, he is per-versely besotted by my family's domesticated heart; and they in turn with him.

And yet tonight, it's hard to know who's more nervous about leaving Millie with Mum and Dad – Tim or me. You see, it's our maiden solo outing since having her. We're off to a dinner party at my best friend Fi's – a beacon of light I've been looking forward to, especially after watching Tim skip out of the front door to work each morning or coming home from one of his many work dos.

I burp Millie, who gets chubbier by the day, and hand her over for Tim to place on the play mat for a kick. As I walk to the bathroom, under Mum's strict instructions to put on a little bit of *colour* (code for 'Go and brush your hair, and make an effort to put on a nice bright lipstick. And a dash of blusher wouldn't go astray, either'), I can hear the ting of the over-hanging bunnies as Millie hits them with her hands – a first today.

I can also hear Tim giving Mum the low-down on my newly stockpiled supply of expressed milk; and a demonstra-tion of his (patented!) middle-of-the-night-broken-down-washing-machine-crossed-with-a-mating-blue-whale drone, which has to be coupled with gently pressing down on Millie's mattress and *always* gets her back off to sleep. And now he's telling her not to forget his 'bonding board' – an A3-sized black-and-white photo of his grinning face that we have to show Millie at *all* awake times. (Something to do with im-planting his image on her visual cortex when he's at work, I think he said.)

Millie doesn't last long on the mat, and is scooped up by Mum for a cuddle. As we make our way to the front door, I give Tim's mobile number to her in giant print, while explain-ing how to use the digital thermometer, where the paracetamol is kept and what the symptoms of meningitis are. And last but not least, I kiss Millie. She already smells like Mum's perfume and gives me a heart-melting smile.

'You go and enjoy yourselves,' says Mum as she snuggles Millie in a blanket and follows us out.

A last-minute rush of panic envelops me.

'But what if she doesn't take the bottle? Although, really, it's just for back-up – she should settle down for a good sleep now. We didn't have time for a proper practice run – it'll only take a few minutes . . .'

'We'll be *fine*.' Mum lightly places her palm in the arch of my back and shuffles us out of the gate.

We're about three blocks from home when my feeble spaghetti brain realises that something bad is afoot. Literally.

'Stop the car!' I shriek.

Tim's relief that smoke isn't billowing from the engine soon transforms into an, 'Oh, for Pete's bloody sake, Jane,' Mars-Venus moment. 'You cannot *seriously* expect me to turn around so that you can change your *shoes*. We're late enough as it is.'

'They're *slippers*.' I ungraciously haul one mammoth-sized sparkly pink Moroccan slipper up on to the dashboard. He cannot do this to me. 'I've been so looking forward to wearing my *special* shoes. This is my *special* night. Remember?' Fi and the girls have organised it in honour of my coming out. 'Life after birth and all that.'

The mere mention of the birth gives me the get-out-of-jail-free card that I need. It's still, thankfully, recent enough for Tim to remember my near-death experience (OK, I only fainted, but it felt like a near-death experience at the time), the blood transfusion and the refashioning operation (and I'm not talking Galliano) that I went through in order to produce our precious princess.

I sneakily omit that the dinner's also to check out Fi's new love target and boyfriend-in-waiting, Marco.

Tim turns the car around grudgingly.

Finally, changed into my black Chanel T-bar stilettos (one of my better shoe-sale purchases) and feeling more than a little relieved and excited, we cruise around the rabbit's warren of Maida Vale streets trying to find a parking space near Fi's mansion flat. A nigh on impossible task on a Friday night.

My eye is immediately drawn to a mum trudging down the street with six grocery bags tied to the handles of a rickety pushchair, a baby rugged up inside it, and a little girl skipping next to her in Barbie-pink Mary Janes with multicoloured tights. (I just adore how little girls bypass the whole walking malarkey.)

I wonder if I'd even have noticed them, pre-Millie?

'Don't you feel the world has changed?' I say. 'Like everything you knew before Millie doesn't count any more? You might as well throw it all out of the window and start again.'

I really have to pinch myself sometimes when I think about the Millie-effect – how she's turned our world head over heels. I can feel the tears well. Damn these hormones.

'Mmm,' Tim ponders, while expertly reversing the car into a space that appears ten times too small. 'Everything seems to make sense now – in a weird sort of way,' he finally responds after a long silence.

'Yes, it *does*, doesn't it?' I say affectionately, and lean across and snatch a kiss from him before he gets out of the car.

Rain suddenly sweeps across the windscreen, and I find myself paralysed from the ankles down. What to do? Click my heels three times and magically fly to Fi's flat?

As I sit and dither, regretting my choice of non-wet-weather shoes, I'm snapped back to reality by Tim tapping on my window. He opens the door wide, and grinning, motions me on to his back, while holding his enormous golf umbrella.

'Well, we can't be getting those *special* shoes wet, can we?'

A tidal-wave smile washes across my face (I always knew he was my knight in shining armour!) and I gratefully jump on board. A black cab whizzing past gives us a couple of cheeky beeps. I break out in a fit of the giggles as I struggle to hold on tight. Which sets Tim off too.

I really can't recall the last time we laughed so much. In a spontaneous, infectious, belly-laugh kind of way. Well, not since Millie was born.

It feels lovely.

3. Fancy Feet

A FULL rain-sodden block later, and finally at Fi's, we follow the waft of vanilla-scented candles up the two flights of stairs to her flat – the last to arrive. Tim fabricates an excuse about working late, which is waved away by Fi, who welcomes us warmly.

We both have a soft spot for Fi – having witnessed many kitchen-table-tea-and-tears sessions over the years. Due mostly to the fact that, gorgeous as she is, she has NO idea when it comes to men.

She leads us straight into the large open living area, which is bursting with dozens of pale-pink helium balloons tied with organza ribbons that hover just above head-height, and giant white lilies in sleek glass vases.

This is a *special* dinner for another reason too: pre-Millie, we girls – Fi, Liz, Rachel and I – would normally meet for lunch or drinks after work. This is one of the rare times that we've brought our partners. And apart from Liz and I, I use the word partner loosely. Very loosely indeed. For vastly different reasons, it's a full-time job keeping up with Fi and Rachel's love lives.

We make our way over to Liz and her husband Harry while Fi sorts out the wet umbrella.

'Wow, man. Congratulations!' Harry earnestly shakes Tim's hand while placing his other on Tim's shoulder. Liz and I embrace.

I can't help but feel unworthy when face to face with Harry and Liz – in their his 'n' hers Tod's loafers. It's common knowledge that they're desperate to have a baby, and have already tried two rounds of IVF without success.

You see, babies were not exactly high on our to-do list a year ago – filed neatly away under 'on-hold'. Falling pregnant as I did (despite the birth control) was a real shock. Such unsolicited relegation from the fashionably childless to the mating masses was not supposed to happen in our iPhone-controlled world.

'How's it been?' Harry asks, as Liz goes to fetch us a drink. The enthusiasm in his eyes is entirely genuine and drives a pang of guilt through me.

'Amazing,' Tim replies without hesitation. My heart swells to bursting point as I notice his heaving chest – testament to his recent conversion to besotted superdaddy. 'The most amazing experience,' he beams.

Amazing, wondrous and joyous, I can't deny. But as I stand here, the lone female between two alpha males, I also find it hard not to begrudge the positively primeval angle to this whole having-a-baby lark too. (I certainly remember wanting to genuflect in front of every mother I passed in the hospital hallway after Millie was born.)

When Liz returns and hands me my drink, I *so* want to tell her that giving birth was more like running the London Marathon while chained to a medieval torture rack, only to be run over by a double-decker bus upon crossing the finishing line. And that I'm barely out of the coma and able to walk in a straight line again.

In fact, if men had to give birth, I'm certain that multinational companies would have poured trillions of pounds into growing babies in plant pots decades ago. Well before nuclear fission, intercontinental ballistic missiles or plasma TV screens, that's for sure.

But when I summon the nerve to meet Liz eye to eye, all I can see is Millie. At once, I break out in a broad smile. And say absolutely nothing – the myth of motherhood remaining firmly and rightfully intact.

As I take Liz by the arm and wander over to the fireplace, where Rachel is holding court, I can't help but feel strangely empowered by childbirth too. Not in a smug, self-congratulatory kind of way. More in a humbling holy-hell-if-I-survived-*that*-I-can-do-*anything* sort of way. And by the look of Rachel's handbag for the evening, I'm going to need to draw upon all the inner strength I can muster.

'Daaarling, congraaatulations,' Rachel schmoozes. It's air kisses all round.

Unlike Fi, who has an invisible tattoo on her forehead saying, 'Doormat: commitment-phobes, love-rats and emotional-vacuums welcome,' Rachel is the man-eater of our group. She took out three student loans at uni and discovered the power of posh clothes and hairdressers over wealthy boys-about-town. Basically, she gets laid a lot. She picks her men with the same strategic zeal as her accessories. A different one for every occasion. Of high quality. Always to complement her. And to attract compliments.

'Hi. I'm Dan.' A preened hulk of a guy in *white* snakeskin loafers removes his arm from Rachel and confidently offers his hand. (What *was* she thinking?) He then takes a drag of his cigarette – exhaling over his right shoulder, and almost straight into the face of the guy next to him (who must be Fi's man, Marco). All the while keeping one eye on his reflection in the mirror above the fireplace.

Within three minutes we know that Dan's just got his helicopter pilot's licence, is a semi-professional snowboarder, a black belt in karate and last but not least a podiatrist. Or rather, as he took great pains to point out, a 'podiatric biomechanist'. (Like we'd know the difference anyway.) In private practice, of course – 'Can't fly like an eagle when you're surrounded by turkeys.' And that if anyone hears a car alarm to be sure to tell him, as it's probably his brand new Porsche whatsamathingy parked outside.

I *really* hope the sex is worth it.

Rachel now has a high-profile job in advertising that affords her a serious shoe habit, and tonight doesn't disappoint. She's in bronze Prada platform spikes with ankle straps – 'the shoes of the season'. Impressive. Come to think of it, the only monogamous relationship Rachel's ever admitted to is with her 'daaarling Enzo' – a shoe-repairer off Marylebone High Street. It's the best kind of relationship as far as she's concerned, with no chance of catching her in the net of neediness and nappies.

I've barely warmed up Marco for my interrogation when Fi snatches him from under my nose and gathers us around the dining table. I make sure to keep close to him though, and jostle for prime position, while Tim chats with Harry and helps to organise drinks.

'Ooh, look at the cloth,' I coo, while stroking the tassels and silky velour. It's stunning and looks like something straight out of *Homes and Gardens*. Fi has placed a crystal bowl overflowing with roses atop an antique mirror as the table's centrepiece. And scattered tea candles in tiny little crystal-encrusted holders around the edge. All the crockery and cutlery is mismatched – so perfectly 'shabby chic' it's almost too good to have come from a charity shop. (Only Fi could pull that off so successfully.) And she has tied a delicate strand of different-coloured antique-glass beads around the stem of each wine glass – so that we know which is ours. 'The love is in the detail,' she always says.

Unfortunately, Fi's gastronomic skills are no match for her interior-design prowess. Especially when nerves and copious glasses of red wine get the better of her. The dinner has gone up in smoke. It's 10 p.m. and Liz, Rachel and I are in the kitchen trying to scrabble together a meal *à la Ready Steady Cook*. While Fi is at the table drinking with the boys. Except for Marco, who doesn't drink because he says it 'dulls the senses'.

'So, what do you think?' Rachel completely ignores Liz's frantic instructions and cuts straight to the chase about Marco.

'I think he's sweet – in an old-fashioned kind of way.'

Liz also thought our simian geography teacher in chocolate-brown desert boots was sweet.

'I Googled him before coming tonight. Not a thing. His surname didn't even register – makes me think he's an ex-crim with a false name,' says Rachel.

The voice of experience?

'At least he didn't come up as a minor-league porn star, like that boyfriend from Merthyr Tydfil with the exceptionally large, err . . . shoes!' I remind everyone with a cackle.

'Oh, you girls,' tuts Liz. 'He's well dressed, polite –'

'And has a hot body!' Rachel can always be relied upon for the essential information. 'Did you see his hands – *yum*.' She rolls the stem of her wine glass wistfully between her fingertips. 'And what about the accent? You can't deny it's bloody horny.'

'He has got that whole tall, dark and handsome Italian thing going for him,' I agree. When he speaks everything's so measured and calm. Almost sensual.

'But he does seem a little on the quiet side – you know, beautiful but boring.' Rachel winks.

'Oh, far from it,' I say. Though admittedly, I did have to go through everything from my pidgin Italian to holiday destinations and supermarket reward schemes before hitting the jackpot. 'He's crazy about shoes. Can you believe it? I couldn't stop him talking about them once he got started – he was *completely* captivating.' Quite honestly, the best dinner party conversation I've ever had.

'He's very attentive towards Fi, too. He practically hangs off her every word,' says Liz proudly. 'And they have a lot in common.'

She's got a point. Marco's quite a departure from Fi's usual fare – no Internet, lonely hearts or speed-dating. She met him in an antique shop in Church Street, while hunting for her latest acquisition. He happens to own the shop and is also an expert on eighteenth-century Venetian mirrors – Fi's Achilles heel. So really, that's about as good a start as she's had in a long time.

'Mmm. I don't know. I'm always suspicious of a good-looking guy in his early forties who says he's single *and* doesn't drink at a dinner party. He *must* be married,' Rachel pushes on. 'Then again, he's so damn polite. And this whole "shoe thing" he's got going – did you notice his shoes? He could be gay.'

Ah, yes. His shoes: John Lobbs. I spotted them a mile away – the luscious caramel swirl of soft brown kid leather, precise stitching and faultless styling.

You see, normally we can guarantee that any boyfriend of Fi's who wears decent shoes is either gay, married or a gangster. (Yes, she has dated them all!) Our theory being that no straight, single, law-abiding guy would fork out that sort of money on shoes – when it could be better spent on stereo speakers or iPods.

'It's a tricky one,' I admit. 'But he told me he's a fifth-generation cobbler from Milan. He's totally passionate about the craftsmanship of a shoe, and I'm sure couldn't care less about the brand or the logo.'

'Well! That clearly throws the gay theory out of the water,' says Rachel.

'He's set his sights on cracking the London shoe scene. He has a studio in the basement of his shop, where he works in-between customers and at night. Plus, he runs weekend shoe-making schools there. The antiques purely bankroll the shoes,' I say, more than impressing the girls with my intelligence-gathering. 'I think he's just a workaholic —'

'Who speaks fluent Italian, French, Spanish and English,' pipes in Liz, his new best friend.

'And speaking of shoes . . .' I'm now laughing at Rachel. 'What's with Dan the he-man and his *white* numbers?'

'Oh. I know.' She grimaces and takes a long drag of her cigarette. 'He's a back-up. Freddie had to fly to New York at the last minute.'

Thank goodness for that. I thought she was losing her touch.

Rachel takes another sip of wine.

'Well, I think Marco's too good to be true.'

The voice of envy?

'He's going to break her heart,' she concludes bleakly.

Mmm, maybe I'll have the Jaffa Cakes and teapot on standby — just in case.

4. Shoedown

Liz does a noble job with the meal. Though there's only so much you *can* do with baby poussin, anchovies, tomato ketchup and Marmite. And nothing can disguise the fact that by now everyone, bar Marco and me, is legless.

Dan has turned out not only to have the shoes of a dentist (albeit a funky one), but the conversational skills of one too. He's completely monopolised the table and finally goes one step too far when he pronounces, 'Women's high-heeled shoes are the scourge of modern-day society,' apparently accountable for an abundance of bodily ills.

Pah! My hackles rise.

'*Reeeeally . . .*'

Tim gives me the evil eye from across the table, and would kick me if he could reach.

'Absolutely. Women's and men's feet have exactly the same bone structure. The high-heeled shoe has no functional value whatsoever. Its sole purpose is to affix a permanent deformity, in order to make walking difficult and tiring.'

Rachel arches a semi-interested eyebrow.

It's shoe-enemy propaganda like this that I blame squarely for Tim's complete heel-neurosis during my pregnancy.

'Why, yes, I'd never thought of it like that before. They're a *safety hazard*,' says Harry, lest we forget, the health and safety officer. 'The stiletto heel decreases the surface area available for the creation of friction – between the foot and the walking surface. It's *so* simple.' He seems blurrily enamoured by his own powers of deduction. 'Slips and trips are the most common cause of major workplace injury in the UK, you know. And can even cause DEATH.'

Fi and Rachel simply burst into fits of laughter at his dramatic punchline, while Liz affectionately rolls her eyes skywards.

'It's no laughing matter,' says Harry. He and Dan frown disapprovingly.

Oh, so *that's* why I bought the pretty little flower-print mules with the scalloped edging and ten-centimetre heels. In order to self-mutilate or, better still, kill myself. Of course! I cannot believe I am hearing this.

'Can I be so bold as to suggest the wild and crazy notion that most shoe-loving women know *exactly* what they're doing when they put on a pair of skyscraper heels or toe-pinching pumps. They *love* them – the way they make them stand, walk, talk and feel.' I'm on a roll now. 'Do you honestly think we're going to be fazed by blisters, bunions or hammer-toes? We have, after all, evolved to survive bloody childbirth.'

'And Brazilian waxes,' Rachel nods ruefully.

I note that these weapons of female mass destruction kindly fund Dan's luxury London lifestyle. I'm furious. For some reason he's really wound me up.

The table is heading towards a full-scale shoe war, when Marco nervously clears his throat and enters the fray, his heavily accented English immediately attention-grabbing amidst the drunken babble.

'The high-heeled shoe: it is *so* much more than a mere physical construct. It is just as much a psychological and emotional extension of a woman's *being*, her *sensuality*, her *essence*,' he says tenderly, and then eyeballs Dan. 'A woman who wears a high-heeled shoe made by an artisan – respectful of the laws of physics and anatomy, fashion and sculpture – need not ever require your services, my friend. Nor should she ever need to, how do I say, *souffrir pour être belle* – suffer to be beautiful.'

Touché. And now he's my new best friend.

Rachel leans over to me and whispers, 'Who'd have thought Fi's new man would be the champion of shoe princesses!' At that, she slowly eases her chair back from the table and brazenly crosses one leg over the other (*à la* Sharon Stone) in front of Dan. The surreptitious flash of the dagger-thin heels executed with the subtlety of a gangster tapping his violin case. Leaving Dan in NO doubt as to where he's getting his dessert tonight.

He backs down like a cobra to its basket.

The last tea candle flickers out and an uneasy silence falls.

'I think we'd better be making a move, Jane,' slurs Tim, reaching for the mobile phone that he's kept in front of him all night like a badge of honour and handing me the car keys.

'Ohmygod.' Fi hiccups and lurches behind her chair. 'Not before we give you this. The girls pitched in and we bought you a little gift.' She hands me an exquisite white box. 'It is after all your coming-out night!' They've gone all sentimental on me? I'm intrigued.

'Something all nursing mothers should have,' Liz says knowledgeably.

It's heavenly. A soft, dusky-pink knitted shawl.

'The new season's must-have,' beams Fi. 'The Stella McCartney cable-knit cape.'

'The shop assistant said The Cat couldn't live without hers,' says Rachel, clearly thrilled by the celebrity endorsement.

Dan's ears prick up and my mood markedly darkens. (I simply don't recall being this emotionally flighty before Millie. Maybe I'm just tired and irritable.) You see, I presume she means The ten-minute-water-birth-my-tattoo-hurt-more-supermodel-supermum Cat. Catriona 'The Cat' — so called because of her impossible and completely natural feline beauty. She's the 'face' of Jolie Naturelle cosmetics and was all over the magazines this week. Most notably in a spread wearing little more than her trademark Christian Louboutin ocelot-print stilettos and her baby, Happy Sunshine (a boy the same age as Millie), sprawled across her bare sun-kissed midriff — completely ruining my mid-morning trash treat.

'It's for breast-feeding in public. You cover *things* up with it.' Rachel vaguely gestures with her hands over the breast area. 'Makes the whole experience more dignified, she said.'

'Hmph. Like she'd know,' I growl under my breath, while picturing Millie puking baby sick on it within two seconds of my wearing it. I can't help but wish they'd given me something useful — like a month's worth of cleaning vouchers. Or offered to do some babysitting, so that I could grab a nap, or get my hair cut.

No — this is not right. I'm an ungrateful cow. It's not their fault. I know I've done exactly the same, pre-Millie — given something deliciously expensive and dry-clean only.

Everyone's a little taken aback by my mean snarl, and I quickly pull my fragile ego into check.

'I love it — really, I do. Thanks.' Bizarrely I feel close to tears. 'It's just that anyone would think The Cat was the only woman on the planet with a baby at the moment. And the whole washboard-stomach-up-for-it-sex-kitten-mothering's-a-doddle thing. . . .'

'Oh! Don't go worrying yourself about *her*.' Fi's relief makes her slur. 'It took a team of four graphic artists fourteen hours to get those photos fit for print – airbrushing, digital touch-ups, you name it. Apparently, she looked more like what the cat dragged in.' She cackles uncontrollably.

I stop dead in my marshmallowy-mummy-tummy tracks.

'How do you know?'

'Trash Queenz,' Fi laughs, as if I've been on another planet. Which technically, I have. 'You know, the blog dedicated to all the behind-the-scenes goss about the trash mags.'

More blank stares from me.

'Everyone at work's hooked on it. First thing we log on to each morning – TrashQueenz.com – with a "z" on the end of Queen. If you put an "s" you'll get some hard-rock band.' This inspires her to do a little air-guitar routine. (Boy, is she going to have one monstrous hangover in the morning.)

I feel a warm glow. Thank God for girlfriends, is all I can say! I vow to rediscover my love of trash magazines armed with the knowledge that the 'dirt' is only a mouse click away.

Dan, meanwhile, is gleefully bringing the boys up to speed on the many 'assets' of The Cat over a glass of port in the lounge.

Rachel's suddenly animated,

'If you're into blogs, I've another that you *must* try: Shoe-Princess.com. Now, I know what you're thinking: every upmarket prostitute worth her salt's doing a blog these days – it's all so dotcom passé. But I assure you, she's divine. Oh, and she's not a prostitute – well, who cares anyway? Just go see.'

Needless to say, I simply cannot wait to meet the Shoe Princess when Millie is asleep tomorrow too.

My happy thoughts are short-lived, though, as I spy Tim motioning frantically across the room at me – slapping his hands against his chest as if he's swatting insects.

Finally, I get it. He wants me to look down – at my chest – or rather at my Dolly-Parton-on-steroids breasts that have taken on a life of their own since Millie. Contrary to all expectations, rather than enjoying my newfound assets, Tim is truly scared of them.

I glance down and see two giant wet lily pads on my pale jersey top. I fear that, with all my expressing today, I must have tricked my breasts into thinking I've now got an enormous baby to feed on the hour. I can't believe this actually happens in *real* life – I was certain it was a joke made up to mock nursing mums. Yet another bizarre bodily experience to add to my growing list.

I'm immediately grateful for the cape's covering-up capabilities and, with every painful minute that passes, wonder if it's physically possible for human breasts to explode. With Millie at the forefront of our minds, Tim and I are suddenly in a rush to leave.

We try to thank Fi for a lovely evening, but she's too busy dancing and singing incoherently to the deafening strains of her favourite Duran Duran CD. Marco manages to nab her as she whizzes by and, drawing her in a close embrace, commences a soft slow waltz. She instantly succumbs to the subtle rhythm and collapses on to his chest – with her eyes closed and an enormous smile from ear to ear.

'You *must* get home to Millie,' says Marco. 'We'll be fine.' He lovingly kisses the top of Fi's head and motions us towards the door.

Dear Liz and Harry offer to stay and help tidy up, while Marco puts Fi to bed. Rachel and Dan head for the clubs. And we beat a hasty retreat homewards.

We're greeted at the front door by a frazzled Mum cradling Millie, who has not slept more than ten minutes, or taken any milk from the bottle all evening.

Oh dear. Oh bloody dear.

I eventually slide into bed next to a comatose Tim, our bodies interlocking in our own human jigsaw. My head is heavy on the pillow as I warm my cold (and unusually sore) feet between his.

I fall asleep quickly – sandwiched between Tim's heavy breathing and Millie's snuffles. Utterly content. And shoeless. Who'd have thought?

Are you a Shoe Princess?

Have You Ever . . .

☐ Been frog-marched into your bedroom by your partner, during heated discussions about finances, to count the number of shoes in your possession?

☐ Displayed your favourite shoes on a mantelpiece or kept your wardrobe doors open so that you could admire them 24/7?

☐ Bought a pair of shoes while on holiday, and ever after referred to them as your 'Berlin shoes' etc?

Do You . . .

☐ Remember more details about the shoes in your wardrobe than the men you've dated?

☐ Find it impossible to walk past a shoe shop with a 'SALE' sign in the window?

☐ Believe that stilettos are not a shoe but a way of life?

☐ Own shoes that you have not worn because you genuinely don't want to spoil them?

☐ Always get given beautiful handmade birthday cards with shoes on them – the favourites of which you keep in a special box?

☐ Find that buying a new pair of shoes always makes you happy?

Would You Rather . . .

☐ Share a toothbrush with a friend than share a pair of your shoes?

☐ Walk barefoot if caught in a sudden rain shower than ruin your shoes – especially if they're suede?

☐ Move house than get rid of any of your shoes?

☐ Have a lifetime of happy shoe memories than a pair of perfect, non-mutilated feet? What are feet for anyway?

If you've ticked ALL of the boxes . . .
Welcome, my darling subject, to my fabulous shoedom!

And remember, if Madonna said that her Manolos are
'as good as sex . . . and last longer', they are.

Email me to share your:

SHOE STORIES – memories; favourites; dreams; dilemmas.
SHOES IN THE NEWS – snippets that catch your eye.
SHOE ALERTS – designer shoe sales; shoe exhibits.

5. Clever Clogs

'IT WAS genius, pure genius,' enthuses Fi, as she thrusts a bottle of bubbly into my arms.

I must admit, it *was* a personal career high point – sending the bid for the Jolie Naturelle contract in a Jimmy Choo shoebox.

For as well as being best friends since school, Fi and I are workmates at the global insurance monolith Asquith & Brown – as client-relationship managers. (All the buzz of wearing smart suits and mock-crock power points, yet none of the tedium of actually being a lawyer.) Fi's been with the company for ages, while I only recently got my well-shod feet under the desk next to hers.

The Jolie Naturelle bid was our first project together and we were determined to make a splash. Ironically, it also became my last hurrah before going on maternity leave – well, four-months-at-home-without-pay maternity break. As I unwittingly signed on the dotted line with Asquith & Brown while two weeks pregnant – failing to qualify for the new paid maternity-leave provisions. (Such rotten luck.)

'Anyway, it was hardly rocket science,' I say. We'd desperately needed to make our bid stand out from the crowd, as it was common knowledge that all the competing insurers had cut their final figures to within millimetres of one another.

And that's where the skill of the client-relationship manager came into play. Of the dozens of staff members at Jolie Naturelle we'd had to schmooze over the months, one thing had become crystal clear. They were mainly female, late twenties to early thirties, bright, well-groomed and ambitious. With a real sense of fun.

I had suggested to Fi that we slash the wording of the bid (without telling the consultants), roll it up in delicious crackly paper, tie it with a crimson, double-satin ribbon, and send it in one of Mr Choo's shoeboxes (from my personal collection, no less). It was do or die.

Now, three months after I left work to have Millie (I can't believe I worked right up to the week before she was born. I really cringe when I think of the tightrope I walked – doing the typical first-time-mum-working-girl thing and refusing to accept that I was different) my willing accomplice is here to tell me that our little shoebox has whizzed through the many layers of hoops at Jolie Naturelle to land us the contract. We won!

I'm over the moon. Truly. It's actually quite nice to be reminded of my pre-Millie job – one thing at least that I know I'm good at.

I come down from my high enough to notice that Fi's looking a little shocked, and I realise that the flat is a tip. Millie's in a washed-out, slightly too small Babygro and I'm in my tracksuit and slippers. The TV's blaring – I'm glued to the home-make-over cable TV channel, to which I've become perversely addicted – and Tim's sprawled on the sofa sleeping off last night's Comedy Club team-bonding session in honour of his new boss, Alex, thanks to a major restructuring programme at the bank. (To be honest, the IT department seems to get a new boss every six months.)

For my part, I'm *more* than a little taken aback to hear that my desk and my entire caseload of clients have been taken over (by Simon, no less). What did I expect, I guess? So much for my fervent belief in my own indispensability.

After filling me in on the finer details of the big Jolie Naturelle win – and of course all the office, Shoe Princess and Trash Queenz goss – for the first time Fi broaches the subject of my return to work in the new year.

'One step at a time,' I reassure her unconvincingly. For while the thought of getting dressed in a suit and heels and reading the newspaper on the tube, followed by sitting at my calm, organised desk with a cup of coffee in hand, is *immensely* appealing, I'm yet to get my brain around the logistics of actually making it happen. It seems nothing short of masochistic to return to work on the sum total of four hours' sleep a night. (No man I've ever worked with would contemplate it, that's for sure.) And then of course there's the small issue of physically leaving Millie . . .

I smokescreen my uncharacteristic fluffiness with a change of topic that's sure to please.

'So, how's Marco, anyway?' I know she's dying to tell. 'Is it official? Are you dating yet?'

'No. Well, at least I don't think so. I don't want to ask him, anyway. Just in case I jinx it.'

'But you see him practically every day, don't you?' And she's always telling me it's the best sex she's ever had.

'Yeah, yeah, yeah. I'm just not sure if he's ready to move on to the next stage yet. I don't want to pressure him.'

'Sure,' I agree reassuringly. I'm simply happy that she's happy.

The doorbell rings and Fi lets Kate in (she's here for her regular aunt's Saturday-morning frolic with Millie) and brings me a letter that had slipped under the hall mat.

I hold the solitary envelope. The air-mail sticker and maple-leaf stamp send a shiver down my spine. It's the first week of December, and our first Christmas card has arrived.

This is no ordinary card, either. It is Aunt Margaret's – the official matriarch and family scribe of the Meadows clan. She is Tim's dad's eldest sister, who emigrated to Canada in 1956. And her card is always the first to arrive.

I will say one thing about Tim's family: they may never win the Waltons' Nuclear Family of the Year Award, but they are prolific and generous correspondents. He's forever getting letters from his mum and dad in Spain (they've got a retirement villa there) and emails from his brother in New York (where he's a museum curator). Must be all those years at boarding school. And thanks to Aunt Margaret's enclosed festive news-letter, we'll know all there is to know about most of Tim's blood relatives. The six-page epic is the pinnacle of her year's meticulous investigative journalism.

I place the card in pride of place at the centre of the mantelpiece, wondering when I am ever going to get around to our cards, let alone Christmas shopping.

Kate does a whizz round with the vacuum cleaner and folds the washing in my bulging basket (she got Mum's cleaning genes that I missed out on), while I gratefully take the oppor-tunity to play ladies with Fi and Millie.

'You really should be putting her on her tummy more,' Kate observes. And then gently rolls Millie over, placing some toys in front of her head as an enticement.

'She's three months now, and needs to develop her neck and upper-body muscles.'

Kate has made a recent point of pulling me kicking and screaming on to the mothering train. Her expertise comes from spending her gap year (and at least one weekend a month there-after) volunteering at a small shelter for homeless single mums.

Fi and I, rather less nobly, chose to spend our year of 'self-discovery and personal development' packing boxes in a tiny shoe village just outside Venice (that's where she developed her antique-mirror fixation too) in exchange for free board, Italian lessons (language, cooking, the lot) and more importantly access to cheap designer shoes. Let's just say we were the only ones on campus to totter along to our first lecture in rhinestone-encrusted slingback stilettos. An impossibly high student shoe standard we were quite unable to sustain.

Though I am rather proud of the fact that at least we didn't squander our gap year in a pair of those hideous rubber-sandal-come-flip-flop things with Velcro fastenings the size of half a Michelin tyre, gamely dodging toenail clippings and verrucas in some festering youth hostel. *Euch.*

Millie's lying face down on her mat and looks like a newborn foal in an animal documentary – valiantly kicking and flailing. Only she doesn't miraculously push up on splayed legs and trot away. She falls flat on her nose, time and again, finally letting out an almighty howl.

I leapfrog Kate's disapproving glare to pick her up, and head for the kitchen.

'Let's have some tea. I made a date cake last night.'

Kate's mildly impressed that I've at least managed to do that.

As I walk out, I notice that Tim's awake and has been watching us. I also can't help but notice his face change from a post-big-night-out liverish greeny-yellow to a ghostly white. And suddenly it all comes rushing back to me . . .

1 a.m. Unmistakable chug of black cab up our street; stops with squeaky brakes outside of flat; husband stumbles out and slams door; black cab chugs off into dead of night; front door opens and closes with the elegance of a hippo on heat; more hippo tiptoeing down hallway; kitchen lights turn on; banging and crashing of doors and plates; ten minutes later husband falls

into bed – pores reeking of alcohol – rambling incoherently that he 'really, really, really, really, really' loves me and Millie . . . with breath that smells of DATE CAKE.

'Well, it technically *was* my dinner,' he says sheepishly.

I am *so* not impressed.

'I tell you what,' says Kate, ever the peacemaker. 'Why don't we all head down to Queen's Park – Tim and I can take Millie for a stroll and see if she'll have a bottle for her next feed, and you and Fi can stop off at the café for a girlie chat.'

She really is an angel.

'That sounds great,' I say, ignoring Tim.

'Oh, before we go, I promised Alison at work that I'd pass this on to you.' Fi produces a crumpled plastic bag and plonks it by Tim on the sofa. 'Though I can't imagine what you'd *ever* want from her.' She laughs heartily.

I don't.

The dull winter duvet of low grey cloud has momentarily given way to a sliver of crisp blue sky, and everyone seems to be making a dash for the park. We walk by rows of prettily painted terraced houses basking in the sun – the net curtains of the old-timers shoulder-to-shoulder with the frosted glass and wooden shutters of their gentrifying neighbours. But the mention of Alison's name has completely thrown me.

Alison worked on the Jolie Naturelle bid, and was by implication important to me. It was my prerogative to know exactly what she was doing and when she was doing it. Alison also irritated me. A lot. Due largely to her heart-stopping ability to scrape through *every* deadline with only milliseconds to spare.

I tolerated her chaotic existence because she's an excellent analyst. The best on the team, by far. But when I think back now to the laughs that Fi and I used to have at her expense, I am ashamed. At our bitchiness. Our basic ignorance.

Our game went something like this: each morning, we would have a bet on Alison. Just between the two of us. (Although it soon became common knowledge on the fourth floor.) The person with the most wins at the end of the week treated the other to a lunchtime sushi the following week. And so it went.

The betting hinged upon Alison's arrival at work, which usually occurred any time after 9.30 a.m. And every day it was the same. The ting of the lift's doorbell would announce the imminent arrival of hurricane Alison. Her detritus of dog-eared files and mishmash of bags and coats led a clumsy trail directly to the desk next to mine and Fi's.

We'd all exchange surreptitious knowing little glances. Of course, we'd been in since 8 a.m. But the best was to come.

The secondary goal of our competition was to be the first to spot the ubiquitous smudge of baby sick, dried milk, jammy fingerprints or honey-glazed snot on the right-back shoulder of her suit jacket (or anywhere else).

A task made increasingly difficult when Fi swore she heard Alison telling our office manager that she didn't dry-clean her suits any more. A fact that nearly made us wretch. (Alison had apparently considered buying out her local dry-cleaner in lieu of her monthly dry-cleaning bills.) So a bonus-point system was introduced for differentiating new from old stains.

The best day, as far as we were concerned, was when she turned up in mismatching shoes. I promise this is true. One black and one navy. *And not even the same style.* We both agreed that we would personally rather have feigned an epileptic seizure in the lift than hobble into the office in such a state.

We dined out on that one for weeks.

And do you know what the genuinely terrifying point to all of this is?

We *really* thought we were clever.

Stiletto Stamina

I'm perplexed by some bad press surrounding stilettos of late. May I gently remind my gorgeous subjects of the important role they play in our lives. Not unlike that of an illicit lover: the melding of two into one is at once irrational, adventurous, exhilarating yet ultimately (and consistently) not for long-term use.

And that is OK.

As my dear Swiss finishing-school tutor always said, 'To avoid disappoint-ment, one should never expect commitment from an electrifying lover nor comfort from a pair of spikes.'

So toughen up and enjoy the ride!

Well-heeled

There's nothing worse than standing behind a SP on an elevator and glancing down to her beautiful shoes, only to notice that the heels are worn through, and the backs are scraped and scuffed. It is strongly suggested that SPs invest in a pair of driving shoes to be left in the car at all times, and make the acquaintance of a skilled shoe-repairer.

6. Arch Enemy

ONCE at the park, Fi takes microsips from the polystyrene coffee cup, as if sampling rat poison. It was always going to be dicey bringing her to a family-friendly café – but I figure she has to be exposed to them sooner or later.

I'm patiently listening to her dissect every word that Marco has ever uttered but my head is on a swivel. Each time a baby cries, I look around thinking it's Millie. Suddenly, I spy Kate marching up the path towards us. Without Tim or Millie. And frowning. My throat dries and my heart goes all fluttery.

'You'd better come. Tim's in a bit of a state. Millie still won't take the bottle and he's talking to some woman who has really put the wind up him.'

We all rush out of the café and follow the sound of Millie's bellowing to where Tim is being held captive by an impeccably groomed woman in a black fur-trimmed Escada ski jacket, and black skinny jeans that are tucked into ultra-pointy-toed, black-leather knee-high boots. She's leaning on a red Bugaboo pushchair with a flock of those psychedelic mobiles that promise future Mensa membership dangling from the hood.

I hurriedly take off my beanie and try to fluff my hair from its matted mass, all the while wishing I'd changed out of my tracksuit. My face feels hot and blotchy from running in the cold.

'This is Victoria,' says Tim. He looks like a deer caught in headlights. 'Her baby girl, Allegra, was born on the same day as Millie.'

'Oh, how lovely,' I say. Tim virtually throws Millie at me as I try to hack a way through my layers of clothes with one hand.

'You're *feeding* her,' Victoria observes, with just the right amount of voice inflection and eyebrow gesticulation – in case I didn't realise this was code for *breast-feeding*. She nods approvingly. 'I couldn't help but notice your husband and sister struggling to give her the bottle – if she won't take it now, she never will. Rod for your own back, I'm afraid.'

Great.

'What centile is Millie on?' Tim asks. 'Allegra's on the eightieth.'

'Ninetieth,' corrects Victoria.

'Um, I don't know. I mean, I'm not sure.' I really can't remember.

'And did you know that there's a new nursery by the park – InfinityPlusOne – for gifted children. Have you got Millie's name down there . . . I think we should put her name down . . .' Tim is almost breathless with panic.

All I care about right now is feeding Millie. Kate's packing away the ill-fated bottle, and Fi's texting Marco – both of them politely keeping out of the eye of the storm.

Victoria asks more questions about teething, neck-control, rolling and sleeping – all of which I seem to be doing wrong – before flying off on her broomstick.

I could weep.

Tim's in full-on rant mode now, and decides to rub my nose in it a little more, bombarding me with questions, stats and more bloody stats.

'Did you know that there is not one nursery within a ten-mile radius of us with a vacancy? Or a waiting list of fewer than thirty kids? And that they're staffed by underpaid sixteen-year-old girls of questionable IQ and body piercings! Victoria's friend in Notting Hill had to provide her nanny with a new Peugeot 206 and a flat for her sole use – otherwise she wouldn't have got anyone decent. We can't compete with that! How have we not thought of this? We need to redo our sums – maybe we *can* survive on just my wage for a year or so . . . Do you use the sling much? Eskimos, whose mothers carry them around in slings for the first two years, have higher than average IQs . . .' Blah de blah de bloody blah.

Fi's in shock.

Kate's holding Tim by the arm and comforting him.

I've zoned out completely.

And Millie, thank goodness, is blissfully asleep on a full tummy of milk.

Bloody Victoria and her bloody perfect baby.

Mmm . . . Maybe I should have taken more notice of Alison's advice on organising childcare, and not spent my entire pregnancy coordinating Millie's nursery with her silver-lamé baby booties?

From:	Jane (home)
To:	Fi (work)
Subject:	RE: Team Xmas dinner – The Cube

Dearest Fi,

Thanks so much for coming and sharing the good news about Jolie Naturelle last Saturday. Really appreciated it. (Sorry haven't emailed earlier – have had run of horror nights!) Thanks too for including me in the team Xmas dinner – thought you'd never ask, in fact. (It's a bit tricksy, being on maternity leave, isn't it?) Needless to say, I would LOVE to come.

Slight problem with the date, though – no one to look after Millie. Tim's in Bangalore for work and rest of family busy with own Christmas functions. So . . . wondering if I could come with Millie for the pre-dinner drinks – should be pretty quiet. And then we'll see how we go after that. If Millie's in fine form, she could very well sleep in her baby capsule (it lies down flat) in the corner of the restaurant or even in her sling.

Jane
xx

I open the front door to take Millie for a walk and find a parcel with a note on it:

Dropped by on way to work, but didn't want to disturb you. My boss thought you might like to borrow this for your team Xmas dinner next week. She said she couldn't have you worshipping at the altar of modern design in your saliva-soaked Baby Björn sling. Enjoy! (And sorry again that I can't help with babysitting.) Kate x

For such a fashion freak my big sister never ceases to amaze me. I'm truly humbled, and open up the parcel.

I cannot believe what I am seeing. There is definitely NO way Kate could have known what was in here.

I hold up what is basically a chunk of incredibly fashionable, extortionately expensive and *very dead* baby lamb. It's gorgeous, and naturally I try it on for size. I can't help but giggle and tell Millie how fabulous she is going to look, bobbing along in her funky designer sling.

I feel almost Cat-like!

There's a little bit of **Shoe Princess** in all of us, my darlings — **Shoe Are You?**

THE SP

This princess (usually an international supermodel, society beauty) totally understands the sexual cocktail of upmarket shoes and good grooming, and uses it to ensnare her impossibly handsome and wealthy husband/lover/partner. She could not tell you how many pairs of shoes she owns — but it would be in the hundreds. Her maid may have a better idea, as she is the only one allowed to touch them. She only ever ambulates cab-to-door and enjoys the jet-set lifestyle. The only 'casual shoes' you will ever spy her in are her high-heeled towelling Jimmy Choo pedicure-wedge flip-flops. She often has personal relationships with some of the biggest shoe designers on the planet, and thinks nothing of having shoes couriered to her home direct from Italy for special occasions. She considers pedicures (French, of course) more important than food.

Cosmo SP

The thoroughly dedicated-to-the-cause, childless working girl who utterly adores shoes. She is known to ring up her best friend on her mobile in the midst of a shoe-sale pandemonium, seeking permission to blow her budget on a must-have pair of silver Sonia Rykiel 3-inch spikes. She always owns a pair of red Dorothy shoes and lucky first-date and job-interview shoes. She takes shoe shopping very seriously, and has been known to shop for 6 hours straight in a quest to find the right pair.

Fashionista SP

Is happy to wear her vertiginous cheetah-print platform wedges with her strapless sundress on a cold and drizzly summer's afternoon in London. All because *Vogue* ran a series of pictures of The Cat wearing them in St Tropez. Her mantra is: 'No pain, no gain.' She has her name on at least three shoe waiting lists at any one time. She doesn't do white trainers — unless at the gym — as it would be like wearing Crimplene trousers.

There's more to come! Or better still, send in your own . . .

7. Click, Clack, Clomp

From: Tim (Bangalore)
To: Jane (home)
Subject: RE: Xmas Cards

We must send Xmas cards. What will Aunt Margaret say? ☺ T

OK. We appear to have a problem.

You see, sending Christmas cards just seems to happen by magic in our relationship. Sort of like the sheets on the bed getting changed. And the black scum line in the bath disappearing.

Hmm . . . He's seen me squat, butt-naked, giving birth to Millie – I think he can handle one more home truth, wife to husband: the Christmas card fairy is a little busy this year.

From: Jane (home)
To: Tim (Bangalore)
Subject: RE: RE: Xmas Cards

Tim, I can't believe I have to spell this out to you: I AM A ZOMBIE.

In case you hadn't noticed, I'm SO exhausted from caring for Millie 24/7 and doing the domestic run of the house, that I have the memory and attention span of a one-celled amoeba. I backed the car into a fence this morning, and put my mobile phone through a cycle of the washing machine. But all is OK – was doing 1 mile/hr in the car at the time, and the phone still works (Ha!). On top of this, I have tonsillitis. And you are in Bangalore, AGAIN.

I believe the armed forces call it torture (or is it death?) by sleep deprivation. Cut me some slack, will you? I simply cannot do the Christmas cards this year. I'm sure people will understand.

Jane

xx

From: Jane (home)
To: Tim (Bangalore)
Subject: RE: RE: RE: Xmas Cards

OK, if you feel that strongly about the bloody cards, why don't YOU do them? I've attached OUR Christmas card list. You can do the necessary edits for this year – changes of address, births, deaths, marriages, divorces, trial separations, reconciliations, new boyfriends/girlfriends, sex changes (and no, I'm not being petulant; remember your dear Uncle Alan who became Aunt Ellen in 2005) – pretty standard stuff.

And then write them – each night after work and in your lunch hour. Polish them off on the flight home from India, perhaps. I like to make sure that I write a personal message in each card – a little summary of the year's events relevant to each person/couple/ family. We normally send out about 60–65 cards.

Don't bother calling tonight, as I'm out at my team Xmas dinner. (Should give me enough time to calm down too.) J

I bid farewell to our trusty chauffeur, Javid, from Reliable Minicabs, and totter off around the corner in my favourite Patrick Coxes with pink-ribbon ties on the sides. My back twitches, but I ignore it and stride confidently along the pavement – Millie in front, baby capsule in one hand and nappy bag in the other.

With each click-clack of my heels and swish of my skirt, I feel alive again. It's great to be back. In decent shoes. In town. I really cannot stop smiling – how proud Clotilde would be if she could see me now.

I kiss Millie on the top of her bobbing downy head. Nothing is going to spoil our night. Not Daddy and his festering festive Christmas cards. Not Mary sodding Poppins the health visitor sticking her gargantuan no-name trainers in our front door, asking why we haven't been to her Birkenstock-wearing-placenta-eating new-mothers' group yet. Not the fact that I look like an actress from an old *Carry On* film squished into my pre-Millie clothes, all rolls-of-fat-poking-through-too-tight-fabric five foot four of me. Not even your explosive poo and complete outfit change in the back of the minicab and accompanying £80 fine for loitering on a yellow line. No, my dear sweet little baby girl, this is *our* night – at The Cube. Your very first experience of a glittering West End restaurant – with your mum.

And what an experience it promises to be. Tim and I had dinner here just before I found out that I was pregnant. It had only been open a few weeks and was the talk of the town – oozing stark white ultra-minimalist chic.

The vibe is palpable before we even enter the building. I desperately want to look around to see if I can see anyone famous, but decide to opt for the casual I-go-to-these-sort-of-places-all-the-time swagger – which is less than convincing with a baby attached to my front.

The double glass doors open and, oh? It's black. Everything's black. Still the odd twinkling of chrome. But no giant plastic Rubik's Cube hanging from the ceiling or enormous white artworks splashed with large multicoloured dots. I do a double-take and wonder if I'm in the right place.

As I leave all the baby gear at reception, my casual investigations reveal that I am indeed in the right place, but that 'black is the new white'. The Rubik's Cube was seen as too Thatcherite for the 'now generation' (is it X, Y or Z?) and is being replaced with an ice-cube sculpture next week. Apparently all part of a rebranding exercise which will also see the name changed to The Ice Cube – representing fluidity, clarity and individuality.

Gosh – I've only been out of circulation for how long? I feel positively ancient.

I make my way down a wide, steep glass staircase into the basement restaurant. All the walls are covered from ceiling to floor with flat computer screens – each one showing a different YouTube clip. A handful of people are seated casually in Philippe Starck Ghost chairs around the sunken (literally – in water) bar in the middle of the room. The bar staff are bopping away to the muffled sounds of an ultra-hip soundtrack, setting up shop for the night.

I spy Fi and the work crew in the far-left corner, and make my way over.

Actually, they're pretty hard to miss – it's 6 p.m. and the guys are on to the tequila already, and having a hilarious time of it.

Simon, already smashed, keeps asking, 'Why did we win Jolie Naturelle?'

And then the others answer in a high-pitched voice, clearly trying to mimic The Cat (from her Jolie Naturelle TV ads), 'Because there's a goddess in all of us!' Accompanied by much pretend flicking of luscious manes of hair, and more hooting and cheering and downing of drinks by all.

(Were it not for our team winning the Jolie Naturelle account, and being crowned the top profit-centre in the company this year, we'd most certainly be enjoying the more downmarket ambience of our usual £10-a-head-Balti-restaurant Christmas bash in Covent Garden.)

Fi rushes over and gives me a huge, wide-armed hug (around Millie's sling).

'I'm SO glad you could make it!' she screeches, before putting a hand over her mouth after noticing that Millie is asleep. 'Ooh, she looks so cute in her scrummy little leather and sheepskin . . .' She's clearly struggling to describe what she's seeing. 'Babybag . . . with straps.'

'It's a sling,' I laugh heartily. 'Bill Amberg, no less. Kate's boss kindly lent it to me.' I do a little twirl for her. She's sufficiently impressed and can't resist stroking Millie's leg, which is dangling like a floppy rabbit's ear out of the corner.

'Jane Meadows. Well, well, well. If my eyes don't deceive me!' Our boss, Richard, grabs a glass of champagne from a passing waiter and gives it to me. 'My star recruit. We thought you'd got lost in nappy valley,' he guffaws. 'You haven't brought little Molly in to see us yet – unlike Alison and her merry gang.' More guffaws.

'Millie. Her name's Millie, actually.' It doesn't seem the moment also to tell him that she's named after the great Emmeline Pankhurst, and is in fact asleep right under his disinterested nose.

Richard is not, shall we say, the most *liberated* of men. As long as his wife has his clothes washed, ironed and laid out for him at the start of the day, and meat 'n' three veg on the table at the end, she is fulfilling her role in society. Paradoxically, he is a really exciting guy to work for − a brilliant mind. And incredibly motivating.

'I've got a lot lined up for you, Jane. This Jolie Naturelle account, it's bigger than big.' It's no secret that his promotion and stock-option package are riding on the back of it too.

He motions the team to gather near Fi and me.

'Everybody, I want to propose a toast − to our dynamic duo − to Jane and Fi!'

'And their bloody brilliant shoebox,' chips in Simon. 'To Jimmy!'

After the toast, it's business as usual.

'Now, ladies . . . I spent the morning with Véronique at Jolie Naturelle HQ yesterday. We've got *big* plans.' Big seems to be the word of the night. Richard pulls out his BlackBerry, checks some emails and then turns to me. 'I want you on the ground running − day one. Do whatever you have to do, to keep Véronique happy. I've upped your travel budget − I want you to cover *all* European work hubs, concentrating on HQ in Paris, of course. No expense spared. By God, if she wants you to floss her teeth or paint her toenails − you'll be there to do it. One hundred and ten per cent − that's our girl!'

Cue more excited squeals and air-punches from the team. (Everyone except Alison, of course, who has made a mad sprint home to sort out the babysitter.)

Now, the old me would have found Richard's little 'call to arms' nothing short of orgasmic. Pinpoint attention to detail, ruthless efficiency and unquestioned commitment were my calling cards. My job was my life.

But the new me feels a little queasy. I can't help wondering exactly how I'm going to wipe Millie's backside and Véronique's at the same time.

Though it seems Véronique is the least of my worries right now. I've just spotted Alison, making her way down the staircase.

Now that the big post-Christmas sales are sneakily starting earlier each year, this is the perfect time for the humble subjects of my shoedom to restock shoe supplies:

The SP Guide to Shoe-sale Shopping

1. Repeat after me: 'I am a (your shoe size). Not a (two sizes bigger) or a (one and a half sizes smaller). Not even a (size smaller). I am a (your shoe size). No matter how divine the shoes. OK, if you really, really love them, buy them no matter what the size. And the matching handbag wouldn't go astray either!

2. Plan your trip wisely, and always arrive early. I know, queue – no matter how common it makes one feel.

3. Wear thin tights and comfy mules or loafers – not glam, but easier when trying on shoes in a hurry.

4. Take a handbag with straps that go across your body – to keep both hands free for shoe-fossicking. And to country mice in town for the day, always pack your Longchamp fold-up travel tote in your handbag – to escort your precious cargo home in.

5. If in a large department store like Harrods (whose shoe sale is phenomenal and an annual must-do for shoe princesses) target key designers, rather than float around aimlessly – you'll get pummelled in the crush otherwise.

6. Always be polite and courteous and never snatch shoes from another shoe princess. Ever.

7. Yes, you really do need satin lime-green stilettos and purple ankle boots.

8. Chant the mantra: 'Why buy one pair of sale shoes when I can technically afford to buy five?'

9. Have fun and hopefully you will find that couture stiletto which you would never have been able to afford otherwise.

10. And, last but not least, have lunch with a girlfriend to ogle and admire your newfound sole mates. (And help justify the amount of money you've spent!)

8. Sidestepping

The team's clearly out for a big night, with food not high on the agenda. My vision of Millie sleeping blissfully in the corner of the restaurant while I delight in the ultimate haute cuisine experience has disintegrated before my very eyes.

Millie's been awake for about an hour now, and shows no sign of going back to sleep. As long as I keep moving, she's happy to stay in the sling. Which is lucky for me. As I've been spending all my time sidestepping and dancing my way around the bar, catching up with people in ever-increasing states of inebriation, in an act of abject cowardice: avoiding Alison.

But eventually, I swivel around in response to a friendly tap on the shoulder, and come unceremoniously face to face with her and her sensible brown rubber-soled court shoes.

'I am *so, so sorry*,' I want to say. But the words get stuck somewhere deep in the toes of my shoes, and I affix a stupid grin to my face.

I *really* want to apologise to her. And tell her that I now understand why she mistakenly put on mismatching shoes: because she has to get up at dawn (and most likely several times throughout the night), dress in the dark, and then single-handedly (her husband has to be at his desk by 7.30 a.m.) shuffle one baby to a childminder, one toddler to nursery and the other child to school, jump on the tube and be seated at her desk sometime around 9.30 a.m. If she's lucky.

But I just stand, frozen with guilt and shame, while Alison makes a huge fuss of how pretty and alert and healthy Millie looks. She's genuinely excited to finally meet her, and is keen to know if I found the small bag of things that she sent with Fi useful.

Oh? I'd completely forgotten about them. They're probably still by the sofa or, most likely, underneath it. I fib, and say they were invaluable.

Alison relieves me of my misery by making a break for a gap in the bar queue, and I unwittingly find myself alone in a sea of suits. I shuffle along and find a quietish spot, and stand still for a moment, gently rocking my hips from side to side to pacify an increasingly fidgety Millie.

As I think about Alison, it all of a sudden dawns on me: maybe Richard isn't the anti-feminist dinosaur, after all? The truth of the matter is he treats us three girls exactly the same as the twelve guys on the team. *Exactly*. He simply couldn't give a toss who has children.

Richard only wants the old me. The Millie-less me who thought she knew it all. And had done it all. Beaten the men at their own game. Lived the corporate lifestyle. The travel, the boozy lunches, the deadlines, the buzz. Who was what her *Cosmo* foremothers had raised her to be. A career girl. A success.

But I hadn't beaten the men. I had just become one.

It's so clear now: I love work, but work doesn't love me – or rather, the-mother-of-a-three-and-a-half-month-old baby-me, returning to work in a few weeks' time. If I don't want to lose my rung on the ladder.

Hell, I even helped to create the Richards of this world.

The war is far from bloody over. (I have a sudden urge to burn any feminist book I own not penned by a mother.)

Then again, maybe Alison is the modern-day Emmeline? And I am a spineless copout, dithering about even getting back to first base. And not sure I particularly want to anyway. I can't believe I am thinking this.

Mmm . . . this is big. And more than a little unsettling.

It's now 8 p.m. and Millie is tired, hungry and irritable. That makes two of us – my head hurts and my throat is sore. Though I'm sure the fact that I've been up since 4.30 a.m. and had nothing more than a glass of champagne and three morsels of sushi since lunchtime isn't helping either.

Unnoticed by the team, Millie and I slip out. It takes us a good ten minutes to hack a path through the jungle of revellers packed cheek to jowl, and filling the whole restaurant and bar.

After I've collected all our bits from the front desk, the concierge walks outside with me to hail a black cab. We're immediately faced with a large number of men in dark anoraks, milling around like an army of ants. Some talking on mobiles. Others huddled in small groups. Quite a few of them are playing cards on the pavement. There are even more across the road.

It's a little intimidating.

The concierge picks up on my anxiety.

'Paparazzi,' he says glibly, and shoos a few of them from the main entrance area.

Of course. Duh! I now notice the massive cameras hanging from their necks.

I've never seen anything like this before.

Must be one *major* celeb for this amount of attention. My mind's ticking overtime with thoughts of who we might run into – Robbie? Elton? Or maybe Sting and Trudy checking into the hotel to practise some tantric sex?

Ooooh, this is SO exciting. I can't wait to tell Fi!

I ask the concierge if he knows who they're here to snap. His eyes widen and he grins broadly.

'The Cat!'

Make my day.

After a long bubble bath and much soul-searching I go to my shoe cupboard and do the blindingly obvious. I pack all my smart, high-heeled work shoes away at the back: 'Goodbye my little friends . . . Parting is such sweet sorrow . . . but remember this is just for now, and definitely not for ever . . .'

From:	Jane (home)
To:	Fi (work)
Subject:	RE: The Cube – What happened to you?

Fi, Wrong time, wrong place for mum with babe in arms! Speaking of which, you're not going to believe what I found in Millie's sling (remember the 'babybag with straps'?): half-eaten sushi; a rolled-up £20 note; and scrunched-up dirty napkins. Did I look like a walking bloody dustbin to you?!

Have a FAB Xmas/New Year break and phone me early Jan with all the Marco goss.

Much Love

Jane

xx

PS. Glad Marco made it to The Cube. And fancy having framed artworks attached to the ceilings directly above the beds . . . only at The Cube! Take Care, J xx

I'm too spineless to tell her that I've just resigned from work.

My first Christmas as a fully-fledged, unemployed 1950s housewife is aptly spent in domestic purgatory – ping-ponging between my mad extended family in Oxfordshire and Tim's barmy clan in Somerset. Millie's so overtired and out of routine we're pretty much back to the bad old days of demand-feeding – sob. And then, there are my gifts:

Tim
(Everything was labelled 'To Mum' – has he forgotten my name?)
- BMA guide to children's health
- Fire-blanket and fire-extinguisher for kitchen
- Carbon-monoxide alarm
- First-aid kit (size of Red Cross field camp)
- Starter home-safety kit of door and drawer latches

(Too much time talking to bloody Harry at Fi's dinner party, it seems.)

Tim's Parents
- Good-housekeeping guide and dinner-party planner
- Set of hot rollers

(Retro-chic gone mad!)

Mum and Dad
- Pinny (*circa* 1953)
- Iron

(Why not throw in a repeat prescription for Prozac for good measure?)

Kate

❤   Twelve-month subscription to *Practical Parenting* (Marginal improvement on last year's PETA gift-aid certificate, in lieu of present. At least I can use it.)

WHAT have I done?

I need a Shoe Princess fix.

New Year's Eve shows all the promise of making up for our completely ordinary festive season, thanks to an invitation to a glittering black-tie ball – hosted by a large client of Tim's company. That is, until Millie breaks out in a frightful fever an hour before Kate's due over for babysitting.

We promptly cancel Kate (who's grateful for the chance to stay at home and quietly meditate the old year out and the new year in) but decide that Tim should still go to the ball. As his boss made it abundantly clear that all of the team should put in an appearance tonight.

Too anxious to sleep, I spend the entire night making copious checks of Millie's temperature and breathing; and looking for any signs of rashes. Filling in the rest of my time on the computer and *finally* mastering the art of blogging, thanks to the wonderful (and patient) help of some fellow Shoe Princess tragics also online. (I wonder if Alison has web friends to help her through her day as well? Nah. Not enough time.)

Just before dawn, Tim stumbles home and finds me asleep at the desk.

Not altogether the best start to the new year. But then again, things can only get better!

A huge thank you for the many stories, especially those from the designer shoe sales – surely the most exhilarating way for a SP to spend her day. Where else could one find office girls clad in jeans and armed with steely determination, side-by-side Gucci handbag-toting, 6-foot-tall Russian mannequins, in full-length (emerald-green!) fur coats? Fabulous!

No doubt everyone's heard of the unsightly commotion at the Manolo Blahnik sale in London – I hope none of my SPs were involved? Although, I will concede that anyone standing on a pavement for 3 hours in Siberian winds has the right to be peeved by 'insiders' taking photos of shoes on their mobile phones for people in the queue *behind you* – and then buying them on their behalf, so that nothing is left when you finally get into the store. Clearly a breach of SP shoe-sale etiquette.

A gem of a **Shoe Sale** story from SP of Manhattan:

The Scene: 11 a.m. Saturday morning. Peak hour at the Saks Fifth Avenue shoe sale.

Two girlfriends are sitting next to each other, trying on several pairs of shoes. Chatting loudly, Girlfriend 1 leans over to Girlfriend 2 and says, 'He stood in the lobby, took ONE look at my new shoes and said accusingly, "I'm not even going to ASK how much they cost!" And I said, "Good! Because neither did I!"'

Cue both girls howling with laughter.

Sound familiar?

9. Tripping

IT seemed like a good idea at the time, giving up corporate life to discover my inner domestic goddess. But to my workmates it was nothing short of absurd. After all, maternal instincts were not something I was particularly known for.

Within a minute of my official resignation letter landing on the desk of 'Patricia the Plague' (head of human resources and so named for the speed at which she can spread anything from memos to STDs) the news of its contents ping-ponged from email to email throughout the entire eight floors of Asquith & Brown. Fi predictably phoned me, demanding the necessary counter-intelligence to keep the gossips at bay. But alas, I could not give her what she wanted. My stellar career at Asquith & Brown had come to an ignominious end.

After I'd detailed my childcare and bottle-feeding fiascos, along with chronic sleep deprivation and the fact that Millie had inconsiderately come into this world without a battery pack and self-help manual, I finally managed to bring Fi round to the fact that she'd be doing solo lunchtime dashes to Russell & Bromley. Well, at least to a point where she's now vaguely supportive of my 'new' job – though I'm sure she thinks it's all skinny lattes and walks in the park. (As is her prerogative as a childless working girl.)

Liz, on the other hand, has been a fantastic pillar of unconditional support. Openly saying that she would give up work in a flash if she were in my position, and that Millie is far more important than any monthly target or business plan. (I have no doubt that she is not just humouring me on this one.)

As for our families, everyone is completely over the moon. Unanimously informing me that these are the best days of my life. It does make me wonder what they would have said if I had gone back to work, though. Would they have feigned approval? Or bitten their tongues?

Nevertheless, I'm trying to think of my current lifestyle change as an adventure – a welcome relief from battling with the daily grind of petty office politics and London transport. Sort of like taking off on a last-minute City Break to a sunny foreign destination, accompanied by Tim and a newly purchased pair of striped canvas espadrilles, with two-and-a-half-inch heels and adorable ankle ties.

The only thing is, I'm quickly starting to feel that maybe Rachel is right: spur-of-the-moment adventures often fizzle horribly after the initial adrenalin rush of escaping. Her response to my big news was peppered with words like 'lifestyle suicide', 'fat', 'boring' and 'penniless'. Oh, and 'sexless'.

But let's be honest, I'm not likely to get an objective reaction from someone who dry-retches at the sight of a car that's not a two-seater sports convertible, am I?

'I'll work again,' I assured Rachel defensively. 'When Millie's a little older. Maybe I'll even do something completely different – something creative.'

'Puh! You'll need to,' she said, looking rather frozen. 'After Simon and his chums finish oiling the rungs on the corporate ladder, you've no hope of climbing back on again. How does night-packing shelves at the supermarket sound? Creative enough for you?'

Hell, she *does* have a point. I'm such a cliché. A gleaming bloody trophy for my team and every misogynistic boss in town to polish and gloat over: 'They're all the same. Once the baby comes along – brains turn to mush. Can't bear to leave the little sproglets. Seen it a hundred times before. No dedication. No work ethic. Blah de blah de blah.'

And I guess that's how I got to today, sitting at my kitchen table with a fractious five-month-old Millie on my lap, frantically scanning the pages of Alison's well-thumbed books – her gifts that are proving to be worth their weight in gold.

And what a truly pathetic sight I am: holding one book on controlled crying in my left hand, another on weaning in my right hand, and the telephone wedged between my ear and raised shoulder – as I enquire about the day and time for the local new-mothers' group.

After all, there's only so much sightseeing one can do without dealing with reality: Tim's been called back to work and I'm adrift in a foreign city, unable to speak the language, and slowly but surely being crippled by my precious new espadrilles.

I need help. Fast!

From:	Fi (work)
To:	Jane (home)
Subject:	Shoe School

Hi Jane

I've decided that the only way to see my two favourite people at weekends is to take matters into my own hands. I've booked you and me into Marco's shoe-making school in 6 weeks' time –

second weekend in March – yeh! (Will also try and rope in Rachel and Liz, as can have up to five in a class.) So consider this prior warning and sort yourself out with Millie – no excuses accepted.

Much Love

Fi

xx

PS. So much for me thinking that spending Christmas with my parents and their respective partners in one big happy dysfunctional family would get me some Brownie points . . . have just heard from Dad that I'm to keep a low profile with Annabel (his third wife). Apparently, they've just spent the night in Casualty after Hector, their 2-year-old, embedded a shoe in his ear from The Barbie Chic Shoe Store (or La Boutique de Chaussures) that I gave his sister for Christmas. (It's SO amazing, by the way: comes complete with no less than ten pairs of shoes, shoeboxes, a Barbie-size seat, a working foot-measurer, display cases, shopping bags, four handbags, a cash register and a mirror. What more could a girl want? Have also put one aside for Millie – couldn't resist.)

Anyway, I thought I was rather clever, making sure that the box said it was for '3 years and over' and that it would be perfect for Charlotte. It didn't even occur to me that Hector would ram the sodding 'tangerine twist' mule in his ear AND narrowly miss perforating his eardrum. Like I was born knowing the bizarre antics of the human 2-year-old?!?! Must dash, Fi xx

From: Liz (work)
To: Fi (work); Jane (home); Rachel (work)
Subject: RE: Shoe School

Ooh, count me in! Perfect timing too, as Harry will be away at a health-and-safety conference all weekend. Please tell me I've done the right thing . . . When Harry saw my VISA bill I got an attack of the guilts about buying 20 (yes!) pairs of shoes at the Selfridges sale (I only went in to buy coffee mugs – promise) and have just sold half of them on eBay. (And even made a small profit!)

   See you soon
   Liz
   xx

From: Rachel (work)
To: Fi (work); Jane (home); Liz (work)
Subject: RE: Shoe School

1. I'm up for it – as long as I don't ruin my nails.
2. Will there be any men there (apart from Marco, of course)?
3. Shame on you Liz – and you call yourself a shoe princess?!
R x

Oh, how I wish a shoe surplus was a problem of mine. Tim's recently banned all new shoe purchases. Not through any particular act of meanness, but more because he has slipped rather too comfortably into Mr 1950s mode, now that he is the sole earner and we are still living in London with a ludicrous mortgage.

He's even taken to calling me from Bangalore, ahead of his flights home, and advising me of his food and laundry needs, before asking about Millie.

Pre-Millie, it would have been hints of a magnum of duty-free champagne, a bottle of expensive perfume and a sexy little number procured from Agent Provocateur. Followed by veiled suggestions of nocturnal activities with a pair of red patent-leather stilettos and fragranced body oil. Now, it seems, I've turned into the catering manager, launderette and chief baby-sitter.

Give me strength. One of the less empowering aspects of my new job, I have to say.

Consider it a date! Tim's back from India that weekend and will delight in minding Millie. Will have to work out how to organise the feeding – but leave it with me, will sort out something. Am really looking forward to it – cabin fever well and truly setting in. Am DESPERATE to get out.

Am actually off to join the local new-mothers' group today – wish me luck. Ha! Am SO nervous – what if it's full of earth-mother fascists and competitive supermums? Anyway, enough of my paranoid ramblings.

Much Love

Jane

xx

PS. Fi, at least Hector chose the funkiest shoes in Barbie's shoe store to embed in his ear!

At the end of yet another day in domestic paradise, I huffily decide that the bulging laundry pile can wait, and make myself a cup of tea and curl up on the sofa to watch some crappy TV, while flicking through my latest trash mag (a small reward I've been saving all day). But an unsightly headline reaches up and grabs me by the throat before I even get the chance to relax: 'Cat Got the Cream'.

It seems that The Cat's not just a pretty face:

Motherhood has unleashed Catriona's creative energies and bold business acumen, and she has great pleasure in announcing her very own organic gourmet cat-food label, Mange Chat. Naturally, her feline clientele will be at the top end of the market. Orders are already streaming in from Europe, the US, Japan and Australia. She sincerely hopes that she can be a role model to all working mothers, as someone who balances brains, beauty and the nurturing of her baby, for the betterment of herself and the world around her.

I think I am going to puke, and I leg it straight to the computer to see what the Trash Queenz have to say about this.

Damn. They confirm it's a done deal. In fact, it's apparently one of the highest single celebrity endorsements *ever* signed, due largely to The Cat's unique household-brand power. It seems the supermodel-supermum has just added superbusinesswoman to her name.

I read on . . . Aha:

> Whispers abound, from credible sources within Mange Chat, that The Cat had absolutely nothing to do with product development and has simply signed her name for a truckload of money.

Now, that's more like it.

I calmly make my way back to the sofa and take up from where I was rudely interrupted: '1960s Soap Star Marries Toyboy Lover in Lavish Star-studded Balinese Ceremony – Exclusive Photos.' *Aahhh, bliss.*

SP Survey Results

Q: Why do heterosexual men think that women's shoes should cost £10, and that any more than one pair in a wardrobe is a heinous crime?

It was extremely tough picking a winner, given that most of you came up with the same answer: something along the lines of the hunter-gatherer conundrum, with men just not 'getting' shoes.

So, I've decided to give the L.K. Bennett gift voucher to SP of Edinburgh who offered a very clever solution to this age-old problem (shoe-shop owners take note!):

A: 'If I owned a shoe shop, I'd call it Fruit 'n' Veg, so that when it came up on VISA statements, my loyal customers' penny-pinching partners would not realise it was shoes.'

A deserving winner, I'm sure you'll agree!

Shoe SOS

I feel it is my civic duty to pass on to the powers that be at L.K. Bennett:

The ex-pat Aussie SPs need you. Desperately!

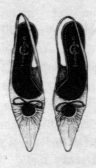

10. Sole Mate

22, 20, 18, 16 . . . 14. No. It can't be. I double-check the address Mary (the health visitor) gave me, which I've scribbled on a scrap of paper, before noticing the sign in the window advertising today's cooking demonstration and talk on weaning. This looks like it.

It strikes me that I must have walked past this building a million times in my pre-Millie morning sprints to the tube. Purposefully clip-clopping along, cappuccino in hand. Funny, I always thought it was a squat. I'm still not convinced, and spend the next few minutes loitering around outside, pretending to fix Millie's hat and blankets.

I spy a likely suspect: a mum with a pushchair slows a little and then stops right next to me, giving me a kindly no-teeth smile. She then puts the brakes on, yanks on her nappy-bag backpack, takes her baby out of the pushchair, folds the pushchair with one arm and one foot, and then gamely carries the whole lot down the steep little moss-covered steps to the basement of the Victorian terraced house.

Blimey! I watch in horror. Could they not make it any more difficult? A moat to swim over, perhaps. Nevertheless, I follow her down, secretly cursing my stupid pushchair and its stupid metal framework for scraping enormous pieces of leather from the tips of my pointy pink mules.

Mary immediately spots me. She latches on to my elbow with an enthusiastic and welcoming tug, and guides me into the heart of the room. I feel eerily like the new girl at school, being dragged into the bowels of hell by a mad woman in size 11 white trainers and *Teletubbies* socks. Whatever am I getting myself into?

I can hardly believe the sight before my eyes: there must be about a dozen women who look *exactly* like me – all with very bad hair, bulging bosoms, puffy eyes and babes in arms – sitting shoulder-to-shoulder in a cosy and familiar circle. I'm gob-smacked to learn from Mary that every one of them lives near by. They shuffle along to make a space for me.

Millie sucks her fist and peeks over my shoulder with interest. Clearly unperturbed by the slightly musty smell and dodgy magnolia paintwork, most of which is stained and peeling from the edges around the radiators. (A far cry from the smart meeting rooms at work.) There is a large hospital sheet on the floor in the middle of the circle, which Mum will be pleased to know Mary washes and starches after each session, and has done so *every* Wednesday for the past thirty years. (Something tells me that nobody elbows in on Mary's patch very easily.)

Some babies are lying on the sheet. Some are with mums being fed or burped, while others are asleep in baby capsules and pushchairs. The room is a simmering, bubbling soup of ani-mated conversation.

I start chatting to the mum in a pair of trendy trainers next to me, though I forget her name as soon as she says it. But I remember the name of her baby – Hugh. (She says she's always had a bit of a crush on Hugh Grant and made sure to ask her husband to agree to the name – which he detests – while at the pinnacle of her labour pains.) Hugh is one month older than Millie, and does have a bit of a cheeky Hugh Grant grin.

She catches me yawning.

'Not getting much sleep, either? Don't worry, you'll soon find we're all obsessed by it – or at least our memories of it.'

'So nice to hear I'm not alone then.' The relief in my voice obvious.

'I complained to my mum only the other day that I felt tired, and she flippantly said that I'd spend the next fifteen years tired,' she says. 'And the scary thing is – she didn't seem to be joking.'

'Well, I think Millie was born with an altimeter in her head. She'll be comatose on my shoulder, but the second I put her down she's like, "I'm awake now!" Wide awake.' I shake my head and give Millie a playful tickle for being such a monkey. She smiles and all is forgiven.

'I *so* know what you mean. Hugh had day and night completely reversed when we came home from hospital. I thought I'd given birth to a vampire. I barely saw my husband for two months.'

'I seem to have spent the last few nights sitting with Millie on the chair in our bedroom – and very gradually sliding down to a semi-horizontal position and transferring her to her crib. And I thought the chair's only purpose was to display my collection of soon-to-be-covered scatter cushions.' I laugh, and then explain how I went through a John Lewis scatter-cushion mania in the last trimester of pregnancy. But failed to get any covered – mostly due to Tim protesting that we could buy a car for the same price.

'Men just don't get scatter cushions, do they? Mine was handbags – the pregnancy mania thing. The only fashion item that truly brought me joy and fitted over any part of my bloated body.' She giggles.

And basically, that's all it took to start us off – sleep, soft furnishings and handbags. Sophie – I soon got to remember her name – and I barely stopped talking, managing to swap horror-birth stories, war wounds, makes of pushchair, colic remedies, addresses, telephone numbers and emails.

It's a truly strange feeling to meet someone at this stage in life that I have so much in common with. And so nice, too.

Mary gathers us around the kitchenette for her cooking demonstration and talk on weaning. A scraggy, handwritten sign instructing us to wash up our cups, and place all food scraps in the bin to prevent rodents (I don't even want to think about it), hangs lopsidedly above the sink.

I must say that Mary's enthusiasm for puréed vegetables and the uses of ice-cube trays is admirable. As is her patience. At the end of it, we're all filled with hope and confidence. I for one am counting on her advice that all Millie needs now is 'something to stick to her sides' and she'll sleep like an angel. *Please, yes.* I make a mental note to walk home via the greengrocer, but need to feed Millie first.

As I stare aimlessly into space holding Millie on my shoulder with one hand while undoing the buttons of my blouse with the other, a voice from behind me says, 'Still *feeding*. Good.'

'Oh, this is –'

'Hi, Victoria,' I interrupt Sophie. I immediately recognise her black boots and clipped voice, though I'd completely missed her in the mix of women in the room.

Bloody hell . . . I knew things were going too smoothly.

'Just having some trouble remembering which side I last fed from.' It's the most cerebral activity I have to perform in my day – and I haven't mastered it particularly well.'

'Oh, I *always* switch my Tiffany bangle from arm to arm

when I've just fed,' Victoria informs me. 'You really must try it – it works a treat.'

The Tiffany bangle would be a nice start.

She then bleats on about how happy she is to have given up her high-profile job with a PR agency, how much she is *loving* being a full-time-stay-at-home mum, and the many virtues of breast-feeding.

Out of the corner of my eye, I spy one of the other mums listening to our conversation as she gives her baby (who looks a little younger than Millie) a bottle. Victoria continues to rabbit on about her voluptuous boobs, how Allegra never gets ill, how she feels so womanly and sexy, and how she has so much milk she feels it is her community duty to donate it to the milk bank at the local hospital. The mum's eyes gradually well up with tears.

I try to sidetrack Victoria by asking whether she's a 'round-, pointy- or square-toed girl' when it comes to shoes.

'Points, of course,' she says matter-of-factly, and somehow manages to steer the conversation back to 'breast is best'.

The mum is now in floods of tears, and Mary leaps across the room to her rescue. They go and find a quiet corner. I think I'm the only one who's noticed.

About twenty minutes pass before they come back, tissue box in hand.

'I think it's time I had a word with my girls,' Mary announces and motions us all to move our chairs closer. 'More of a little pep talk,' she brightly informs us.

'I've learnt a lesson today.' She glints and turns briefly to the mum, whose eyes start to glaze over again. 'And I want to share it with you all. See this.' She holds up a piece of paper between the tip of her right index finger and thumb with disdain. It appears to be a certificate of some sort. 'Bureaucracy gone mad,' she says, and gleefully rips it up into tiny shreds.

'What is it?' I ask nervously.

'It's a declaration – on the benefits of breast-feeding – which I'm to get you to sign (in triplicate – hah) before letting you bottle-feed your babies. It's in your new-mothers' pack.' Mary smiles and pauses thoughtfully. 'Now, I know for a fact how hard every single one of you has tried to breast-feed. Some with greater ease than others.'

She is suddenly earnest.

'All of you are good mums. Trying your very best, day and night, for your babies. Don't you *ever* let anyone make you think otherwise. You hear me now.' She makes a point of trying to catch each one of us in the eye.

We nod meekly.

'I'll have none of it.'

'No wonder women get post-natal depression,' Sophie drily whispers to me as we sit and try to digest what's just happened. 'How *moronically* insensitive. The sort of tick-list-league-table-trash only a *male* bureaucrat could have initiated,' she hisses.

'More like Nanny State gone mad,' I add.

'My friend has a theory that all first-time mums get PND to some degree. Notwithstanding the really serious stuff, the whole thing sort of strikes me as something that should be relabelled from being an illness to an entirely normal coping reaction,' Sophie says.

'What do you mean?'

'Well, maybe it's a natural reaction to finding yourself in extraordinary circumstances,' she reflects. 'Paddling like crazy to stay afloat with one arm, keeping the baby afloat with the other, whilst grappling with your husband (with what free arm?) to save him from drifting away in the tide of flotsam and jetsam that is your new life.'

At least I don't have to worry about Tim – he's been so incredibly supportive of my need to devote myself to Millie in these early months.

'It's true, though,' I say, as I reflect on it a little more. 'Especially for us modern-day girls – who often have no contact with babies before our own.' Certainly not a day passes that I don't think I've been given the chief executive's job of being a mum, without the barest trace of skills and experience on my CV to back up my appointment.

Sophie wistfully strokes Hugh's chubby, mottled cheeks.

'Before Hugh, the sum total of my exposure to babies was watching two-year-olds unravelling rolls of loo paper with Labrador pups in TV ads. But don't get me started . . .' And we break out into a fit of the giggles and laugh until our sides hurt.

I think I've just found a soul mate. Well, a new best-mum-friend and ranting mate at the very least.

As I push Millie up the hill towards home, there's a distinct new spring in my step. Quite frankly, I am beside myself with excitement as I think about Sophie and the motley crew of mums. Even full-on Victoria has an entertainment factor – I almost felt like I was back in the office. I wish not only that I had gone months earlier, but that it was held twice a week – wild horses couldn't keep me from it.

But most incredibly, I smile to myself in disbelief when I think of my newfound adoration of Mary. Maybe there *is* room in a shoe princess's life for squeaky, smelly white trainers after all.

Shoe Catastrophe

First-time-mum SPs beware: Do not under any circumstances be tricked into wearing flat wide shoes either before or just after the birth. Unless you wish to go up a full (yes!) shoe size and consign your hard-earned shoe collection to a dusty death at the back of your wardrobe.

It's all to do with an overzealous little hormone that makes ligaments supple in preparation for childbirth (ha!). Regrettably, it takes the scattergun approach and softens all ligaments — and your feet are full of them.

Boxing Clever

For the legion of SPs that love a good shoebox, here are two special commendations:

Emma Hope's shoeboxes in high-gloss white, with black-embossed logo on the lid: 'Regalia for Feet'. Pretty much says it all, doesn't it? Wonderful.

Prada's multicoloured shoeboxes for their ballet slippers; and peep-toe and cut-away flats. Using different combinations of vibrant shades of cerise, purple, emerald, yellow and cobalt for the boxes and lids. Covetable.

11. No Mean Feet

KATE holds my A4 page entitled 'Millie's Day' and studies it closely.

'It's a great little routine for a six-and-a-half-month-old,' she finally says. I'm mildly spooked by her approving tone, so unused am I to hearing it. 'Two sleeps – mid-morning, mid-afternoon; four milk feeds; nice variety of foods – chunky, not puréed; play time; quiet time. She's even taking drinks from a trainer cup now – fantastic.'

Yes, it is, actually. Achieved through much perseverance. And the carrot of this weekend's shoe school with the girls may have helped a teeny bit too.

Kate's here with Mum and Dad to give Tim a hand looking after Millie.

'She's even sleeping through a lot more too,' says Mum, who's listening in on Kate and me. 'I knew she'd get the hang of it.'

I'm glad she was so sure. But yes, I will for ever love sweet potatoes. Truly madly deeply.

As I watch Millie sitting and playing with her toys, I can't help but be enchanted by how she's blossomed. When she spots me she breaks into a gummy smile, and then blows a sloppy raspberry. We all burst into fits of laughter, which, naturally, heralds an encore.

I'm sure this is nature's reward for all the hard graft of the early months – a socially engaging, utterly adorable bear cub.

The shoe school starts at 10 a.m. and Kate, feeling adventurous in light of the mild spell of weather, suggests that she and Millie join me for the short bus ride to Marco's studio. This is lucky for Tim, as it enables him to spend the first morning of his 'father–daughter bonding weekend' flat out in bed (after having arrived from India late last night) in the warm knowledge that a fully cooked breakfast from Mum awaits him, as well as a comprehensive selection of weekend newspapers, courtesy of Dad. I'm sure he'd have been more than capable of looking after Millie himself – though I believe my family's rally to his side is what he likes to call a win-win situation.

The only glitch to the journey so far has been nearly giving myself a hernia by lugging Millie's pushchair on to the bus, while Kate nursed Millie. Oh, and then having to sit directly on top of The Cat's pert breasts – yes – due to her neck-to-toe gold Lycra cat-suited body stretching the entire length of the bus's upper deck in her new Mange Chat advertisement.

Once off the bus, we duck and dive our way down to the far end of Church Street, where the hubbub of the noisy market traders gives way to the more serene antique shops. I leave Kate and Millie, making Kate promise to come and see me before heading home, and follow the signs for the shoe school down to the basement of Marco's Antique Mirrors.

I feel strangely lost not carrying seventeen bags, a baby and a pushchair, yet wonderfully liberated too. Fi is busy showing off her new toy – a 3G iPhone with inbuilt video camera (courtesy of Jolie Naturelle) – to a completely captivated Liz. Fi's been emailing me videos of shoes all week from her lunchtime jaunts. (It's almost like old times.)

Marco is speaking to a sandy-haired and not that unattractive (I really do need to get out more) guy, when Rachel makes her trademark grand entrance, a fashionable ten minutes late.

Fi immediately spots her metallic-silver ballet flats.

'Ooh, do you like?' says Rachel. 'Trust me, they're the next *big* thing.'

I'm bewildered. There's not a knitting-needle-thin heel in sight. Though admittedly Rachel was way ahead with the wedge. And legend has it that Sienna and Kate saw *her* in Ugg boots on Ledbury Road – kick-starting the now infamous West London Ugg Boot shortage of Christmas 2003.

Marco, in his usual studied silence, moves across to put the finishing touches to our workstations at a large antique wooden table. There are five spots laid out – each with pliers, hammer, nails, scissors, heat gun and glue pots.

'I see we're already running a little late,' he says, self-consciously fiddling with his watch. 'If we could do the introductions and then get started. We'll need all the time we can get this weekend.'

The sandy-haired guy takes up Marco's lead.

'Hi, I'm Ben.' He flashes a boyish smile. Rachel X-rays his trendily tight long-sleeved T-shirt, baggy jeans and Converse trainers with a glimmer in her eye. He's very young – maybe early twenties.

'I'm a set designer. And before you ask, no, I'm not here to make a pair of shoes for myself. I'd like to try and make a pair of shoes for my girlfriend – actually, fiancée – as a special birthday gift.'

Blimey, Tim wouldn't even know my shoe size, let alone make me a pair of shoes. A collective sigh of admiration ripples around the table.

'Does she like shoes, then – your fiancée?' Liz asks in awe.

'Oh, yes. They're her one real passion in life – apart from the kids at work. She's a paediatric intensive-care nurse. I always like to do something special for her birthday – really spoil her.'

'What else have you done?' I ask. Tim is going to hear about this.

'Um, let me think. Well, last year I did the Pru Leith cooking school and surprised her with a dinner party for her best friends. The year before that I did an Emma Bridgewater pottery workshop and hand-painted a teacup and teapot set. I always like to do something with my hands for her.' He holds up a pair of large, muscular, veined hands.

Rachel is practically salivating beside me, and I fear she may faint.

'*Oooh! Come to Mamma,*' she whispers wickedly in my ear.

I shoot her a disapproving glare – for all it's worth.

Marco seems a little flustered by our rather lengthy introductions and obsession with asking Ben all about his fiancée, and tries to redirect us back to the business of shoe-making. He firstly gives us a short talk on the history of the shoe and its various components, which I find totally fascinating. He then explains that we have a choice of two styles – both mules, as backs and straps are too complicated for beginners – one with a heel and the other flat. Rachel and I choose to make flats (sadly not because I'm a slave to her big fashion prediction, but because that's all I have the need to wear these days), while Fi and Liz stick steadfastly to heels.

We select insole plates and a pair of plastic foot moulds (or lasts) in our shoe size. Marco proudly shows us some newly arrived leathers that we can use for the upper (the outside material of the shoe front) as well as some exquisitely soft pigskins in gorgeous colours like cherry and turquoise for the linings – which will give the shoes a distinctly upmarket look and feel. He brings out some sample shoes and photos from previous classes to inspire us – I can't believe how professional they look. Definitely good enough to be shop-bought.

We all gather around an enormous antique sea chest with yet more pieces of leather and fabric to choose from – in every conceivable colour and pattern. The choice is too much and we dither about for some time, before I settle upon a textured fabric with a sort of lineny, raw-silk feel.

I get up from kneeling by the chest and am straightening my clothes when Rachel gasps alarmingly, 'Jane!'

I jump a mile. What on earth.

'What is it?'

She puts her hand to her mouth and points at my waist.

'*Eeeelastic.*' She spits the word out and then says in monosyllabic bursts, 'Waistband. E-las-tic. Oh, Jane, do be careful.'

'Well, I'm hardly going to fit into a pair of skinny jeans, am I?'

'You don't see The Cat in elastic, post-bambino, do you?'

I consider pulling her up on a technicality, in light of the gold Lycra cat-suit, but bite my tongue, sensing it could easily backfire on me.

'One very slippery slope, my darling. Next it'll be the three Ts.' She's already given me several lectures on these: T-shirts, tracksuits and trainers. 'And then it's, "Hello, mistress."'

'Oh, seriously.' Liz pooh-poohs Rachel's drama-queenness. 'Not all married men have mistresses, you know.'

Rachel purses her lips. Her silence is discomfiting.

'And anyway, *real* mums don't have multimillion-pound slush funds to spend on nutritionists and personal trainers.' I suddenly find my fight.

'OR tummy tucks and boob jobs,' says Fi, winking and quoting the latest Trash Queenz bombshell about The Cat.

'Excuses. I'm just hearing excuses, girls,' Rachel reprimands, and I know she's not joking.

A little crestfallen, I skulk back to the table, where Ben is patiently waiting for us. He brought his own fabric along today – a microfibre that looks and feels uncannily like leather, in a pretty shade of pink. His fiancée is a devout vegetarian. He's also got a suitable lining material and his own vegan glue.

'Who's his fiancée? Stella McCartney's secret twin sister,' whispers Rachel slyly before sidling up next to Ben, and coquettishly fiddling with her materials.

My first challenge turns out to be pattern cutting. I've already been given a gentle rap on the knuckles by Marco for wasting material – he's extremely professional. I'm left with no doubt that this is no token craft class for bored housewives, and that in less than forty-eight hours the jigsaw pieces in front of me will resemble a gorgeous pair of shoes. I have a feeling it's going to be no mean feat, though.

Kate and Millie take me by surprise when they peek into the studio an hour later, providing a welcome interruption to the gluing and sewing. I frantically motion to Kate not to come in, keen as I know she is to get a glimpse of Marco. But the fumes from the glue are headache-inducing and far too strong for Millie. I excuse myself and go upstairs with them. Fi promptly follows us with her wretched video phone and takes aim at Millie. She's like a kid with a new toy today – I've already had to take numerous movies of her and Marco 'making shoes together'. Though I should think it's more 'Marco making her shoes' – she's really showed minimal interest in the mechanics of it, preferring to dote on Marco instead.

When I get back, I'm surprised to find that Ben has finished off sewing one of my uppers – so that I don't fall behind. He seems to be taking to shoe-making like a duck to water. And is similarly at ease with his handling of Rachel's outrageous flirtations – politely humouring her and taking it in his stride.

The room is bustling with activity and shoe chatter, and Ben and Marco soon become privy to all of our girlie ramblings. Fi has tried to convert us to Iyengar yoga – as part of her New Year's resolution to harmonise body, mind and soul. Hah!

We've dissected the Shoe Princess's latest words of wisdom, as well as expanded our vocabularies, thanks to blogs posted by fellow SPs, with the likes of 'choogasm' (when one's nirvana comes from wearing upmarket high-heeled shoes) and 'sparklers' (gold- or silver-lamé shoes worn in group sex so one knows where one's feet are – Rachel, of course, obliging us with the logistics).

The table is unanimous on one topic, though – my sister's choice of footwear. Ghastly! Unfortunately, Fi messed up on the video of Millie and managed to get Kate's feet in *every* frame. I'm so embarrassed. They look uncannily like King Kong's – and she's not even wearing fur-trimmed Ugg boots.

After my slightly shaky start, I've become entirely engrossed in the work at hand, and am surprised to see that it's 2 p.m. when Marco lets us out for a short break. (But not before chatting to each of us and inspecting our workstations to make sure we've made sufficient progress.) Much to Fi's disappointment, Marco declines to join us at the local café – instead holding a meeting with some clients. He's been in and out of the class all morning, talking to various people both in the studio and upstairs in the shop. Needless to say, Rachel and Fi have made great use of Ben in Marco's absence, for all manner of queries. Rachel, for her part, is so outrageously transparent.

The afternoon session, Marco informs us, is the hardest part of all – joining the upper to the insole plate. We should get one complete today, and the other tomorrow. The trick is in getting the insole plate correctly positioned on the last (aha, so that's what it's for) and then shaping and tacking the upper to it. Followed by gluing it all into place.

I now know why the shoemaker left all the work for the elves – it is *so* labour-intensive. My fingertips are burning from all the nailing and tacking, and I'm finding it hard to manoeuvre everything perfectly into place.

Marco, sensing my frustration, offers to help me. He positions himself directly behind me – with one leg placed either side of me and both arms around me – leaning forward in order to reach the last.

Ohhh-K. Not *quite* what I had expected. The skin on my neck rapidly turns into a blotchy mulberry Turkish rug that creeps to the tips of my burning ears. My stomach does a complete flip. I guess it's not every day a six-foot-plus Italian hunk engulfs me!

Marco then proceeds to finger the leather – kneading and cajoling it onto the last with the dexterous skill of a masseur crossed with a concert violinist. I'm trying to take careful note of how he's doing it, but am finding it a smidge difficult to concentrate. Not helped in the least by the fact that he reeks of the most sublime aftershave – a light, citrusy mix with a woody vanilla undertone. I'm completely haunted by the smell. And then it occurs to me that it's very like one I used to buy Tim when we first met – it brings back wild, delicious memories. A far cry from today, ironically, when we're hardly in the same room (or country!) long enough for me to smell his aftershave. Sadly, I can't even remember if he wears one these days.

I'm snapped from my daydream by the touch of Marco's hand on my shoulder.

'That should give you a good start. See how you go.'

'Great. Thanks.' I can barely meet him in the eye. *Oh, get a grip, Jane.* I'm a happily married woman. And a mother. Not a giddy fourteen-year-old schoolgirl. This is most peculiar. Not to mention completely mortifying – given that he's also my best friend's much longed-for boyfriend.

Liz has obviously witnessed the whole thing, and is standing open-mouthed and a little scarlet-faced next to me.

That's it – from now on, when I need any help, I'll be fighting Rachel for Ben.

The Marco incident has rattled me, and I'm anxious to leave on the dot of 6 p.m. to get home.

Rachel is clearly hoping for the elves to come in overnight and finish off her shoe, as she's been seated at Marco's desk for the past hour getting an emergency nail repair from Ben. He did a French polish course for his fiancée's Christmas present and happened to have all the gear in his backpack. Why can't Kate find a guy like him?

Fi nuzzles up to Marco.

'Any exciting plans for tonight?' she asks us.

'My fiancée's on night shift – from 8 p.m. to 8 a.m. – so it's pizza and a video for me,' Ben says glumly.

Liz and I look at each other in alarm. And then at Rachel. Unfortunately, we know *exactly* what she's thinking.

Shoe Are You?

You can run, princesses, but you can't hide . . .

Common Garden Variety SP

This princess is genuinely interested in looking smart and stylish, and has a knack for buying mid-range shoes that can instantly update last season's outfits. She is more likely to be spotted in a kitten heel than a 3-inch designer stiletto, and has serious shoe-credibility issues when it comes to spurning fake plastic imports – think Pied-à-Terre rather than Payless Shoes. She has years of shoe-buying experience behind her. And as she hits her mid-30s she's finding it harder to get shoes that are wide enough (especially post-childbirth) or have sufficient padding under the balls of her feet. She bemoans always having to apply a non-slip rubber sole to her new shoes, and don't even get her started on the total uselessness of plastic heel tips. She wishes that designers would bring out her favourite shoe styles, updated ever so slightly each season. She will *always* be able to justify blowing her shoe budget for a very special occasion!

Persecuted SP

Princesses with particularly small or large feet, who often find it impossible to get smart, fashionable, well-fitting shoes in their size. When they do come across either a supplier or a style of shoe that fits them, they will buy several pairs of the same shoe, often in different colours. These princesses always need container ships to store their shoe collections in. The **Persecuted SP** with large feet is quite adept at arm-wrestling transvestites for shoe bargains in the upmarket shoe sales.

Petite SP

Very high heels are a way of life for this vertically challenged princess. She would rather die than be seen in anything with less than a 3-inch heel. Her calf muscles are so shortened that even her slippers have heels. Her partner has never seen her barefoot, and she could easily run a marathon in stilettos. Her mantra is: 'Why go to the gym when you can wear stilettos?' Role models are Posh Spice and Carrie from *Sex and the City*.

12. Twinkle-Toes

IN a rather cheery fashion, Mum's always told Kate and me to expect the unexpected. As if by greeting the unfamiliar as the familiar we'll deny it the full force of its intended blow.

The only thing is, I keep forgetting to do it.

It's Sunday morning, and Millie is covered head-to-toe in spots. Actually, not spots, but a pulsing river of angry red pustules that the on-call doctor at the hospital last night assured us was a textbook case of chickenpox. Yes, her first major childhood illness. Coinciding with my first solo escape from domestic servitude.

What else should I have expected, right?

And now Tim, whose only form of daily exercise ever since I've known him has been walking to and from the tube and lifting a pint of lager, is lying face down in bed doing something he assures me is 'the cobra'. A yoga asana that involves gently pushing up on straightened arms and arching his back and head, while breathing heavily. He's eulogising the same mind–body–soul sound bites as Fi. I'm dumb-founded.

Not that I'm complaining, mind you. If last night between the sheets (before our sprint to the hospital) was anything to go by, I'm all for these asanas, or whatever they are. Scrummy.

He told me that the yoga's one of the perks of the staff wellness programme in Bangalore. That was just before he dropped the bombshell that he'll be working a rota of one week in London and three weeks in Bangalore for the foreseeable future.

Why not?

Honestly, his career has gone into overdrive since Millie was born – what with the overseas travel, longer hours and corporate dinners. Never mind the 'bonding board' – I should think he'll need to make Millie a life-sized bloody papier mâché dummy now.

My offer of applying for single-parent benefit was greeted with a major sense-of-humour-failure. As if my pathetic housewife brain couldn't understand the demands of the big bad corporate world any more.

The trouble is, I understand them only too well.

I blearily step over Tim's half-opened suitcase and start pulling myself together for today's shoe school. Where to begin? I can barely think straight after numerous bumping-into-walls sprints to Millie's room in the dead of night. I don't exactly know how I do it, but I'm vertical and halfway down the hall within a hair's breadth of her first muffled cries. And last night, there were many.

When I did manage to get back into bed and knit a few worried power naps into a continuous blanket of sleep, I was woken by Dad squirrelling up and down the hall between the spare room and the kitchen – tracking the course of tropical cyclone Dennis live on an Internet weather channel on his laptop as it hurtled into some remote Coral Sea island. The man's positively mad. He has the *option* of uninterrupted sleep, and he *chooses* to wake every two hours. Ever since he and Mum joined the Silver Surfers Internet Club, they seem to be permanently wired to their computers.

Mum volleys my suggestion of not going to the final day of the shoe school today straight back. Reminding me that she has two very healthy adult daughters to her credit, before jettisoning me out of the front door.

I force myself to focus on the clip-cloppy rhythm of my feet as I march mechanically to the end of the street. Desperately trying to ignore Millie's wailing that blasts through the still morning air like an Exocet missile into my ears – completely scrambling my brain.

A few minutes into the bus journey, I hurriedly release my white-knuckled clutch of my mobile phone to read the text message: *All gd. Hv a gr8 day.* T ☺

Phew. I did not enjoy that one little bit.

As I stare out of the bus window, my mind wanders to Alison and how she does this every day. With three kids. And then turns up to work. Only to be sniggered at behind her back for being neurotic.

You see, Alison *always* seemed to be fretting over some drama, whether it was Joseph's temperature and recurring middle-ear infection ('The nursery will notify me if he comes out in a rash, won't they?' 'How can I get him to the doctor after work to see if he needs another round of antibiotics?'), Lucy's nits ('It's a national plague, didn't you know?'), Tom's diarrhoea ('Could he have a food allergy? Or maybe a reaction to the MMR?' 'I hope the childminder's giving him enough fluids'), or some other deadly infection they had contracted.

Sue, in front reception, was the only person mildly receptive to her obsessing. Due largely to the fact that she was a mother herself, and completely understood the need to offload such concerns.

But you know what? Alison *never* complained.

Not even when I supported the decision to refuse her (quite legitimately) a week's leave without pay for a summer holiday. Because she'd just used up the final three weeks of her annual leave, when all three kids got chickenpox one after the other. (I needed her for the Jolie Naturelle bid, for goodness sake.)

So, no prizes for guessing my New Year's resolution: apologise to Alison. Profusely. (After my feeble effort at the Christmas party.)

Whether I have the backbone to follow it through this time is another thing entirely.

It looks like I needn't have worried about sprinting to Marco's studio in my high heels, nearly spraining my ankles (I'm so out of practice) – only Fi and Ben are here. Along with Marco, of course.

'Here's the periodical I was telling you about,' says Marco, handing me a thick glossy magazine with a shoe on the front. 'Everyone in the trade buys it – it should give you a good idea of what's out there.' With Millie's illness and everything going on at home, I'd completely forgotten that I'd asked him (almost in passing, actually) about learning some more about shoe-making. It really is very sweet of him to follow it up. And so quickly too.

I'm also pleased to say that yesterday's embarrassing mini-case of wanderlust is history. Thanks to the well-timed return of my cobra.

Fi hands me a welcome double espresso from the coffee machine she's set up by Marco's small sink. (She nearly died yesterday without a decent coffee under her belt.) The rush of caffeine also helps me suddenly remember the whole Rachelgagging-to-bed-the-spunky-young-and-engaged-set-designer scenario.

'Where are the girls?'

'Oh, Rachel called to say that she'll be late,' says Marco. 'She said to start without her – but she won't be long.'

I immediately dart my gaze over to Ben, and study him closely. He's either very sneaky or very cool. (Or very innocent, I guess?) As he hasn't flinched a muscle at the mention of Rachel's name. Apart from a lazy yawn, which, given that it's Sunday morning, I'll let him get away with.

Normally, I'd bet my last penny on my granny's grave that Rachel's shagged him senseless, and is at this moment indulging in a post-sleep-in bubble bath and home-delivered Patisserie Valerie croissants (courtesy of a young, hunky pastry chef whom she 'treats' every now and then too). Rachel usually gets what Rachel wants.

'And Liz called to say that she won't be coming in at all,' says Fi.

'Why? What's wrong?'

'She didn't really say. Just that she couldn't make it.'

That's strange, because Harry's away at a conference too.

'Did she sound poorly?' Ben's concern seems genuine.

'No. Not really. A little tired, I guess.'

When I think about it, she was pale and drawn yesterday. The stress of trying for a baby is so all-encompassing. Every now and then it catches up with her – mentally and physically.

'Well, the least I can do is finish her shoes for her.' Ben goes over and collects her materials. He really is a darling.

In fact, Ben turns out to be our saviour, practically tutoring us the whole morning, while Marco meets yet more clients up in the shop. If Fi's miffed by her plan to spend the weekend with Marco being scuppered by all these meetings, she's certainly not showing it.

During our break, I ask her tentatively who the clients are. 'I don't mean to be rude, but they all seem to be, um . . .'

'Disabled,' she says, matter-of-factly.

'Well, yes.'

'He's making their shoes for a special one-off performance of *A Midsummer Night's Dream*, at the Open Air Theatre in Regent's Park. They're from a disabled theatre company – every one of the actors has been affected in some way by a motor-vehicle accident. Marco's doing it all for free. It's going to be out of this world. You should see the designs he's come up with – sort of Zandra Rhodes glam rock meets *The Wizard of Oz*!' Fi's glowing with pride.

Well, I never. Marco Delaserio – the intelligent, handsome shoe designer – now with a social conscience. Fi has *truly* hit the jackpot!

'And Ben's kindly offered to help out with the set designs too,' she says excitedly.

I would expect nothing less.

Ugg Boot Survey

The results are in! And I have to say that it was a keenly fought battle between the European and Australian SPs as to who had the strongest views on the subject.

The Australians, and in particular the Sydney SPs, assure me that only 'Westies' (from an allegedly outer-suburban fashion-challenged region) wear 'Uggies'. And that no amount of 'talking them up' in *Vogue* is going to change their minds. A definite NO vote there.

Meanwhile, the European SPs are happily toasting their tootsies from the King's Road to St Moritz – a winter-wardrobe winner that I'm afraid seems to be here to stay. And with enough votes to push the poll result to a resounding win for the Yeti YES team!

Shoe Shopping Hot Spot

Tokyo is officially this month's winner. Its star status achieved by hundreds of SP reports of shoe shops to die for! And not only is the shopping great, but the shoe-spotting is out of this world. The girls there are mad about shoes – especially platforms or prettily patterned shoes.

And for my legion of SPs constantly complaining about shoes not being wide enough, the Japanese shoes are also made with more generous widths too.

So, what are you waiting for . . .

13. Kick the Boot In

RACHEL graces us with her company just before midday, with a pounding headache and dark sunglasses. She vows that Liz gave her and Ben a lift home last night – dropping her off first. And alone. Ben corroborates the chain of events wholeheartedly. (In fact, he seems so clueless as to my line of questioning that I feel a tad embarrassed to have implicated him in the first place.)

I start to smell a rat, though, when Rachel says that she's late because she's had a huge night with a guy from work. Rachel's always insisted that she'd sooner go hiking in Tibet than sleep with someone from work.

'You've got a statistically higher chance of finding your life partner at work these days,' says Fi, no doubt quoting from one of her trash-mag surveys.

'Well, I can't argue with that,' says Ben with a smile. 'I met my fiancée at the hospital when I was doing some volunteer work for the children's ward.'

Rachel's face turns even greener than it already is. And naturally, Fi and I quiz Ben some more about his fateful meeting with his fiancée.

'I really think we should be getting on with things,' says Marco anxiously, doing his best to jolly Fi and I along a bit, and leave poor Ben alone. I take his cue, and set straight back to work.

With Marco not racing off to a client meeting, Fi takes the opportunity to get some more video footage of them, and thrusts her phone into Ben's hands. Marco looks slightly ill at ease, while I've never seen Fi looking so radiant. Rachel's spirits suddenly rise too, as she takes delivery of a dozen red roses (with a raunchy little note that she won't let us read) from her new lover. She's floating on cloud nine.

Happily, we all settle down to a relaxed and quietly in-dustrious session. I'm thoroughly enjoying the craft of cobbling today, now that I've really got the knack of it. And when we stop for a late lunch, and I've checked with Mum and Tim that all is OK at home, I even allow myself a little indulgence – I take up Ben's offer of a French manicure. I made a special effort in the clothing department today too – *just* managing to squeeze into a pair of low-rise jeans (with the top button undone but cleverly covered by my knitted wrap top) and of course my high heels. Rachel and Fi are most approving.

By the afternoon's end, and much to our collective delight, we're admiring our very own pairs of handmade shoes. All in all, it's been a brilliant weekend. Fi points out that, if we were to put our shoes side by side on the table, we'd be staring at mini versions of ourselves. And she's not wrong: Rachel's are in red satin leopardskin print, with gold-lamé lining. Fi's are a funky denim, with fuchsia pigskin lining. And mine are mint-coloured with a flower sewn on to the side – a Cath Kidstony-type fabric contrasted with crimson pigskin lining.

And thankfully, with Rachel's attentions elsewhere, Ben's

had time to finish Liz's shoes. He's done a lovely job on them too – they're a beautiful cream calfskin, with classic cream lining. She'll be thrilled.

I'm now more convinced than ever that shoes are worth every penny we pay for them. I'll certainly not be able to look at a pair in the same way again.

'You've got a good eye for shoe-making, Jane,' says Marco, holding up my shoes and examining them closely.

'Really?'

'Yes. I'm serious. I've seen several other students use this fabric – but none so cleverly. And you've made very few mistakes – not easy for a novice. Well done.'

I'm embarrassed, yet completely chuffed.

'If you ever want to make more shoes, you're very welcome to use my studio.'

'Thanks. But I don't really have the time at the moment.'

'Don't be so sure about that,' says Marco supportively. 'You can take the materials home if that suits you best. I made my first pair at my mother's kitchen table.'

'I guess I can't quite justify bespoke shoes in my wardrobe these days, either.'

'Well, make them for other people instead,' pipes in Fi enthusiastically. 'You could sell them – make some "shoe money" for yourself. Marco, tell her about the scouts – from the large French fashion house – who bought the entire Portobello Road market-stall collection from one of your students last year.'

'It's true,' he nods.

'Gosh, that's amazing.' Now that I think about it, Sophie and the mums at my mothers' group are always complaining about a lack of fashionable, yet wearable, mum shoes.

'Actually, you've all done magnificently,' says Marco. 'And thank you to Ben, too. I don't know what I would have done without you this weekend. Extraordinary circumstances – I do apologise.' Marco glances over in the direction of his own worktable, which is buried under sketches and shoes he's making for the play.

Ben stares at the floor bashfully. He's already boxed up his fiancée's pretty pink mules in their crackly paper. Oh yes, Marco provides us with the icing for our cakes as well!

I'm still on a high when I get home. And excitedly tell everyone about Marco saying that I was the next Manolo Blahnik – OK not quite. But still . . .

Unfortunately, Tim is about as receptive as a damp squid to Marco's suggestion that I make shoes – openly querying the 'business plan' behind such a 'folly'. He could have at least given me twenty-four hours to bask in glory before bursting my bubble. (He's not normally so horrid.) I suspect he's worried I'll slip up on my 'house duties', now that he's got me manacled in apron strings.

Mum, of course, is hugely impressed by my efforts. And even Dad urges me not to give up on any aspirations to make some funky mum shoes.

Folly, indeed . . . I'll show him!

And now, to top things off, it's 10 p.m., and I'm home alone *again* thanks to Tim taking a call from work. He's gone in to fix a system-test failure that his boss Alex says needs to be sorted by start of play tomorrow.

To be honest, I'm quietly glad to see the back of him. So much for radiating inner peace and harmony.

From:	Sophie (home)
To:	Jane (home)
Subject:	RE: Saturday Night – Chickenpox Alert

Hi Jane

Thanks so much for letting me know about Millie – poor little darling. And poor you too with your shoe school – Murphy's Law. Will be watching Hugh with baited breath now.

Feel like we didn't get the chance to speak much last Wednesday. I seemed to be constantly chasing after Hugh or dragging him off the tops of tables – how civilised our mothers' group used to be when they all stayed in one spot. I sometimes wonder if we're ever going to finish a conversation again. Thank goodness for email, is all I can say.

I did have the unfortunate pleasure of sitting next to Victoria, though. I know Mary tells us that she means no harm. (Mary would tell us to give a convicted murderer standing with a blood-soaked axe the benefit of the doubt!) But seriously, WHAT is her story? She drove me insane, telling me how fantastic Allegra is – how she's such an easy baby (is there such a thing?). And how she can't wait until Allegra is old enough to bake cakes with her. All hell broke loose when she found out that I was going back to work.

I'm due back in a few weeks (really can't afford to stay out of the loop too much longer). They gave me the option of 4 days per week, so I jumped at it. Must admit, I've been looking forward to and dreading this 'next big step' in equal measure. Victoria made me feel so damn guilty, though. I don't know what her husband does, but the bills at our place certainly can't be paid by my husband's town-planning salary much beyond April. (Nor can my sanity stay intact much beyond then either!)

Have been sitting at the computer all weekend, trawling the Internet for any hints on how to choose the best nanny. Mind you, not sure it's such a good idea, as have been totally transfixed by horror stories posted on noticeboards about nannies that steal your clothes and lock your kids in cupboards etc – have worked myself up into a real state. Have interviewed quite a few already –

what an experience. Only proving that I can confidently advise board members of multinational companies, yet am reduced to a whimpering, indecisive idiot when it comes to who looks after our son.

Had I gone back to work earlier, would I have found it easier letting go? Who knows? I guess it's never easy. (Am constantly having these guilt-ridden rhetorical conversations with myself.)

But I do know I'm being held to ransom by these nannies – all of them have 'requested' they be paid cash-in-hand. I'm so confused. Have fallen for the charms of the friendly and capable Oz/Kiwi/SA girls – but big drawback is their transience. I just want a simple life!

Can't wait to catch up and see your bespoke shoes – you clever thing. Hope Millie's on the mend soon

Sophie xx

Blimey, she sprang that one on me.

From:	Jane (home)
To:	Sophie (home)
Subject:	Sunday Night

Sophie . . . you can't leave me with Victoria . . . Aaaaargh! Am starting to get a complex – as of tomorrow Tim's spending 3 weeks out of 4 in Bangalore. (He's been having a hellish time of it lately, ever since his new boss came on board. Sadly, no end in sight.) Can't say I'm looking forward to yet more time flying solo with young bub at home. But we do what we have to do, I guess.

Am amazed, actually, at how physically shattered yet mentally invigorated I feel, just from my weekend of shoe-making – ready to tackle the demands of mothering again. Am SO proud of my creations!

Millie is soldiering on. Just difficult stopping her from itching, and keeping her indoors for now. See you in a week or so when she's spot-free. And good luck with the nannies!

Hugs to Hugh

Jane xx

New Year's resolution mark two: Get a life.

I'd like to go out on a limb and share with you a **shoe poem**, sent in by SP of Dublin. If only for the sake of helping to mend a broken heart! (And as any self-respecting SP knows, there is no better remedy than a new pair of shoes.) OK, here goes . . .

An Ode to Shoes
I love you more than cherry pies,
You never betray me and go straight to my thighs,
Or leave me once you've had your fun,
Without explanation or so much as a so long.
(*All will become clear soon . . .*)

The smell of your new leather, cheery colour and delectable touch . . .
Your illicit purchase brings no comparable rush.
(*I'm guessing cherry-red Marc Jacobs pumps?*)

Gobshite two-timing boyfriends may come and go,
But we'll be together for ever, I know.
Ah, how I looooove shoes!

14. Soft Shoe Shuffle

From: Sophie (work)
To: Jane (home)
Subject: RE: Fallen off the Radar

Hi Jane

So sorry I haven't been in touch for ages. All is good, thanks. But have just survived my first nanny crisis – a mere 4 weeks back at work. Sharelle got a severe bout of gastro and had to take a week off! Thankfully, James has a brilliant boss who let him take 2 days off work (unpaid) to look after Hugh, then Mum came down from Cheshire and covered 1 day before dashing back for a specialist's appointment, and I took a sick day. Felt like such a fraud – but was left with no other option.

Then Sharelle called to say that she'd broken up with her boyfriend and was going back to NZ – the next day. Cue me taking the whole next week off work (from my holidays – who needs them) to interview more nannies and find one that could start straight away. (And I didn't believe the agency when they said Sharelle would be the first, but definitely not the last, nanny I would ever hire.) Hence, my silence.

The irony of all of this is that I'm really enjoying being back at work. Although can't believe how efficient I am these days. No after-work drinks and pats on the back – just want to get my job done and get home as fast as I can (and hopefully catch Hugh before bed). James gets home before me and helps out with meals and bathtime. Which is fantastic – their special time together. (Doesn't mean I don't worry or still feel guilty – but I can't be in two places at once, right?)

Anyway, we've now got Rhiannon – who I'm happy to say is very single and very mature. She had the cleanest and most sensible shoes too – you've made me paranoid now about everyone's shoes.

Here's hoping that the rest of May will be hassle-free for all of us.

Hope to catch up soon (miss our Wednesday girlie chats) and much love to Millie

S xx

PS. How's Mary and Victoria and the gang? xx

Ah, what a difference a couple of months can make. The gang has all but disbanded. Mary's new-mothers' group is just that – full of new mothers again. Every one of the old-timers, bar Victoria and me, has gone back to some form of work. And we were politely told to move on and arrange our own get-together.

Which Victoria obligingly did.

So now, each Wednesday, Millie and I sit on the rug with an assortment of nannies in the front room of Victoria's massive double-fronted house overlooking Queen's Park, while she runs her Musical Maestros group. (We had to make up numbers by placing an ad on the noticeboard at the park café.) And I must say, even though Victoria makes me feel hugely inadequate, she does a fantastic job of the group.

Each week she chooses a different composer and does a little spiel on why his (yes, unfortunately no females yet) music is good for infant-brain development. Usually quoting one of her notorious 'research studies' linking, for example, early exposure to classical music with increased spatial-reasoning abilities. (Something Victoria *assures* me Millie will need if she's half a chance of getting into a decent school – not that I've thought that far ahead yet.)

The music group doesn't have the same battle-scarred camaraderie as our old mums' group, but the babies love it. And Millie and Allegra have become great friends too. Meanwhile, I think I've made friends with every white-van man in London – signing for an endless stream of home-delivered groceries, furniture, toys, designer shoes and chic French baby clothes for Victoria. She's an Internet/catalogue fanatic. Call me old-fashioned, but I like to shop – the thrill of the chase and all that!

Outside music group, Millie and I muddle along in our own little way. Mostly involving rain-sodden jaunts around the park and trips to the high street and supermarket. (As well as a newly discovered affection for wellie boots.)

But we always seem to be busy. And I always seem to be in a permanent state of exhaustion. (We haven't fully cracked the night-time sleep thing yet.) I sometimes think that it's the constant second-guessing that frazzles my brain the most: is it teething (isn't it always?); too much sleep; not enough sleep; dairy; immunisations; hungry; thirsty; too hot; too cold? I thought by now, at least, I'd have a grip on this mothering business. But it's proving to be a little more slippery than that. What with the relentless pace of growth and change in this first year, I no sooner think I've got the hang of things and the goal-posts move again.

Mum and Dad are busier than ever, and only manage to pop down to London now and then. And Kate's taken up a new philosophy course on Saturdays, so she doesn't see as much of Millie as she used to either.

I also haven't seen much of the girls since the shoe-making weekend back in March. When Fi's not busy with work she's surgically attached to Marco – they both seem very happy (an all-time record). I never did take Marco up on his kind offer to use his studio to make my mum shoes – though I think about it often. (The story of my life at the moment.) Liz's gone under-ground – maybe starting another round of IVF? Not sure and not game to ask. And Rachel's still slinking off to the stationery cupboard with her work lover – yet another record.

Oh, yes, and Tim. My husband. He's also kind of deserted us. He phones daily when he's in Bangalore (still three weeks out of four) and has set up a webcam on the computer for Millie. Poor little sweetheart, she's gone from thinking her father's a 'bond-ing board' to an interactive computer game. I do miss him terribly, but the sad thing is, we're quite set in our own little routines now and actually getting quite used to it.

But that doesn't mean we haven't made some new friends too. There's Florence, my ninety-two-year-old neighbour – a true local, who was born in her tiny terraced house and went on to raise six children there. I can't believe I'd lived here for three years and barely said hello to her before now. Florence is always good for a pot of tea and a chat. As well as a gentle reminder of the layer of privilege that encompasses modern-day life, which is brought forcefully home when she recounts stories of far too many babies and relatives lost to disease and war.

And then, lest I forget, that wonderful world of daytime TV, where my home-makeover obsession is now in fierce competition with *The Wiggles*, which Millie adores. (I must admit the tunes are quite catchy.) And then there's *Brunch with Britain* – bursting at the seams with bickering and subliminal power-plays between the deliciously vacuous (and quite handsome) Gavin and the perma-tanned, perma-surprised (Botox-overdosed?) Tamsin. Live theatre at its best! Sophie used to call them our daily G & T – sufficiently mind-numbing, yet pleasantly addictive.

Thankfully, I've still got my faithful royal web family – the Shoe Princess and Trash Queenz. Florence can't quite get her head around me needing to talk to women in cyberspace, especially when she had her entire extended family living within a one-mile radius. But they truly are a lifeline.

As is Mary the health visitor, I have to say. Ever since she found out about Tim being away so much, she's made a concerted effort to pop in and say hello when she's on her morning rounds. She'll often call in to us at the end of her clinic days too and stop for a proper chat. I hadn't realised just how much I looked forward to her visits until she took a few days off recently – I really missed her smiling face and genuine concern for our well-being. And, of course, Millie adores her.

So, what does all of this add up to? Well, that largely depends upon which day and which hour of that day the question's asked: Lucky. Suffocated. Awestruck. Invisible. Proud. Bittersweet. Happy. Tired. Lonely. Content. Bored. Humble. Guilty. Challenged. Loved. Very, very loved. And in love. With Millie.

'Jane, pick up the phone. It's Fi. You have to be home. It's 9.30 a.m. Friday morning. Please tell me you're not at a baby group. Well, if you are, you're becoming a . . . a . . . playgroup junkie. It can't be good for Millie – all this Mozart whatsamathingy. Goodness knows, all we used to do was crawl around our mothers' legs and play with pegs while she hung out the washing – and we turned out all right. Oh, come on. Pick. Up. The. Phone.'

'Fi, hi. Lovely to hear from you. Where are you?'

'I'm in the car. On my way back into London – I've had a week away with client meetings and –'

'Great,' I cut in. 'You won't believe what we're watching? G & T got the big interview with The Cat.' The nation's been holding its collective breath over her 'alleged' split from Jeremy Jones, the football hero turned celebrity chef. (And incidentally, not Happy Sunshine's father.)

'Ohmy god. Even the Trash Queenz couldn't scoop this. Do tell,' Fi says excitedly.

'Tamsin's asking all the probing questions. And wait for it . . . Blimey, yes, they've officially split. She says, "The single-mother life is best for me." And while she can't "confirm or deny" any rumours, she is "loving life" and looking forward to "juggling full-time motherhood" with her "business career".'

'Wow. He *did* sleep with her nanny!' Fi can hardly contain her excitement. 'And they were only crowned the new It couple last week.' The curse of *Hello!* rides again.

'The minx!' I yelp. 'She's plonked Happy Sunshine on to Gavin's lap and is now giving a pole-dancing demonstration. Coincidentally, a DVD called *Cat-a-Pole the Pounds Away: From Mummy to Scrummy in Three Easy Weeks* will be in the shops tomorrow.'

Damn, she's good too.

'And she's wearing that bloody cat-suit again. It's borderline soft porn. Gavin's hyperventilating. Maybe I should turn it off – for Millie's sake.'

'Noooooo! She won't remember it when she's older. And if she does, I'll pay for her psychotherapy.'

'Oh, Fi. MAJOR Cat-astrophe. Happy Sunshine's wriggled off Gavin's lap on to the floor, picked up his half-finished mug of cold coffee, and tipped it *all over* Tamsin's cream suede Manolos. I can't watch.'

I don't know whether to laugh or cry. Poor Tamsin.

'Euuw. Is she absolutely throttling Gavin?'

'No. Not only has she picked up Happy Sunshine and placed him on *her* lap, but she's kept smiling as if *nothing* happened. What a pro!'

'Well, I wouldn't like to be in Gavin's size 10s after the show today.'

'Nor would I. Not in a million years.'

After The Cat slinks out of the studio and we've calmed down, Fi eventually tells me that she's phoned to coerce Millie and me into going to a shoe exhibition with her and Marco today. It's at a hip warehouse down by Tate Modern, and is being staged by one of Marco's old classmates from the Ars Arpel Shoe School in Milan.

'But shouldn't you be at work?'

'Oh, don't worry – I can afford to take the rest of the day off. I'm the new golden girl – thanks to all the income I've been generating on the Jolie Naturelle account.' I feel a pang as I remember that Richard was certainly good like that – never a clock-watcher. '. . . Sorry, sweetie, for mentioning Jolie Naturelle,' Fi says awkwardly.

'Don't be silly. I'm OK. Really.' Well, sort of. I still have the occasional moment of regret when I see Fi glowing with success. (Particularly if I'm up to my elbows in poo!) But the harsh reality that, if I was on the Jolie Naturelle account, I'd never be able to care for Millie (let alone know or understand her as well as I do) is enough to put on hold any fanciful notions of smart shoes and PowerPoint presentations. For now.

'And in any case, Alison can cover. She's been doing some unbelievable work for Jolie Naturelle lately. They adore her.'

Oh, bollocks, she's still there. Still stretched like elastic, no doubt. Still tolerating the banal antics of men and the childless, fertility-controlled females (the old me). Still very good at her job, it seems. And *still* without an apology from me.

'And don't worry about money either, it's Aunt Fi's shout.' Fi's well aware of my new pauper status.

She also tells me that an email–alert came through this morning on Shoe Princess, saying that a portion of the entrance fees will be donated to charity – as long as we're wearing red shoes. So we have to go.

'And I know you've got at least forty pairs of red shoes to choose from, Jane Meadows. And so has Millie, for that matter. It will be good for her see the creative toils of a living genius for a change.'

I mumble something about sleeps and routine, but Fi's having none of it.

'We'll drop by your place around midday.'

Gain Without Pain

If your days of dancing till dawn in stilettos are fading fast, yet you want a statement-making high heel for a special occasion, go for a stiletto with a small **platform sole**. It makes for a much more comfortable ride.

Most designers from the high street to Chanel have embraced the platform sole this season, so there is an abundance of style variations to choose from. They work particularly well with round toes and peep-toes, in satin for the evening. And a strappy sandal with a full-wedge platform sole is great for summer sundresses.

But beware, SPs, if you're over 35 years old the platform sole must not be higher than 1–1.5 cm to achieve the desired elegant silhouette. Any higher and we're teetering into pole-dancing territory! Quite literally, given the propensity of PVC and perspex platforms on the shelves at the moment.

Only younger SPs can get away with the glam, ridiculously high platform wedges with a bit more attitude – think purple luminescent Miu Miu party shoes!

Pump Up the Volume

A SP can never have too many pairs of shoes. The more you have, the longer they'll last. Remember the three golden rules of shoe wearing: rotation, rotation, rotation.

15. Heel Heaven

SOMETHING'S been bothering me about Fi since we arrived at the exhibition. And when she lifts her trousers to present her red ballet pumps to the ticket attendant (who indeed gives us a special Shoe Princess ticket, emblazoned with the name of a charity) it hits me: she's wearing *flat* shoes.

I haven't seen her in flat shoes since about 1985. It's almost unnerving. She was adamant that she wasn't going to succumb to the fad, too. And at least Rachel has the legs of a giraffe to carry them off, whereas Fi simply looks like me now – plain, short old Jane.

'So,' I quiz, 'what's with the shoes?'

'My yoga guru says that my stilettos are interfering with my mind–body energies. I need to be more "grounded".'

Oh, not the yoga still. I was so sure she'd have tired of it by now.

'Since when?' I ask.

'Last night. Today's my maiden voyage,' she says with mock trepidation and playfully pretends to lose balance.

As if it wasn't bad enough back in March, when she gave up hair dye and 'the world of illusion'. Her guru assuring her that mousy brown, also *circa* 1985, was more conducive to inner balance and harmony than golden blonde.

I glance over to Marco to gauge his reaction. His continuing affection is, after all, the goal of Fi's whole yoga farce. And try as I might, I just can't get my head around the logic of seducing the demi-god of stilettos by waddling along like a flat-footed penguin. But then again, he clearly adores her, no matter what her hair colour or shoe style. There's no telling Fi this, of course.

I'm mortified when Marco catches my eye, and gives me a cheeky smile and a wink, as if he knows exactly what I'm thinking.

As I watch him take Fi by the hand and walk up the small staircase with her, it suddenly strikes me: maybe this flat-shoed folly *will* work. She's certainly more needy and dependent on him, now that her centre of gravity's entirely evaporated. Let's hope so. Because I'd hate her to be trying to fix something that isn't broken, particularly as it seems to be going so well between them.

We pull aside a heavy gold-mesh curtain in order to enter the exhibition, and the 'wow factor' hits us immediately. I feel like we've been entombed – or at least gone to heel heaven! The whole room is darkened and all I can see is a twelve-foot-high wall of perspex shoeboxes, stacked together like brickwork, and containing glittering shoes of every colour of the rainbow. Similar shoebox-walls separate each section.

I'm so glad Fi enticed me out of my Kilburn safe haven. It's impossible not to be mesmerised by the vast showcase of colours, music, books, hand-drawn sketches and of course many, many pairs of shoes in countless styles and heel shapes, and not to forget fabrics. I really don't know which way to look first.

Millie's squealing with delight and pulling at the straps of her pushchair, trying to get out. Now that she's crawling, she's not so happy to be strapped in for very long. Plus, I know exactly what she wants to do – play with the shoes. Her favourite pastime at home and a definite no-no here.

After my humble foray into basic shoe-making with Marco, I can tell just how masterfully these shoes have been made. My favourite parts are undoubtedly the embellishments: jewels, fringing, fur, rivets, bells, eyelets, appliqués, pompoms, shells, ribbons, feathers, the list is endless. The shoes positively dance with the energy of imagination. It's completely inspiring and fills me with a rush of enthusiasm for my mum shoes project. I stop to jot down a few ideas on the back of a scrap of paper I find in Millie's nappy bag.

Marco spots me.

'Ah! The sign of a true designer,' he says enthusiastically. 'I never go anywhere without my notebook.' He holds up a battered leather-bound diary that he's been sketching in too. We both laugh.

'I'll be seeing you in the studio soon, then,' he says.

'Maybe,' I blush. And then Fi catches up to us and shuffles us along.

We've now done a full loop of the exhibition, and find ourselves back near the entrance in a darkened lounge area, where there is an enormous bright-red sofa along with a continuous screening of Carrie's shoe-thief scene from *Sex and the City* on the opposite wall. Fi, Marco and I settle on to the sofa to watch it, with Millie beside us in her pushchair, when Fi suddenly spots Ben from our shoe school.

'Ben, yoo-hoo! Ben!' Subtlety has never been one of Fi's finer points.

He's with a group of women and has his arm around a slightly podgy, plain-looking girl. Funny, I'd always imagined his fiancée to be a bit more glam. And a bit younger. But that's just like Ben, I guess, to go for personality over looks. He really is so mature for a guy his age.

Anyway, I always get a thrill, in a city the size of London, to run into someone I know. And Ben is definitely surprised to see us, hurriedly making his way over.

We both immediately spy his shiny red trainers.

'You didn't tell us you were a Shoe Princess convert,' I tease. Fi cackles and we're shushed by everyone reverentially waiting for the video clip to begin again.

We hastily agree a rendezvous at a nearby café before he goes off to rejoin his party and we skulk back on to the sofa. Marco's decidedly unmoved when we gloat to him about our imminent meeting with Ben's much-talked-about fiancée. I always sense that he frowns upon our overenthusiastic interest in her. He certainly never seemed to talk to Ben about her at the shoe-school weekend – but maybe that's just a bloke thing.

Marco decides to leave us alone to watch Carrie, and darts off to do another quick round of the exhibition.

Fi and I had both forgotten how completely fabulous the shoe skit was. We're sitting discussing whether to stay and watch it a second time when Marco returns, seemingly rather pleased with himself.

'He leans down and, placing his hand on my forearm, says, 'Jane, have you got a moment? There's an excellent book on display I've just found – I'd love to show you.'

'Ohhh-K?' I glance at Fi.

'It was a text that I used in my studies at Ars Arpel in Milan. I think it would be very good for you – if you're serious about shoe-making.'

Fi relaxes back into the sofa and kindly offers to sit with Millie through another rerun while I quickly go and check out this book. Luckily she's not the least bit interested in shoe textbooks or shoe-making, for that matter – Marco and Ben practically made her shoes for her on our weekend school – so at least I don't feel guilty.

The book is back in the middle of the exhibition but, as it turns out, it's well worth the trek. I love seeing it and hearing Marco talk avidly of his student days at Ars Arpel. He also tells me how he now goes back to give tutorials – arranging them to coincide with his visits home to see his mum and siblings – and that he could easily get me in on one of his classes, if I wanted. Dare I even dream!

As we make our way back to Fi we're stunned to run straight into her – holding Millie on her hip – barging through the mesh curtain with all the grace of a bank robber.

'Don't say anything. Jane, follow me. Marco, go inside and get Ben to help,' she says calmly yet purposefully.

We both know her well enough not to ask any questions.

Finally, out on the riverbank and well away from the exhibition, we stop. And Fi explains.

With Marco and I taking a little longer than expected, Millie started to get restless, so Fi thought she'd let her out of the pushchair for a stretch. Of course, in a split-second, Millie crawled straight over to the shoeboxes and with one dainty nudge caused the entire entrance wall to collapse. Leaving the remainder of the shoebox-walls wobbling precariously like the San Andreas Fault.

Total chaos erupted. Security guards streamed in and Fi and Millie slipped out.

We burst into fits of laughter and make our way back across the footbridge; the Thames' dark inky water flowing strongly beneath us. I'm sure it's seen worse crimes in its time than an inquisitive eight-and-a-half-month-old tumbling a few hundred shoeboxes!

Ben, I'm told, managed to use his best set-design skills to reconstruct the shoebox-wall. Aunt Fi needed a strong drink and a lie-down after almost crippling herself by running in flat shoes. And Marco stealthily took home the incriminating evidence – Millie's pushchair – hand-delivering it back to me the next day.

Oh Millie. What a story to tell on your twenty-first birthday!

My spies at the exhibition on Friday tell me it was a resounding success — despite the small shoebox earthquake! So thank you to all of my loyal subjects who went along, and helped to raise an astonishing amount of money for charity.

Shoe Shame

Like many of you, I find some of the images in the media these days very disturbing, and yesterday was no exception: I opened my newspaper to the horror-vision of The Cat sitting on the edge of a pool with her A-list Sardinian crowd — feet dangling in the water with her **stilettos still on**. Has this Cat creature no respect for the sanctity of shoes? She may as well have been holding her child's head underwater. I had to tear the offending page out and banish it to the bin.

And on the other side of the Atlantic, I'm hearing stories of shoe valets at pool parties in the Hamptons. Where they apparently take your bejewelled beauties from your feet and provide everyone with identical pool shoes.

I don't know what's worse . . . If I want to attend a party looking like every other person in the room, wearing standard-issue clogs, I'll book into prison.

Vive la différence!

Footnote

Not that a SP needs an excuse, but . . .
If a shoe is available for retail purchase, it is technically 'on sale'.

16. Tread Carefully

I AM aware that I'm a freak. Not a weirdo-harm-to-society freak, but definitely an on-the-edge-of-mainstream kind of freak.

Like wearing vintage black-and-white polka-dot platforms to my free-dress day at school, aged eleven. Or being the only person in the City not doing coke on a Friday night (kiss of death to the shoe fund). But I have to say, this stay-at-home-mum gig (not the *most* fashionable lifestyle choice these days) is *really* testing my mettle.

So it's no surprise that I jumped at Marco's offer to pay me 'in kind' (a pair of shoes of my choice from his collection) for helping him to finish the shoes for *A Midsummer Night's Dream* – as Ben's snowed under with the set designs and unable to lend him a hand. And with a strict five-day deadline that coincided perfectly with Tim's week home from India, it was too good to refuse.

Of course, Tim thinks I'm insane, slaving all day at home with Millie and then again late into the evening at Marco's studio, and keeps moaning that we barely see each other. His hypocrisy is not completely lost on me – given the enormous amount of time I'm left on my own when he's working. Plus it's all good experience for me. Especially if I'm ever to get my mum shoes project off the ground.

Fi annoyingly greeted the news of my job with lukewarm enthusiasm. As if I was somehow trying to sabotage her precious 'alone time' with Marco. Her insecurity radars are on full alert at present, due to the fact that she's in uncharted waters. This is the most serious relationship she's ever been involved in, by far. And while I've always been hugely tolerant of Fi and her dating neuroses – diligently patching and fluffing up her ego and sending her back out into the fray – I just don't seem to have the emotional capacity for them these days. Particularly as this is something that I *really* want to do, and an opportunity not to be missed.

Thankfully, Fi found a way out of her melancholy and has reinvented herself as Marco's PA for the project. (Marco's organisational skills are akin to those of a nutty professor, which is possibly why he's in this predicament in the first place.) She's absolutely thrown herself into the project – arranging fittings, and ferrying materials, shoes and people all over London each evening. Not a stone's been left unturned.

In spite of Tim and Fi, my own slightly flagging spirits have been greatly boosted by Marco's faith in my abilities. I'd almost forgotten how enjoyable it is to work on a project – with a team and a pressing deadline. I feel like the fire in my belly has been reignited.

My main task has been to make the shoes for Puck, the mischievous fairy helper – who's incidentally being played by a woman. During her shoe fittings she's spoken openly to me about losing her left leg (above the knee) in a car accident eight years ago. (She was twenty-three and hit by an oncoming car on her way to work.) She's super-excited about showing off her new state-of-the-art false limb in her shoes too. The money from her legal case has just come through, which has allowed her to ditch her NHS tree-stump and get some glam shoes made at the last minute. They're a slightly more difficult version of the mules that we made at shoe school – in white patent leather, with a Louis heel and large red sequinned bow on the front – and quite a challenge for me; but nonetheless exciting too.

Mum, Dad, Kate, Tim and Millie have all come along this evening to the Open Air Theatre, appropriately on midsummer's eve, to admire the fruits of our labours. And after the fiasco at the shoe exhibition, they've been given strict instructions to keep Millie out of mischief – even if it involves Dad taking her for a walk around the entire Regent's Park. I don't want any extras on stage tonight.

Once seated, we find ourselves cocooned in an enchanted wood of lush green trees, rose-perfumed air and evening birdsong. The occasional hovering jumbo jet or distant siren the only clues to the bustling city beyond.

With only minutes to go until the start, my thoughts wander to the actors as well as to Marco, Ben and Fi all working frantically backstage. I can't help but smile when I think about Puck, and how she will most definitely be creating havoc in the woods tonight. She's a real pocket dynamo, and an inspiration.

'Now remind me, what's the play about?' Tim poorly disguises the cloud of impending boredom looming over him.

'Being with the one you love. Oh, and fairies. But mostly the power of imagination!' I can barely contain my excitement, as this is one of my all-time favourite plays. Though I fully appreciate the latter two concepts may be a little left-of-field for my darling computer nerd of a husband.

With a wry smile, Tim kisses me and places his arm around me, squeezing me tenderly.

'Let the magic begin, then.'

Mum gives us a little wink. She and Dad are sitting on a rug on the grassed section beside us, with Millie nestled in her lap – heavy-lidded and glazy-eyed in the mottled twilight.

As a wave of hush rolls across the audience, I spot Liz and Harry hurriedly making their way over to us.

A few weeks back, after months of little contact from Liz, I summoned the courage to keep calling until her answer machine was full and she had no choice but to pick up the phone. Sometimes that's what friends are for, isn't it?

Anyway, she dropped the bombshell that she and Harry had been having a terrible time of it – their relationship disintegrating under the pressure of IVF the past year or so. This news *really* rocked us. We'd always envisioned Liz and Harry as the sweet old couple walking arm in arm along Brighton Pier. It was a given.

I guess, as Liz said, 'Nothing turns you off sex more than *having* to do it.'

But tonight Liz blushes uncontrollably when I whisper that I'm glad they could make it out of their bedroom to come along. For in a happy twist, they reached a watershed a few months back, and have been 'going for it' with little time for anyone, or anything else.

Harry's beaming and I'm so completely chuffed for them.

In such a surreal setting, and with my loved ones around me, I can't help but openly count my blessings. I turn and kiss Tim's hand as he gently caresses my shoulder. It's hard to think how life could get any better.

A warm breeze swirls around our feet and the play begins.

While I've been looking forward to seeing Puck perform, I've also been really nervous for her too. As she also suffered a mild head injury from the accident which affects her ability to plan and organise her thoughts. But she assured me that she'd been taught loads of tricks by the occupational therapists on how to memorise her lines. A gaggle of them are here tonight cheering her on from the front row.

I needn't have worried. Puck's a stand-out star! And if she has missed any lines no one is the wiser, as her stage presence and energy is infectious. In fact, all the actors have done a superb job, and by the interval the atmosphere is electric.

Tim, Liz, Harry, Kate and I are standing in the bar area when Fi comes rushing over.

'Oh, Jane, great! We need you ASAP. It's Oberon. He's having a *major* muscle spasm and I can't get his boots back on. It's at least a two-person job, and we can't have the King of the Fairies *sans* boots. Everything's gone haywire back there. Marco and Ben are *frantic*.'

I glance quickly at Tim, who, seeing my eyes light up with the thrill of being needed for a shoe emergency, nudges me towards Fi.

'I'll be back as soon as possible,' I promise.

'Actually, Liz, I think we'll need your help too,' says Fi.

Liz splutters and chokes a little on her champagne.

'Oh, I don't know. I didn't even finish my shoes at shoe school, remember. I won't be much help.'

Her response gives Fi a visible shock; it's most unlike Liz not to offer help. But then again, I notice her clutching Harry's hand like a newlywed and it seems almost criminal to separate them.

Fi clearly doesn't have time for polite parley and turns desperately to Kate, who is on her way backstage with us without even needing to be asked.

'Oh my!' Fi wasn't wrong when she said it was chaos back here. She immediately darts over to Ben and the other set designers, who are in a complete tizz. It looks like some fairy lights have singed the props for the next scene.

Marco quickly nabs me, giving me instructions on how to restitch one of the gold-leather ties on Titania's stilettos. Kate and I then help him get Oberon's boots on, while he chats animatedly, seemingly elated by how well his shoes have fared. I'm *so* pleased for him and can't help but give him a congratulatory hug and peck on the cheek.

After a couple more frenzied jobs, and still high from the adrenalin of our backstage visit, we make our way to the audience. The next act's due to start any minute.

'So that's THE Marco?' Kate says inquisitively.

'Yes, indeed.' I keep forgetting that she hasn't met Fi's man yet.

'Who you've been spending all the time with in the studio – making shoes.'

'Uhuh,' I nod. Though I'm not sure I like her tone and am curious as to where she's heading with this.

She purses her lips and mutters a feeble, 'Mmm.' I *really* hate it when she does this.

'What?' I say a little defensively. She's giving me the spooks.

'And Tim's OK with this?'

'Oh, bloody hell, Kate. It's not Saudi Arabia. I don't need my husband's *permission* to work with a man, you know.'

'A very handsome man, who you certainly get on well with.'

'Meaning . . .'

'All the hugging and kissing.'

This is slightly ridiculous.

'He's Italian. He's very tactile. It means *nothing* to him. And in any case, I was genuinely happy for him.'

'Well, I'm just saying you looked a little *flirty*,' she says.

'Oh, get a grip Kate,' I say in exasperation. She, of all people, should know that I had a sufficiently misspent youth, and am hardly the most likely candidate for a miniskirts-and-disco-ball midlife crisis. No matter how often my husband buggers off to India.

'And don't you think Fi seemed odd too?' she pushes on.

I have to say I've sort of got used to Fi being a little strung-out lately, what with the whole yoga-no-high-heels-no-hair-dye-uncharted-waters thing. And in any case, she's got good reason to be stressed out tonight.

'You know what Fi's like when she's under pressure. She's so desperate to impress Marco and wants everything to be perfect.'

'My point exactly. Fi's your best friend, Jane. And Tim's the best thing that ever happened to you. Tread carefully.'

I don't even dignify that with a response.

The hazy twilight suddenly gives way to an ominous shroud of darkness and we march back to our seats in stony silence – only for me to find Tim's empty.

Oh.

Liz leans over and whispers, 'Tim got an urgent call from work – Alex or someone or other. There's a major computer glitch. He said it'll probably be a late one, and not to wait up for him.'

Just great. I swear, ever since Alex came on the scene, Tim's taken on the role of executive dogsbody, ready to jump at his every beck and call.

More than a little dejected, I jostle my way over to the grassed section and snuggle up on the rug with Mum, Dad and Millie. As I watch the remainder of the play, I can only conclude that Puck's been rubbing pansy juice in Kate's eyes too. I can't believe she had me explaining myself about something that doesn't even exist.

I am not attracted to Marco.

Am I?

OK, I won't deny that he is quite *fanciable*. And there was that little *frisson* at shoe school. But I purely enjoy his company for our shared passion for shoes. That's it.

Right?

Well . . . he *has* featured in the odd X-rated daydream. But who doesn't have fantasies? Maybe not ones involving their best friend's boyfriend, I admit. (If it's any consolation, Tim was in them too.)

And Marco most certainly does not fancy me.

Does he?

Nah. This is real life, not theatre – people don't magically switch affections.

Do they?

I suddenly feel a little uneasy.

Bloody Kate.

Puck delivers the final lines to rapturous applause:

If we shadows have offended,
Think but this, and all is mended,
That you have but slumber'd here,
While these visions did appear . . .

Yes, that's it. I'll wake up next to Tim tomorrow and this will have been nothing but a bad dream. And we'll all live happily ever after.

I might just suss out Fi, though . . .

Shoe Are You?

Cinderella SP

The poor little overworked and underpaid housewife who can no longer afford to buy whatever shoes take her fancy. She sees her rapidly diminishing shoe collection as a metaphor of her current life horizons, yet takes meticulous care of the shoes she does have. Is mostly spotted in pram shoes (ugly with scuffed toes) or sensible flat driving shoes (school run). She has been known to skimp on household food items and transfer assets to a 'secret shoe fund'. She asks her family to give her money at Christmas to spend at the shoe sales in lieu of presents. The **Cinderella SP** has several pairs of unworn, expensive high-heeled evening shoes in boxes — just in case she gets whisked away to that five-Michelin-starred restaurant for her wedding anniversary. (Ha!)

Court Jester SP

A close cousin of the **Cinderella SP**. So named because of the juggling act this working mum maintains. She spends so much money on childcare she can't justify keeping up with the latest trends in footwear. Her shoes are usually purchased solely from sale racks and are comically out of date compared to those of the **Cosmo** and **Fashionista SPs**.

Politically Correct SP

This princess has strong socio-political beliefs which are reflected in her footwear; she will, for example, only wear non-animal products on her feet. She either has a keen and often quirky sense of style, or no style at all. She has been known to morph into the **Earth SP** and will only wear Birkenstocks or elfin handmade sandals from Neil's Yard.

Pauper SP

Clever and resourceful student princess who scours funky and obscure flea markets for up-to-the-minute shoes or links up with fashion-design-student friends and makes her own. This princess can't wait to earn real money and start investing in a proper shoe collection. But in the meantime, she's happy to make do with cheap imitations and ALWAYS looks gorgeous.

17. Toe the Line

From: Fi (work)
To: Jane (home)
Subject: RE: Play

Hi Jane

It was a FABULOUS evening, wasn't it! Marco's still on a high.

Your instincts were spot on, of course. Sorry if I seemed a little weird. There's something I've been wanting to tell you face to face but, with everything going on and Kate being in the way, the right opportunity never came up. So, here goes . . .

I'm really, really, really sorry, but when you next log on to Shoe Princess, please don't be cross with me. You may recognise a YouTube video clip (with music from the *King Kong* soundtrack!) of a certain person's feet: Kate's. (Remember from the day at shoe school.)

I entered her in the **Eliza Shoelittle** competition, not thinking that it would go any further. But alas, I (or rather Kate) has just won a pair of designer shoes, plus a bonus 12 months' worth of waxing and pedicure vouchers. (The Shoe Princess said she'd never seen anyone so badly in need of shoe therapy before!)

I know it was very naughty of me – but I couldn't resist.

Must dash, chat soon

Fi xx

PS. Do you think I should fess up to Kate and share the prize? Then again, we could take Liz's lead and sell the shoes on eBay (they're an exquisite classic Salvatore Ferragamo court) and go out for a girlie lunch to a posh restaurant? F x

Phew.

From:	Rachel (work)
To:	Jane (home)
Subject:	RE: Play

Darling

Sorry I couldn't make it – don't do pagan festivals. Actually, got caught up at work. Glad all went well though, and that hunky Marco's shoes were star attractions.

You won't believe it – have been seconded to Edinburgh office for 4–6 months with Mr X. An all-expenses-paid sex-a-thon. Not sure if will find it too suffocating though, without his wife to go home to each evening?

Will see.

R xx

Wife? Oh, Rachel.

From:	Fi (work)
To:	Jane (home)
Subject:	FW: Fat Cat

I really will do some work today . . . this just came in. xx

TrashQueenz e-lert

Fat Cat: Which supermodel-supermum (pictured) has been spotted frolicking in the park with her baby, looking decidedly chunky?

The photo's grainy, but there's no denying the feline: it's The Cat. Or rather, The Fat Cat. She's *very* big. This is disastrous. (And yet more than a teeny bit enjoyable, too!)

I've barely had time to bask in the glory of The Cat's calorific blow-out when an annoying Kate-thought bubbles to the surface and niggles at my conscience: *Is it truly gracious to get morbid delight from someone else's weight gain?*

But after a nanosecond of contemplation, I decide that The Cat and I are about even. It serves her right for brazenly flaunting her way into my living room as a size zero immediately after Happy Sunshine was born, making me feel so bad.

Doesn't it?

From: Sophie (work)
To: Jane (home)
Subject: RE: Nanny Contract

Hi Jane

Here's a copy of Rhiannon's contract – good luck with it all. I didn't realise you were looking for a nanny. (Does this mean things have settled down with Tim, and he's back in London?) Trust me, you won't regret it. Going back to work has been like plugging my brain back into the National Grid. And Hugh's totally in love with Rhiannon – actually, we all are!

S xx

Sophie, you star! Though my request has nothing to do with a return to work *just* yet (nor is a nanny ever likely to be an option on my salary – ha). And it's regrettably nothing to do with Tim ditching Bangalore either. (Far from it, in fact.) No, I need this to crib for Dad's Home Parent Assistant contract. Mum and Kate want me to babysit him next month while they go off on their indulgent little August holidays (Kate, naturally, on a carbon-neutral biking tour of the Lake District with her philosophy group; and Mum to a cooking school in Tuscany) so I am going to set some ground rules.

You see, no matter how good it will be to have Dad to stay (given that Tim will now be in Bangalore for the entire month of August, thanks to the interminable Alex and that bloody company) I've already got one baby to look after, and that is quite enough. In fact, if it weren't for the upcoming treat of a night with Tim at his annual luxury team-building conference in Oxfordshire, just before he jets back to Bangalore, I think I'd be in a complete state of denial about the summer altogether.

Home Parent Assistant (HPA) Contract

Employee	Dad (HPA)
Employer	Jane – Home parent (HP)
Place of Work	Meadows' residence, Kilburn, London NW6
Duration	The month of August
Hours	24 hours per day, 7 days per week
Remuneration	As per the basic salary, overtime, pension, incapacity, sickness and holiday entitlements of the home parent: NIL

Duties and Benefits

1. The HPA will be transported to the Meadows' residence when the HP returns to London from her husband's

team-building conference in Oxfordshire. The HPA will be provided with free board and lodging for the duration of the contract, but is strongly reminded that he is **not on holiday** and, in the absence of the HPA's wife, is responsible for looking after his own health, safety and well-being.

2. The HPA shall carry out any duties deemed reasonably appropriate by the HP, including: playing with Millie and taking her for walks (especially between 10 and 11 a.m. and the 'witching hour' of 4.30 to 5.30 p.m); keeping the workplace clean and tidy (the vacuum cleaner is in the cupboard next to the cooker). **NB:** The HPA will not be expected to change dirty nappies, unless in an emergency – in which case a brief training period will be provided.

3. The HPA shall be allowed reasonable and responsible use of the family television (inclusive of cable channels), **except during *Brunch with Britain*, *The Wiggles*, *Desperate Housewives*, *House*, and ALL reruns of *Sex and the City* and *What Not to Wear***. The television benefit may be withdrawn if excessive viewing of the following occurs: **Antiques Roadshow, The Weather Channel, The History Channel** or **ANY sports channel** (in particular, cricket).

4. The HPA will be allowed to bring his dog Pierre for the duration of the contract, and will be responsible for all feeding, hygiene, exercise and related tasks. If said dog destroys ONE pair of the HP's shoes, he will be relocated to the nearest pound.

Exclusions

The HPA is forbidden to:

Bring more than one computer for personal use into the

work premises, or perform any physics experiments in said premises (especially kitchen and bathroom); start up discussions with the HP on topics related to the meaning of life and the existence of anti-matter; count or criticise the number of shoes he may come across in the workplace; give Millie chocolates, Twiglets or any other sweets, unless expressly approved by the HP.

I agree and accept the terms and conditions set out in this contract,

Home Parent Assistant   Home parent
(Signature and date)   (Signature and date)

Brilliant! A happy summer shall be had by all.

Manolo Blahnik Moments of Madness

I get sent so many Manolo stories, here's my **Top 10** (in no particular order):

1. Full marks for initiative to junior SP of Hong Kong, aged 9 years, who sawed off the 9cm heels on her mother's Manolos so that she could wear them.

2. Why not? SPs at Manolo Blahnik shopping 'events' in the US routinely buy two sets of the same pair of shoes – one to wear and the other (autographed) to display on their mantelpiece.

3. A popular London daytime TV personality reportedly renewed her contract with the network at the 11th hour, thanks to the inclusion of a 'shoe clause' – to feed her Manolo habit.

4. Go, Sister! A Spanish nun was sentenced to community service after embezzling school-library funds and spending them on 30 pairs of Manolos.

5. SP of Paris only ever wears skyscraper Manolos and drinks champagne during long-haul flights. Vowing that it prevents jetlag and always makes the destination city look more interesting.

6. Manolo rules the waves! SP of Shanghai was spied confidently strutting along a narrow gangway to a river-boat in a pair of towering alligator-skin party shoes.

7. Respect to SP of Toronto, who gave birth in 10cm Manolos — in stirrups.

8. Feng Shoey! SP of Los Angeles sued her (now ex-) boyfriend for emotional distress and material damages when he mistook her shoe-cupboard door for her bathroom door after a big night out — caking her many pairs of Manolos in vomit. (Surely death row would have been more appropriate!)

9. SP of St Petersburg highly recommends Manolos to inject spice into love-making — ever since her boyfriend started wearing them.

10. It must be love! Cape Town model and SP put 200 pairs of Manolos up for sale on eBay after her boyfriend refused to move in with her unless she halved her shoe collection.

18. Buckle Up

SATURDAY evening mega-pack for luxury team-building extravaganza: red patent-leather loafers – for car journey and motorway pit stops (must be able to withstand possible baby vomit and changing Millie on floor of grotty loo). Check. Sparkly slides and woven-mesh carry-all – perfect for antique fossicking in charming Oxfordshire village, post-baby-drop-off at Mum and Dad's. Check. Hot pink-and-white gingham lace-ups, Jackie-O sunglasses and wide-brimmed hat – just in case we venture into a field. Check. Zebra-print pony-hair peep-toe wedges – to jazz up afternoon tea. Check. Satin jewel-trimmed slippers – for languishing post-love-making (with gin and tonic and girlie trash novel in hand) while Tim slumbers. Check. Cherry-and-lilac paisley-patterned wellie boots – for pre-dinner clay-pigeon shooting (that's what they do at manor houses, isn't it?). Check. Gold-chain-linked T-bar platform stilettos – for welcome dinner. Mmm, maybe a tad too 'out there' for Tim's geeky IT crowd? Will take classic black three-inch court shoes as a fall-back. Check. Check. Now to pack my clothes and make-up, and we're done.

6.30 a.m. Sunday morning: I'm fully dressed and sitting at the kitchen table waiting for Tim and Millie to wake up – a first for me. All our bags are lined up down the hallway, ready for the drive. Words cannot describe how excited I am about getting out of London and having some precious alone time with Tim. And not to mention *finally* getting to meet his new boss Alex and the rest of the guys he's been spending so much time with in Bangalore.

Tim's suitcase was pretty easy to organise, as he's just flown in from Bangalore, where they now, thankfully, have a full laundering service – so have merely added a few more casual clothes and shoes for good measure. He's staying on at the manor house for a week, doing more team-building things, and then going straight back to Bangalore for four weeks. (Just our luck that August is near enough to a five-week month this year.) But I'm trying not to think about that right now, imagining instead the fabulously decadent time we are going to have together in the lap of five-star luxury.

This is rather an auspicious occasion too. It's the first time *ever* that 'partners' have been allowed to come to one of Tim's conferences – albeit for just one night and the welcome dinner. And from what he's told me of previous years, they are quite opulent affairs – very much a staff reward. And goodness knows they deserve it this year, with all the travelling that they've been doing.

It takes two hours for Tim to get out of bed, do his yoga (I guarantee he's more evangelical about it than Fi), have a shower, read the paper, play with Millie, take copious photos of Millie, get Millie fed and changed, and pack the car before we're finally en route to the motorway. And after only one turn-back (not my fault this time – Tim forgot a work CD-Rom) we are still on schedule to drop Millie off at my parents' house before checking in mid-afternoon. (And maybe taking full advantage of the four-poster bed and a cheeky bubble bath, pre-dinner.)

As we settle into the rhythm of the motorway, I can almost feel the car stretching its limbs as it flees the shackles of stop-start inner-city traffic. And though it's nice to be zooming along on the open road, it has to be said that I am also a little on edge, thanks to talking to all the people from Marco's play. I guess it's not until you're faced with the reality of motor-vehicle accidents that you think about them. My incessant nagging about Tim's driving justified, in my mind at least, by the added responsibility of Millie asleep in the back.

Horror-road-smash-paranoia aside, I'm loving being co-cooned with Tim and Millie in our tiny car capsule. (Our little trio – together at last!) Listening to the radio. Daydreaming. For a brief moment, it feels like the old us. Of free-flowing busy lives that intersected for mid-week dinner dates and lost weekends away. The us that talked non-stop about work projects and current affairs.

Speaking of current affairs, albeit local, I fill Tim in on the latest news.

'Mary's clinic is being renovated. Sophie saw it being boarded up the other day on her way to work – with loads of builders in there.' Hoorah. 'It's only thirty years overdue.' The last time I got Millie weighed, the central heating had come on (in mid-July) and wasn't able to be turned off. It was practically sub-Saharan. 'And while they're at it, maybe they'll get Mary an assistant. She's always late because she has so many house visits to do. The mere thought of her gridlocked waiting room is enough to give me heart palpitations.' Her first-come, first-served appointment system often leads to buggy-rage in the corridor.

Tim appears annoyingly unmoved by my news, and is clearly more interested in the stream of texts and emails that have just announced their arrival on his BlackBerry. (Work, of course.) He's permanently got one ear and eye tuned in to that bloody phone – he even sleeps with it under his pillow.

'You shouldn't be doing that, you know,' I chastise maybe a little curtly as he checks the messages while driving. What could be so important that it can't wait until the next stop?

A little piqued by Tim's distant mood, I decide to flick through the latest *Hello!* and come across an advertisement with a very cute baby. I'm instantly reminded of Victoria's latest triumph, which I mention to him.

'Allegra's going to be the new Johnson's baby.' An old PR colleague of hers asked if they could use a photo of Allegra for their pitch – and they won. 'Mind you, Allegra is an incredibly beautiful baby in that perfect baby-commercial sort of way.' I'm guessing Millie's flame-red Mohican hairdo (from Tim's side of the family) and double chin (my side, unfortunately) wouldn't quite fit the bill. 'Victoria's going to be insufferable after this.'

Admittedly, I'm still in shock after seeing Allegra's baby album yesterday. (Victoria showed it off at Bambini Yogalini – another of the many groups I've been bullied into joining at her house, for fear of damaging Millie's future chances in life.) I have never seen anything so beautiful. Ever. I tell Tim how Victoria's done an album page for each week of Allegra's life to date. (I'm serious – each week.) She's decorated it with solid silver angels and antique French lace. It's truly an heirloom. There are at least two A4 pages of diary writing per week too – saying how privileged she is to be a mother; and how she relishes just sitting and watching the dreams roll across Allegra's face as she frowns and smiles in her sleep in the shadow of the morning sun, blah de blah de blah.

I still have all of Millie's photos, since the day she was born, on the digital camera. And haven't a clue how to get them to the PC, let alone edited, printed and put in an album. Blogging is the sum total of my technical prowess. (I'm truly bowled over when I see my contributions make it on to Shoe Princess; and I've even joined the Funky Mammas SP sub-group.) Tim's been promising me he'll sort out the photos, but we get so little shared time these days – it's just one of the many jobs that never seem to get done. I don't like to badger him about it, as the fraction of time we do have together is spent paying bills and balancing the books – it's stressful enough.

Tim's so tired when he gets back from Bangalore. He invariably spends the weekend in bed sleeping off jetlag and exhaustion (they work horrifically long hours), and the week working like crazy to catch up with everything in the London office. And then it's back to Bangalore again on Sunday afternoon. We have no social life to speak of. Honestly, I've almost given up on being a normal couple. (Though I will concede the yoga continues to expand Tim's prowess in the bedroom.)

But I guess I mustn't grumble – it's not like he's working on an oil rig in the North Sea or serving in a war zone. He's *always* at the end of a computer or a phone, and that in itself is comforting. Plus, I've become quite the home handywoman – am now rather a dab hand at regrouting tiles and fixing plumbing problems!

I've no idea how Victoria gets the time for the album, though. For like Tim, her husband works very long hours, with lots of business travel. But then again even Sophie, the ardent anti-fuss mum, has put together a memory box for Hugh.

'Poor Millie, she'll not only grow up thinking that her dad's a 2-D image on a computer screen, but that her mum was a slummy mummy too bone lazy to collate a baby album,' I lament.

I'm waiting for Tim to jump in about Millie's undeniable beauty and what an outstanding job I'm doing in the mothering department, but am met by a cone of silence. He's completely zoned out.

I suddenly feel quite aggrieved.

'You haven't listened to a word I've said, have you?'

'What? . . . Yes . . . Yes I have,' he says with an indignant bristle. I'm not convinced.

'OK. Name three words from my last three sentences.' This should be good.

'Millie,' he whips back without a second thought.

Mmm, well, that one's not rocket science.

'Err . . . baby. And . . . mums,' he finishes triumphantly.

Heck – am I that predictable?

'All right then, but what was I actually talking about?'

'Ah, yes.' He straightens himself in the car seat and, in a voice that's clearly supposed to mimic mine (and isn't particularly complimentary), quotes verbatim my very own (and according to him, dubiously derived) theory: 'The genetically predisposed inequality of life as a woman and mother in the modern capitalist world. As evidential proof of Darwin's theory of natural selection, transposed as a model for male power attainment and world domination, and female social exclusion.'

Well, it's a theory. And one admittedly more likely to have been derived by Kate than me. (But I thought it sounded quite good at the time.) I don't know whether to be offended or flattered, as I never truly think he's listening when I go off on my hobby horse. (Usually on the phone, towards the end of his third week in Bangalore, when my emotional and physical reserves for solo-parenting of a baby are perilously low.)

The speedometer suddenly increases in unison with Tim's ire and I realise that he's really worked up.

'Do you think that I'm particularly *excited* about staring down the barrel of sixty-plus-hour working weeks, deep in the bowels of middle management, for the rest of my life? Constantly hassled by the financial stresses of mortgages, school fees and retirement funds. Oh, and with the added bonus, if I'm *really* lucky, of a heart attack, or a stroke, by the age of sixty-five.'

A distinct air of bitterness fills the car.

'But surely the best part of my most excellent *male* life' – blimey, if he spits that out any more spitefully he *will* have a stroke – 'must be the prospect of never having the time to form a relationship with Millie. Having her see me as a walking, talking wallet that appears sporadically at mealtimes, weekends and school-concert nights. With a wife who resents me because all I do is work and not help enough with the chores.'

I'm now completely exasperated (and a little stung) by his outburst.

'Don't you get it? I'm not the enemy here. As long as most jobs that men perform get paid more than women's, things will *never* change. If my pay was nearer to yours, for example, and we were both able to work flexitime, we could both split our week between caring for Millie and participating in paid work outside the home – with the same net income.'

'Ah, my lovely wife the closet socialist. Shall we call in the removal men and go and live on a kibbutz, then?'

'Don't make fun of me, Tim.' His highbrow tone smacks of patriarchy and is really winding me up. 'If couples shared the burdens of finance, child-rearing and domestic chores more *equally*, men like you might, God willing, just live a few years longer with the aid of healthier arteries; and not to mention have more nurturing relationships with your kids . . . and less bickering from your wife.'

'Let's play the cards we've been dealt, Jane. You're living in la-la land.'

I'm *furious* that he's so dismissive.

'Oh, I get it. Just because a situation *exists*, that makes it right, does it?'

'Look, you know I don't think it's right.'

'No, I don't, actually. You never acknowledge how hard it is for *me* – being at home with Millie. Especially with you being away so much.'

'Oh, I do – all the time. You just don't want to hear it.'

'Rubbish! We live in parallel universes, Tim: work and home. Not to mention different bloody *continents*! Apart from now, you haven't said very much to me about it at all, actually.' My voice falters a little and I feel quite teary all of a sudden.

'Look,' he says, clearly trying to make amends, 'as much as I'd *love* to change the world, I'm just saying that we're mortgaged up to our eyeballs, we have other bills to pay and I have a job to do to pay them while you're at home caring for Millie. That's the choice *we* made – for Millie. And it is hard right now. For *both* of us. But we'll get through it.'

'*I suppose . . .*' I mumble belligerently, and turn and stare out of the car window. Where, incidentally, I don't see a mass rally of men with placards demanding equal rights for pay, flexitime, housework and home-parenting. Funny that.

Following the uneasily brokered truce in our game of my-life-is-harder-than-yours we sit in silence, with seemingly little else of mutual interest to talk about, for the remainder of the drive to my parents' house.

After a rather awkward lunch and handover of Millie, and the obligatory check of Tim's phone, we're back on the road again for the short drive to the manor house – with sadly no time to spare for any stops at quaint antique shops.

Tim suddenly cranes his neck at an obscure angle to gawp at a roadside poster – of The Cat, no less. She's in a new series of advertisements for Mange Chat. This time in a gold-lamé bikini (that really leaves little to the imagination), strategically covered by a perspex cape with satin leopardprint trim, gold platform wedges and dark, oversized sunglasses.

So much for The Fat Cat. She looks jaw-droppingly amazing – I'd say she must have shed about two stone in two weeks. I guess that old Cat-a-Pole has been getting a workout of late.

'You're ogling, Tim Meadows!'

'I am not,' he huffs. 'And since when did you become the fun police, anyway?'

Ever since I went up two dress sizes.

I try to lighten the mood a little.

'I'm just sick of seeing The Cat this week, that's all.' Her PR team obviously want us to know that she's not The Fat Cat any more. 'She's got a huge spread of "exclusive secret photos" in the trash mags.' I hold up my *Hello!* with the front-page picture of her frolicking on a Sardinian beach with Happy Sunshine, wearing those bloody giant black sunglasses again – which are incidentally bigger than her micro-bikini. 'It was all completely orchestrated, anyway.'

'How do you know?'

'Trash Queenz – they said that she paid for the flights of the photographer.'

'Hah! And you believe everything you read on a blog.' He can hardly disguise his contempt. 'You never used to be this gullible. Or cynical.'

'Well, what about the drunken nightclubbing shots sent in to Trash Queenz from someone's phone camera the following evening? Are you saying they made them up, too?' It's pathetic that she gets paid loads of money for being the so-called model mum, at home knitting mittens and baking cakes.

'Why can't you just be happy for her? She put on weight, she lost it. So what if she had a big night out. You've become obsessed with this whole conspiracy-theory-feminist-band-wagon of late.'

Have I just.

So far, NOT so good.

Toe Tips

If you're shorter than 5'5" and do not wish to be mistaken for a garden gnome, then it's strongly advised that you never wear flat shoes with a pointed toe. If you insist on wearing flat shoes, try a square toe – it's much more becoming.

And while we're covering toes, there are two important rules for round-toed shoes: only ever wear them if they have high heels or if they're complete flats (e.g., Chanel ballet slipper). Never wear a round-toed shoe with a mid-heel height – think Minnie Mouse!

SP Star Summer City

It is my great pleasure to announce that the award goes to Copenhagen. Any city where it's normal practice to ride bicycles in stilettos is a shoe princess's kind of city!

Walk Tall

Classic courts with a medium to high heel height elongate the leg and flatter the ankles. Only wear ankle straps and T-bars if you can afford to cut a foot off your height.

And in the summertime, wear light-beige (nude) high-heeled courts with sundresses or jeans (A-list actresses and the Scandinavian royals do it all the time) to give height and poise, yet not draw the eye down. You'll be amazed at how much taller you appear!

19. Stilettos at Dawn

Tᴵᴹ and I quarrel the remainder of the way to the manor house, only to arrive and find that it is no longer a luxury five-star country estate but a clean, green, spartan wellness centre that Kate would most surely approve of: No caffeine. No carbs. No meat. No fat. No smoking. No alcohol. No TV. No shoes. (I'm *deadly* serious – everyone seems to be walking about barefoot.)

What have I done to deserve this? My very own living hell!

To make matters worse, Tim has just remembered to give me the schedule for the partners' welcome session: We are to assemble in the main foyer in half an hour, where we will be led by none other than Tim's illustrious boss Alex in a session called Facing Your Fears – at the indoor three-metre-spring-board diving complex.

I didn't pack my swimsuit. What a brilliant stroke of luck – as I'm terrified of heights, not to mention the idea of baring my blubber in public.

We run into a familiar face – Hannah, the wife of Tim's long-time colleague, Charlie. She tells me that if I don't participate in the diving session it won't be just Tim who loses points, but the whole team. Apparently, they're going to spend the week accruing points, as part of a corporate incentive scheme. Whoever wins gets the chance to share the prize of their choice with the team. But only if they beat the scores of the other twelve teams in the company. The sky's the limit.

Charlie's already put his name down for a heli-ski trip to Colorado. I wistfully think that, if Tim won, I'd convince him to book everyone (including partners) into the Savoy for a fortnight – so I could catch up on a year's worth of sleep.

Hannah also tells me that she's been in training for the diving for months – ever since Charlie told her about it.

'After all, it's such an important occasion for them.'

I could kill Tim. I *really* could kill him.

But I'll be damned if I'm going to lose any of their precious points.

A mad dash to the inhouse shop reveals that it's closed Sunday afternoons. And no amount of pleading and bribing seems to be able to sway the sinewy little lentil-eating manager to open up. So that leaves only one option . . .

Cue me getting back in the car and breaking the land-speed record to my parents' house. Making a hasty choice between my mother's post-mastectomy orange, purple and lime-green floral swimsuit, and a chlorine-eaten bikini I last wore when I was fourteen. The floral wins hands down. Dry-shaving my bikini line with Dad's razor, throwing a homespun beaded kaftan (one of Mum's latest sewing projects) on top of the swimsuit. Caking my excruciatingly itchy and sore bikini line with Millie's zinc nappy cream (which I find in my handbag) while stopped at the traffic lights en route back to the hellhole. And arriving back in time for the diving session. With seconds to spare.

But it gets worse.

At long last, I come face to face with Alex.

The 'Alex' that Tim spends most of his living hours with at work in Bangalore and London. The 'Alex' that he and the boys went out with for a riotous New Year's Eve ball, while I stayed at home with a feverish Millie. The 'Alex' that calls him into work at all times of the day and night to fix system-test failures. 'Alex' bloody 'Alexandra', the most exquisitely beautiful, articulate, intelligent woman I have *ever* met. An Indian bloody beauty queen in a black halter-neck swimsuit with an impossibly small cinched waist.

Why had Tim failed to mention that Alex was not a bloke? It's always, 'Alex and the guys this . . . Alex and the guys that . . .'

'Jane, it's *so* lovely to meet you,' she says with a plummy accent and offers her perfectly manicured hand. 'Tim's told me *so* much about you and Millie. He talks about you *all* the time.' How much time do they get to talk, exactly? I don't know if I want her knowing about me and Millie. At all.

I feel stupidly uneasy.

But most of all, I feel *stupid*.

The instructor pronounces Alex a natural at diving. She emerges from the pool like Ursula Andress from the sea in *Dr No* and slinks straight over to Tim's side. I note that her waterproof make-up has remained immaculate, along with her chestnut-brown ponytail. It's downright criminal to look so good without shoes on.

Alex credits her flexibility and calmness up on the three-metre springboard to the yoga that she teaches at the staff wellness centre in Bangalore.

'It's my own form of yoga, which has been passed down from my great-great-grandmother – sort of yoga-meets-Kama Sutra. I can do most of the positions from the comfort of my bed,' she purrs.

Blimey, she makes Rachel look like the international leader of the Christian Youth Chastity Foundation.

I lock a piercing gaze on Tim, who has conveniently yet to meet me in the eye, and wonder if his startling new bedroom skills are more to do with Alex than the yoga per se.

Please, no.

And naturally, when it's my turn to stand atop of the three-metre springboard, I remove my kaftan to reveal visibly trembling legs and GIANT globules of nappy cream. My only option is to dive into the pool as quickly as possible.

But alas, dive is too dignified a word. I leap – the most awkward, ungracious kamikaze leap humanly possible. Crashing into the water in a lopsided jumble of arms and legs. While underwater, I pray desperately that the lost city of Atlantis will suddenly appear and whisk me away from this living nightmare. But to no avail.

I emerge from the pool with a thumping headache and a nasty red mark down the entire right side of my body.

But at least Tim and his team got their bloody points.

And oh, did I face my fears!

Tim and I don't talk much before dinner. Or during dinner, for that matter. With the no-shoe rule waived, the seating is arranged so that Alex and her pythonskin platform stilettos are at the head of the table, with her two managers, Tim and Charlie, on either side of her. Alex's partner is conveniently at a conference in Belgium this weekend.

'No children,' Hannah whispers cautiously, when I ask her. I should have guessed Alex is one half of a 'power couple'.

Hannah and I have been banished to the lower end of the table alongside the junior computer programmers and their partners. I'm *really* peeved. Hannah, though a little more distracted than usual, is perfectly fine with this. But then she would be, because she is one of the nicest, most self-effacing people I know.

As it turns out, Hannah seems to be on familiar terms with most of the programmers, and is also 'in' on most of their work stories and jokes from Bangalore. As each conversation goes over my head, I can't help but feel totally out of the loop, and eventually give up on asking Hannah to explain things to me. I simply sit in silence, looking achingly inadequate and boring.

And to top things off, Tim's wearing new shoes that Alex, of course, helped him to buy. (I've always bought his shoes – I may as well hand over my wedding ring right now.) Actually, the whole team has new shoes (courtesy of a factory near Bangalore that's relocated from Norwich) as well as Hollywood-whitened teeth. All perks in their cheap-as-chips staff wellness programme.

I wish Trinny and Susannah would come and give *me* a makeover.

I spend the evening in a complete fog. With every wild drinking story from Bangalore that Tim and Alex are seemingly at the centre of, I'm increasingly frozen with uncertainty and mistrust.

I no longer hear words – just loud noises blurring into one another. The macrobiotic, biodynamic feast is wasted on me too. My mouth is so dry I can hardly chew, let alone swallow. And even if I did manage to eat anything, it would most certainly not get past the enormous lump lodged in my burning throat.

Time stands still, and yet goes on for ever.

I gather every ounce of dignity I can muster not to burst into tears.

It's now 5 a.m. The bed is empty beside me. I can just hear, above the morning birdsong, the faint creak of the door being carefully opened. Tim takes off his clothes and shoes, and trips over my stilettos before sliding into bed. All I can smell is the unmistakable scent of Chanel No. 5.

I wear Issey Miyake.

My stomach turns.

We don't touch.

I want to find Alex and tell her to keep away from my husband. But I think back over the car journey and my embarrassing performance at the diving centre. And I wonder if, just maybe, I'm doing a fine enough job of driving him to her myself.

Perfect Match

I read in a magazine recently that we're supposedly attracted to life partners with similar facial features to our own. Naturally, I prefer to think that people are far more likely to be compatible if they wear similar shoes! A cursory glance around the airport, en route to the first-class lounge, revealed the following **Shoe Couples**:

Hikers – matching mountain boots and Gore-tex backpacks.

Celebs – stylist-coordinated his 'n' hers designer shoes in complementary colours.

Funkies – concerted effort to wear green or purple shoes of individualistic styling.

Conservatives – high-quality brogues and flat mules or kittens.

Glamazons – white shiny heels, and LOTS of bling.

Mums 'n' dads – sensible loafers and lace-ups, or matching white trainers.

Trendy trainer sneaker freaks – say no more.

Mirrors – same shoes, same sex.

Hippies – flip-flops, ankle ties and bells; felt vegetable-dyed moccasins.

Sasquatches – big and comfy shoes. The collective style of a sack of potatoes.

Bikers – black-leather biker boots.

Cowboys 'n' cowgirls – matching, well-worn tan leather cowboy boots.

London Calling

Q: How does a SP know she's in London and not Manhattan?

A: A gruff cabbie will mutter a stream of expletives under his breath during the whole three blocks you've asked him to take you in your skyscraper stilettos. And, if you happen to be in W1, he declines to pick you up altogether, assuming you're a high-class call girl.

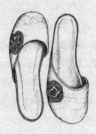

20. Flat Out

From: Sophie (work)
To: Jane (home)
Subject: RE: Woof Woof I am a DOG!

Sophie is out of the office today on holiday, and I am taking care of
her emails. Perhaps she could contact you when she returns.
   Very best
   Edward

Oh dear. Stupid, stupid me.

I guess it was bound to happen, sooner or later. Given how
much Sophie and I correspond via her work email. But why
this email? Why couldn't we have been discussing the morality
of the Iraq invasion? Or the deep and meaningful insights from
our latest reading of Proust (in French, of course)? Why her
boss? Oh, I hope I haven't got her into trouble. She's always
telling me how they're just about tolerating her at work these
days. I'll give her a call when Millie goes down for her sleep

today – as I'm positive that 'holiday' is code for staying-at-home-to-look-after-Hugh because of Rhiannon's recurring bronchitis.

I blame it all squarely on Trinny. You see, I certainly did get the makeover that I so desperately wanted. It's just that she shouldn't have told me (OK, maybe not me *personally*, but a pear-shaped, fat-ankled housewife *exactly like me*) that greasy, lank hair dribbling down each side of one's face to one's shoulders resembles a dog's ears – a spaniel's to be exact.

But possibly the most depressing thing is that my hair is just the tip of the proverbial iceberg. I've been through my entire wardrobe (again with Trinny and Susannah's help) and concluded that it has, in the space of just one post-baby year, become entirely sexless. (And yes, I hate it when Rachel's so bloody right!)

Little wonder my husband has fallen into the arms of a temptress.

I'm busy pondering my future life as a bona fide single parent, when an incoming email takes me by surprise. Oh, great. Just what I need – Aunt Margaret's joined the twenty-first century:

From	Tim (work)
To	Jane (home)
Subject:	FW: Family News Update

fyi. T

My Dearest Tim, Jane and Emmeline

Please forgive this intrusion into your busy lives. (Tim, your parents kindly gave me your work email address.) Now that I have mastered the email and World Wide Web, I am taking the liberty of collating a mid-year update from family members to expedite the writing of my Christmas letter.

We're all most anxious to learn of your news, especially since we didn't hear from you last year.

I have had the pleasure of my niece Penelope and her husband Mike from Norfolk staying this past week. They send their love. (Do you remember playing Knights and Queens with Penelope in my garden when you were six, Tim?) Their baby Libby is almost one, and an absolute treasure – sleeping through the night and walking. Mike has been promoted to partner at work, and Penelope has just completed her Ph.D. – in record time.

I hope this small note finds you happy and healthy.

Yours in haste

Aunt Margaret

Oh, sod off, you nosy old cow.

I sit and stare blankly at the computer screen, my head in my hands. Aunt Margaret's email forces me to think about the year that has been: the most exhilarating, challenging and enlightening year of my life – without doubt. A year that I have a feeling is going to end with a *very* big bang.

At that, I also allow myself to think about Tim. Something I've been blocking, since the diabolical wellness centre last weekend, where I managed to play the role of insecure, paranoid housewife to a tee. We had an enormous row late on Monday afternoon before I left – probably our worst ever – where Tim got completely frustrated and mortally offended by my absurd and petty (according to him) questions about Alex and Bangalore.

He rather annoyingly pointed out that I used to have a male boss and predominantly male work colleagues, whom I spent significant amounts of time with, pre-Millie. But I, of course, reminded him that I didn't *hide* the fact that they were men from him. To which he said he hadn't misled me about Alex 'intentionally'.

I found this hard to swallow.

And so it went.

Mum sensed that all was not right the moment I got out of the car to pick up Dad, Millie and Pierre (on dog good-behaviour bond) for the return to London. My jolly-hock-ey-sticks demeanour was probably my biggest giveaway. I quickly changed tack, and blamed an allergic reaction to the incense at the wellness centre for my puffy eyes; and my foray on the three-metre springboard for my migraine. No wonder I appeared a little out of sorts.

I think she *just* about bought it.

This forwarded email of Aunt Margaret's is the first contact Tim and I have had, so to speak, in a week. And of course we can't even meet to patch things up, because he's running away with Alex tonight to Bangalore, for four weeks – returning in time for Millie's birthday.

I feel ill simply thinking about it.

My Home Parent Assistant has been with me for just over a week now, and I can honestly say that the whole experience of living together has been a real eye-opener – for both of us. Possibly it's the praise Dad lavishly heaps on me (never forth-coming from Tim) that I enjoy the most. His favourite mantra at the moment is: 'Young mums are the unsung heroines of the world.' Though I constantly remind him I'm not doing any-thing that Mum didn't do. In fact, I think Mum had it a lot harder than me, being without the luxury of disposable nappies, a tumble dryer or even a car. Let alone a computer and the World Wide Web.

But most of all, Dad seems to be fascinated by the effects of a baby on domestic life. In particular, how the rhythm of each day (and night) is relentlessly the same, yet with variable notes that can change at any time (and usually without warning) to result in a completely different melody by day's end. A melody that's just as likely to be dotted with flourishes of heart-warming joy as it is with dips of pure frustration – and always tempered by vast oceans of patience. He's even been jotting down little theorems and algorithms to try and map it out. Much to my amusement!

Dad truly can't put a foot wrong at the moment, though. He's not only done a brilliant job of completely 'Millie proof-ing' the flat for us, but I can almost feel the layers of stress peel away with every precious baby-free snippet of head space he gives me. Speaking of which, he and Millie have just popped out for their regular morning stroll down to the high street to see what's been left under the council's 'No Dumping' sign overnight. They'll be at least an hour – rummaging through the lounge suites, cookers and toasters for something to claim. And, of course, chatting to all the homeless people, passing mums and babies, and elderly folk.

Dad will only be happy when he finds something to bring back to the garden shed to fix – so that he can give me a lecture on the throwaway nature of today's society. You see, he sneakily 'interpreted' the terms of his HPA contract to allow the use of the garden shed (technically not part of the 'work premises' and therefore exempt from restrictions) to house his laptops, physics experiments and repair projects. He's lucky that the shed's so big, actually. We bought our flat from a notorious local landlord – and legend has it that he used to house about ten Antipodean backpackers in there for extra income.

I take the opportunity to get some chores done while Dad and Millie are out, and am halfway through stuffing a load of clothes into the washing machine (how is it that one tiny scrap of a baby human can produce the same amount of laundry each day as a rugby team after a rain-sodden game?) when the doorbell rings.

It's Florence. She's popped in to hand me some mail that's mistakenly made its way into her pile.

'I think it must be from your charming friend Marco,' she says innocently enough.

I look at the postcard emblazoned with Italian stamps, and confirm that it is indeed from Marco – and Fi. They're on a romantic summer holiday in Sicily. Yet another important milestone for Fi. Mind you, she was so excited and nervous about the trip that she worked herself into a complete twist and broke out in hives the day before they left. Thankfully, the postcard reveals that all is now good and they're having a magical time together.

As for my 'charming friend Marco' – I was *so* embarrassed when Florence walked in on me with him a little while back. Not because we were *in flagrante delicto* or anything. (Wouldn't that have been fun!) No, it was all extremely above board. Marco was dropping off Millie's pushchair after that shoe-exhibition fiasco (fiascos seem to be a recurring theme in my life of late). The front door was left ajar, because he was literally just dropping the pushchair off, and Florence was coming in for our planned afternoon tea while Millie was asleep.

But you see, the thing is, I was in Marco's embrace – sobbing uncontrollably on his shoulder.

I honestly had no intention of blubbering all over him. It's just that he's so damn understanding. He asked me how I was coping with being on my own with Millie so much. (His dad died when he was ten, and he helped his mum raise his four younger siblings – he's really in tune with the demands of childcare.) Just being asked made the tears sort of explode out of me like a geyser.

I shocked even myself.

Marco kindly stayed and took tea with Florence and me – charming her in his polite, gentlemanly fashion by being completely attentive to both of us. And of course, he made an extra effort to cheer me up by telling Florence all about my commendable shoe-making abilities.

Florence is also a bit of a shoe princess (or should that be shoe queen, given her age?) and truly delighted in meeting an artisan like Marco. She has since taken a keen interest in my still-as-yet-to-happen mum shoes project, even offering her services to crochet flowers for embellishments. And provided they're done with the right coloured and textured thread (like super-fine silver lamé), they could actually go down a treat with the fashionistas in my Funky Mammas SP subgroup – now that foho is the new boho (think funky yet folksy).

I finger the curved edge of the postcard and smile warmly at the thought of Marco. I really do like thinking about him . . . it certainly helps take the sting from my thoughts of Tim and Alex. But like any drug of dependence, the effect wears off quicker each time. And I'm left to think of Fi. And feel ashamed.

Oh, what a muddle I'm in.

Shop Like a Princess

I'm constantly amazed by the stories from our princesses in the US – where they genuinely seem to understand the art of retail therapy. Many shoe shops have VIP rooms for private viewings; luxurious lounges and spacious seating; onsite shoe repairs; free foot massages and pedicures for multiple purchases of shoes; plus tea, coffee, cake and champagne as part of the shoe-shopping experience. Who wouldn't want to walk away in a pair of glass slippers after such pampering? One can only hope it catches on this side of the Atlantic.

Shoe Moment

My 3½-year-old niece recently asked me to buy her a pair of "black little girls' shoes with long sticks".

I'm soooo proud! (from SP of São Paulo)

As we are too, SP!

Footnote

I've been asked many times why I never use the term 'shoeaholic' in my blog. It's quite simple: far from having an affliction that needs to be cured by a 12 Step Programme, Shoe Princesses are passionate lovers and appreciators of shoes. Footwear connoisseurs!

21. Mind the Step

WITH Dad and Millie still out, Florence decides to stay and join me for a pot of tea and *Brunch with Britain* (our whole day is practically planned around it).

'Welcome back to our special item this week on marital well-being,' announces Tamsin earnestly.

Why is everybody so hung up on bloody well-being, wellness, well this, well that, well, well, bloody well . . .?

'If you think that your partner spending long hours at work, and not at the pub, will protect your marriage from the ever-present temptation of the extra-marital affair – think again.'

I'm thinking. And I don't like it.

'Marriage counsellors the length and breadth of the country are predicting an epidemic of something potentially more serious than physical infidelity – emotional infidelity. Or what's becoming known as **mind sex**: the intimate, blatantly open, non-physical bond between two individuals. Yes, Gavin, this cocktail is dynamite to the modern marriage.'

'But how does someone know if their partner is having mind sex? Or is maybe a candidate for mind sex?' Gavin asks, wide-eyed.

Yes, do tell.

'Marjorie Moore – marriage guidance counsellor, industrial psychologist and leading authority on mind sex at work – is here to walk us through **the five deadly Ts.** Welcome, Marjorie.' Tamsin guides Marjorie and her beige brogues to the silk-covered sofa.

'Thank you,' she says gravely. 'The first and biggest risk factor is **time**. *Lots and lots* of time spent away from the spouse in the company of like-minded individuals.'

'So what's your view then on work functions, like, say . . . the annual conference – which often requires employees to live closely together in hotels or boot camp environments?' says Tamsin.

A bright-red rash spreads rapidly northwards from my chest.

Marjorie slaps her hands together to make two thunderous claps at the same time as saying. 'Double! Trouble!' Florence and I both flinch. 'Competition-driven environments are the *worst* offenders: their very nature is to encourage strong bonds between work colleagues, who are often placed in high-stress situations together. I call them **mind–sex multipliers**: one week at conference equals one year in the office. It's quite astonishing.'

I squirm uneasily.

'So, is mind sex the same as a fantasy?' says Gavin.

'I'm glad you asked that, Gavin. In short, no, it's not. With a fantasy, something that's missing from a relationship (be it emotional or physical) is transposed on to a person one rarely spends time with – like a celebrity or a handsome shop assistant. With mind sex, the workers are attracted to each other *and* are constantly together. So the lure of the unfulfilled 'what if' scenario is the sexual electricity that powers their day. And that's our second risk factor: **tension**.'

Mmm.

'The third is: **tools.** Willing accomplices in the workplace war against monogamy are email, text and MSN, just to name a few. The immediacy with which the straying spouse can get a fix of their forbidden fruit is unprecedented. A common give-away is a partner's preoccupation with work emails and texts, which they keep private.'

Bloody hell. Three out of three.

'The fourth risk factor is **tedium**. What we're finding is that the straying spouse is almost always attracted to an individual at work who does not obsess about the mundane pressures of child-rearing and family life. For example, no matter how essential the housewife may feel it to express how hard done by she is as an unpaid domestic slave, he will find it a major turn-off. With the husband often disengaging completely, and saving his interesting conversations for the mind-sex partner.'

Gulp.

'This is particularly dangerous, because emotional bonding is an essential ingredient in the physical relationship for women. So the quality of the marital sexual relationship soon begins to suffer. In turn, making the lure of the mind-sex partner even more intoxicating. A wandering eye is a good indicator of a wandering mind.'

I'm doomed.

'And last but not least, **treachery**. If mind sex is left unchecked for too long, the final step in the path to physical infidelity is *almost always* taken.'

'Thank you, Marjorie,' says Tamsin earnestly. 'You've cer-tainly given us a lot to think about.' That's an understatement. Shall I call in the lawyers now? 'Tomorrow, we follow the same theme but move our attentions further afield, to India. Where a seemingly innocent motivational culture of play-while-you-work at multinational-owned call centres has been rocked by allegations of lurid sexual shenanigans and binge drinking amongst employees. Bangalore is alleged to be the hub of such activities – with its well-equipped technical parks offering twenty-four-hour office facilities combined with alfresco dining, retail outlets, health clubs and social clubs galore.'

The camera pans over to Gavin and zooms in to his furrowed brow.

'Join us tomorrow for our exclusive exposé, and we'll let *you* be the judge.'

There's clearly a conspiracy that I don't know about. I thought Gavin and Tamsin were supposed to be on *my* side. I turn off the television in dismay.

Where did I put those Jaffa Cakes?

Florence has clearly picked up on my discomfort and was conspicuously quiet throughout the entire item, and now makes a polite excuse to leave.

My thoughts wander to Aunt Margaret's email requesting all our 'family news', which has been hanging over my head ever since it came in. I mentally draft my reply:

Dear Aunt Margaret, What a year we've had to date. Most notably, Tim, your butter-wouldn't-melt-in-his-mouth nephew, has abandoned Millie and me for, at best, a mind-sex affair and, at worst, a full-blown illicit affair, with a malnourished Indian beauty queen IT director, whom he now practically lives with.

Coincidentally, one of my good friends is also having a steamy affair with a married work colleague. And quite frankly, I'm not that amused by it any more, and can't bring myself to answer her emails.

As for me, I'm having increasingly lustful dreams involving me and my best friend's boyfriend. And I wonder, does this prevent me from taking up his kind invitation to go to

Milan with him for the day in early October? (Without my best friend.) So that I can attend one of his tutorials at the Ars Arpel Shoe School and further my own fanciful notion of venturing into shoe-making — considering that it's something I actually seem to have an aptitude for, and may even be able to fit around the demands of stay-at-home parenting. (And hopefully make some money out of too.)

Oh, forget it. Aunt Margaret can wait . . . I may as well do a quick check of the computer before Dad and Millie get back:

TrashQueenz e-lert
Catnap: There's been a sighting of The Cat, passed out in the back of her limo with her minders, after yet another wild night out clubbing in the West End. Still with her dark sunglasses on. The tabloids are now running with the story too. At this stage, there is no comment from her management.
Stay tuned . . .

Hah! So much for Tim thinking I'm gullible.

From:	Sophie (work)
To:	Jane (home)
Subject:	RE: RE: Woof Woof I am a DOG!

Don't worry, at all. Truly. Edward will get over it. He needs my support in his bid against David for divisional head, so am pretty confident he'll keep mum on our mum-chats. And for the record, you look NOTHING like a spaniel.

I did get your phone message, and so sorry I haven't got back to you earlier. I actually was on holiday for a change. James has just earned Husband of the Year Award for whisking me away on Eurostar for the day, to Paris, for our wedding anniversary.

Absolutely indulgent and completely magical. Speaking of get-aways, how was your lux country house? Did you go for the whole pamper package? Seems like ages since we've had a catch-up girlie chat. Can't wait to hear all.

Though will have to wait a little bit longer, as we're off now on holiday for the next two weeks – Greece!

S xx

I wish I *had* a husband at the moment, let alone a Husband of the Year. I wonder if Tim will be able to drag himself away from Alex's lair in Bangalore to celebrate our anniversary this year.

Where did it all go so horribly wrong?

From	Jane (home)
To	Aunt Margaret (home)
Subject:	RE: Family News Update

Dear Aunt Margaret

It is so lovely to hear from you. Will write very soon when my new email address is up and running.

With All Best Wishes

Jane, Tim and Millie

It's not quite the fob-off that it seems. I really do need to change my hotmail address, as I'm drowning in a sea of porn spam at the moment. But I need Tim to help me change it. Oh, hell, that's if he ever talks to me again. If I was Alex, I could no doubt do it all myself *and* print off the baby photos *and* have the most wonderful baby album on the planet.

I'm yet again pondering the prospect of solo-parenthood, when I notice that a picture frame on the desk has fallen face down. And by the look of the dust on it, it's been like this for a few months (my housewifery standards have slipped to an all-time low of late). I flip it over and immediately choke up with tears: it's a photo that Kate took on her camera, during one of her Saturday visits, and had framed for me for Mother's Day. I'm sitting on our sofa, holding Millie on my lap. And Tim's behind, embracing the two of us with his huge arms while he nuzzles his face into my neck. I'm wincing with an enormous half-annoyed-but-really-enjoying-it-very-much smile from one ear to the other.

I remember it as if it was yesterday.

Tim was clowning around and pretending to give me love-bites – making large raspberry-like sounds. Millie must have been about four months old and has her head turned towards us – clearly delighted by all the noise and fuss. But what's most striking is not just the aura of collective happiness that radiates from the photo, but the look of absolute love and admiration in Millie's sparkling eyes – directed *entirely* towards Tim.

Mmm . . . This little baby girl needs her daddy back. And I clearly need to find the pre-Millie me, if I've half a chance of releasing Tim from Alex's fragrant spell.

I'll be damned if I'm going to stand by and let my beloved little family disintegrate.

Crocs Survey

Well, the results of the survey are in and I must say I've had a dismal response — at best.

One can only assume that either you're all away on summer holiday, or, like me, you feel the only use for 'real' reptiles is flattened and stitched into a boot or bag, and that any self-respecting SP would not be seen dead in these cloggy, spongy, goofy affronts to the senses.

However, there were just enough positive responses for me to concede a rare middle ground, and deem that crocs may be worn by SPs strictly in the garden and/or the short distance between pool / sea / spa and towel. That's it.

Heel Virgins

A heinous state of affairs has recently been brought to my attention: some of the women nearest and dearest to us have never — not ever — worn stiletto heels. (I know, as hard as it is to imagine.)

I urge all of my loyal subjects to put an end to this unacceptable social injustice, and make it your goal this month to introduce one girlfriend/sister/mother/cousin to spikes. Even if you have to escort them personally to the shoe shop. Or better still, give them a pair of gorgeous high heels as a friendship gift — with some walking-training thrown in for good measure, of course. What are SP friends for anyway?

Footnote

Cracked heels and yellow toenails are never a good look. Foot maintenance is just as important as shoe maintenance.

22. Hop to It

I EMBARK upon the task of finding the pre-Millie me with nothing less than the strategic zeal of a Harvey Nicks shoe-sale offensive. And with time being of the essence, I quickly gather my wits about me – cunning, persistence, agility, finesse – and begin. . .

Step One: Face and Body
This is insane. Absolute madness. I'm looking, of course, at the recipe I've diligently formulated, from a dozen or so trash mags:

Essentials: Gym membership, jogging, yoga, swimming, Pilates, Yogalates, spinning, acupuncture, face waxing, body waxing (including Brazilian), face firming/anti-ageing creams, manicure, pedicure, massage – full body, spray tan – full body, starvation diet, teeth-whitening, toners (hip, thigh and buttocks).

Desirables: Personal trainer, detox, Botox (face AND buttocks), crystals, reiki, reflexology, day spa, glycolic-acid

face peels, pigmentation-spot laser therapy, laser hair removal, microdermabrasion, seaweed wrap, eye-liner tatoo-
ing, eyelash dyeing, silk eyelash extensions, collagen fills,
liposuction/body sculpting, teeth reshaping, surgery (tummy tuck, boob job, nose job, neck lift, eyelid lift), fine-line
laser treatment, spider-vein removal, colonic irrigation.

I can't imagine *anyone* going through all of this palaver. I
certainly couldn't, pre-Millie. Bar the leg waxes and pedicures, of course. Plus, I've always considered shoe shopping
to be a much more civilised form of exercise than working
out in stinky old gyms. But the thought of Alex-the-alluring-
waif throwing herself at my husband quickly returns me to
the task in hand. As does the knowledge of my tracksuit
bottoms being an inch higher off the ground, thanks to an
extra two inches of fat around my girth. (It's just my luck to
get the middle-aged spread at the same time as post-baby
blubber.)

I'm mulling over the fact that I can't afford even a fraction of
these treatments (let alone find the time for them) as I sort
through the morning post. And for the first time *ever*, I open
one of the seven letters from banks that I get each day –
encouraging me to sign a pre-approved application for instant
credit.

It's soooo tempting. Maybe credit-card debt is a small price to
pay for saving my marriage? After all, desperate times call for
desperate measures.

Am I *completely* crazy? Tim's favourite pastime is scouring our
VISA card statement and doing his best Basil Fawlty imperso-
nation when he comes across my purchases. If he found out
about a hidden mountain of debt, that would surely put another
nail in the coffin.

No, I'm going to have to be *much* cleverer than that . . .

Step Two: Mind and Spirit

I think back to when Tim and I were happiest. When he wanted me. Undressed me with one fleeting glance. Devoured me.

I was working. Always busy – in an inspired, positive sort of way. And ambitious.

It's clear that now is the time for my mum shoes project (really just a very simple variation on the flat mules that I made at shoe school) to see the light of day. I pull together all my ideas and sketches on scraps of paper from the top drawer of the desk, and set about getting the wheels in motion.

I firstly phone Marco's studio, and am surprised when Ben answers the phone.

'Ben, hi. Is Marco there, thanks?'

'He's still in Italy with Fi. They've extended their stay, remember.'

Damn.

'Oh, of course! How silly of me.'

In my haste to get started I'd forgotten about Fi and Marco throwing caution to the wind. She forwarded me an email that she sent to work, saying that they'd decided to lend a hand on an 'eco-friendly thermal-energy project' at Mount Etna – till the end of the month. This was entirely fabricated, of course. The closest she and Marco have come to thermal energy at Mount Etna is the sauna in the nearby five-star resort. Unbelievably, human resources not only bought into her little scam, but gave her a 'special commendation' on her staff file for participating in a project of 'global and/or community significance'. (They get extra EU funding in return.) Good on her for being canny enough to pull it off – she certainly deserves to be having the time of her life with Marco.

'Can I help you with anything – I'm taking care of the shop and studio for Marco? A bit of a lull in set-design work,' says Ben.

That's strange, Marco and Fi never said anything to me about Ben holding the fort. Oh well . . .

'Um, yes, actually.' I tell him all about my mum shoes – how I want them to be funky and fashionable, yet comfortable enough to cope with fallen arches and bunions, and sturdy enough for a walk around the block or the school run. And of course, not extortionately priced.

'What a *great* idea. Come into the studio any time you like.'

Well, that is a stroke of luck. As is the fact that he's got Marco's contact details and can find out for me what materials he has in stock and what sort of an outlay I need to get started.

Ben phones back the next morning with Marco's cost estimate for enough raw materials to make my first batch of mum shoes (about seven to ten pairs, depending on how well I go). It's not as much as I expected – though I'm sure Marco's giving everything to me at a discounted rate. That's just so like him. Marco also gets Ben to open some packages of gorgeous, super-soft leathers for me – in chocolate, crimson, charcoal and teal. They'll be perfect.

Fi then drops me a quick email, saying that Marco insists I take as many materials and tools home as I like, instead of having to go into the studio with Ben. That's very kind of him, but of course completely unnecessary – now that I've got Dad's welcome help with Millie (and in truth is the only reason this project's remotely doable in the first place).

My next obvious hurdle is paying Marco for the raw materials. Fortunately, my trusty Home Parent Assistant has not only been behind my mum shoes project from the beginning, but he's also been living with me long enough now to pick up on the strain of Tim being away and my need to get my groove back – if not even for the sake of the marriage, but simply for me. We put our heads together and, in light of the Shoe Princess's Heel Virgins campaign, come up with a rather ingenious plan to raise funds: shoe pimping. (I promise it's not as dodgy as it sounds.)

I gather a small selection of what-on-earth-was-I-thinking-about-at-the-time-impossibly-high-stiletto-heeled shoes (still in original shoeboxes and mostly unworn) from the back of my wardrobe, write a series of provocatively irresistible descriptions about them, and then post them, along with a photo, for sale on the Shoe Princess noticeboard. (I'm quite computer-savvy now, thanks to Dad's technical help.)

The stilettos sell out within a few days – and I'm suddenly in the shoe-making business!

I spend the remainder of August dashing between Marco's studio and home – generally going in after lunch (when Millie has her afternoon sleep) to do all the gluing, stitching and hammering. And then coming home late afternoon, thanks to Dad taking Millie for a walk and play at Queen's Park when she wakes up. They've had a truly magical time together and, by all accounts, the other toddlers have relished having a rare, older male figure around too – Dad proudly telling me that he's the newly crowned Pied Piper of the sandpit.

I finish off the shoes in the garden shed during Millie's morning sleep, and then embellish them with my own funky/retro designs made from material, ribbon and leather remnants, as well as Florence's gorgeous little crocheted flowers. Plus, most evenings I take advantage of the long twilight and return to the studio for a few hours, once Millie's gone down and Dad's settled in front of the TV. All thanks to Ben's generous offer of opening up for me. I don't feel too guilty about it, as he seemed genuinely glad of the company, given that his fiancée is away on her annual stint volunteering at a Romanian orphanage.

Actually, Ben's proven to be something of an angel in disguise this summer. Not only has he been helpful with the odd technical issue with the shoes, but he's also been a real emotional crutch. You see, with only the two of us in the studio for long stretches, one thing led to another, and before I knew it, I was pouring out my heart and soul to him – about Tim. I told him everything, right up to the horrid time at the wellness centre. And I have to say that it was nothing short of liberating. 'A problem shared is a problem halved,' and all that. He's such a patient and natural listener. And not judgemental in the slightest.

Tim and I have at least spoken – but crucially not about Alex. I've not been game to, for fear of pushing him further away. And he seems to have just swept it under the rug, as if there's nothing to talk about. All he does talk about is coming home to be with Millie on her first birthday. And for that, at least, I'm grateful.

Step Three: Clothing, Hair and Make-up

I'm so happy with my first batch of mum shoes that I post them for sale on the Shoe Princess noticeboard straight away, and am absolutely staggered (and ecstatic) when they sell out within hours to the loyal members of my Funky Mammas subgroup (plus one or two outsiders). In turn, raising enough money for me to splash out on some trendy new high-rise jeans (thank goodness they're back in fashion), a chic new haircut, colour and sassy highlights, and invest in a good-quality cleanser, tinted moisturiser, mascara and lip gloss.

All of my grooming advice has been gleaned from the 'mistress of mistresses' – Rachel (who's still in Scotland). I'll do anything at this stage of the game to get ahead of the enemy – even fraternising with them. But of course I didn't tell her about my own dilemma, just that I needed to claw myself out of dumpy mumsville on a *very* tight budget. Naturally, she was only too happy to oblige with the secret formula.

My only regret about this incredibly hectic summer of shoe-making is that I haven't seen as much of Mary as I normally do. And bar the odd friendly greeting across the street, I haven't spoken to her at all. As one of us was always in a mad rush. But I know she'll understand, especially when I tell her about this exciting new direction I've found with shoes – which, I must say, feels *wonderful*.

In fact, I'm so inspired by the success of my mum shoes sales that I rekindle the idea of going to Milan with Marco in October and visiting the Ars Arpel Shoe School – given that it coincides with when Tim's due to be in London. He can look after Millie for one day, surely?

The minute I sound this idea out with Ben, he insists that I go. Even saying that he'd like to join us, as there's a new interior design store he'd like to visit. And in the light of Fi's neuroses about Marco (and indeed Marco's appearances in my own little err . . . subconscious wanderings) it seems like the perfect plan. Ben can be my chaperone. (Or vice versa, seeing as though I'm practically old enough to be his mother.) That's it sorted then: two students off to Milan for the day, with their teacher. Superb!

Except that I don't have any money left from my mum shoes sales to pay for the air fare.

Unbelievably, Ben offers to pay for my easyJet ticket now – saying that I can pay him back as soon as I make my next batch of shoes. I waver, throwing all kinds of excuses his way about

Millie needing me, and my shoe-making skills perhaps not being quite good enough to warrant a spot in an Ars Arpel class. But he's insistent, and books the tickets anyway.

I'm immediately hugely indebted to him. But with Dad about to go home, I'm also only too aware that I won't be able to make another big batch of mum shoes any time soon.

What to do?

Of course, it's so obvious: It's time for the shoe pimp to broaden her clientele beyond SP bloggers and move into the *big* league.

I do a gigantic clean-out of all my what-on-earth-was-I-thinking-of-at-the-time shoes plus my pre-Millie-not-a-chance-in-hell-of-fitting-me-ever-again shoes that are still in good condition, collecting about fifty pairs.

And now for a computer lesson on all things eBay. From the addict herself, Liz.

Shoe Are You?

Claytons SP

This princess, usually a lawyer or senior executive, protests that she's not into shoes for fear of chinking her feminist armour. But she has very strong views on what shoes she will (sensible, high-quality Italian leather work shoes with a low to medium heel) and won't (stilettos or any shoe with ribboned adornment or colour other than black and brown) wear. She detests it when the inner on her shoes goes all wrinkly and smelly and out of shape.

Trendy Trainer SP

A close relative of the **Claytons SP.** She likes to think that she is no frivolous fashionista, but does have very strict views on what brand, shape, colour and style of trainer she will be seen in. Often has many, many pairs of trainers.

Practical SP

Will only wear comfortable shoes with no or low heels. Is not the least bit concerned with fashion trends, fabric, brand or quality of shoes. A close cousin to her is the **White Trainer SP** — usually the SP who has completely given in to comfort over style. The most extreme form of the **Practical SP** is the **Anti-SP**, who sees feet merely as the bothersome yet necessary means of transport, and completely undeserving of embellishment. She would happily do away with shoes altogether if the pavements were not so littered with dog poo.

Shoe Queen

Usually the octogenarian granny who genuinely adores shoes and has a lifetime of happy 'shoe memories' to her credit. She constantly complains about the lack of comfortable yet stylish shoes available for women of her age. Genuinely enjoys keeping up to date with her granddaughter's shoe collection, and viewing the fashion spreads in newspapers and magazines.

Still haven't found yourself? Keep looking!

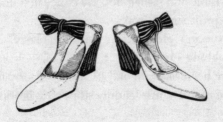

23. Goody Two Shoes

I T ' S Sunday, and the last day of Dad's summer stay. Millie's having her afternoon sleep, Dad's in the garden shed packing away his computers, jumble of experiments and half-finished repair projects (that were supposed to have been done days age), and Liz and I are in the study getting me set up on eBay. She's just returned from her and Harry's summer holiday in Menorca and kindly answered my SOS as soon as she got it (eBay being just a smidge out of Dad's computer-skills league).

'My! You've certainly been super busy, haven't you?' Liz is clicking through the photos of my mum shoes on my digital camera. 'They're divine!' She pauses and then ventures a little hesitantly, 'Can I put in an order for a pair – even if I'm not a fully-fledged mum, *just* yet?'

I immediately stop what I'm doing and swing round to look her in the eye. She's crying. And smiling.

'I'm fourteen weeks today,' she manages to say.

'Oh, Liz! This is the *best* news. Ever!' I say, hugging her. And then, of course, I start crying too. 'How are you? How have you been feeling?'

'Good. So far, so good,' she says amidst the tears, and then stands up proudly to show off her bump. Which is, I have to say, only barely visible and rather cleverly concealed under her foho chic Liberty print smock top.

'I'm just sooooo pleased for you and Harry!' We're both practically sobbing now.

'But I have been *hideously* ill.' Liz pulls a funny face and tries to lighten the mood a little. 'I only stopped vomiting a few days ago.'

'Don't worry, hopefully that's the end of it – and you'll soon be basking in the radiant glow of the second trimester,' I reassure her, as I too try to pull myself together. 'I was *exactly* the same with Millie.' Though oddly enough, as I think about it now, I can barely remember that awful feeling of all-day seasickness that I was certain would be etched on my brain for ever. It's a bit like the birth – a rather distant, fuzzy recollection now. (And without doubt Mother Nature's sneaky little way of making sure we go back for more.)

'Great. I very much like the sound of *glowing* – a lot,' she says. 'Actually, Menorca was just what the doctor ordered: magical weather and beaches. All very relaxing. Oh, and you would have *loved* the shoe shopping.'

'I know – ever since I saw the SP Holiday Hot Spot recommendation I've been daydreaming about how I can get there. I'm so jealous.'

'I did a deal with Harry, and we drove to the Jaime Mascaró shoe-factory outlet in exchange for him doing a whole day of golf. The new range of ballet flats are to die for, by the way. I'm now a convert – and have an excess-baggage fine to prove it!' She gently rubs her belly and then glances at the computer screen. 'And of course, I've already furnished my whole nursery from eBay.'

When we're finally finished, some two hours later, and I've taken down all the details I need for Liz's mum shoes (I will delight in making them for her as a pregnancy gift), she heads home. Millie wakes up soon after, and she and Dad and I settle in the garden for our last-afternoon tea together. An occasion tinged with much sadness (at seeing him go), fondness (at having got to know him better) but most of all gratitude. As he's undoubtedly helped me turn my life around this past month – in so many ways. And for that, I will *always* be truly grateful. I bring out some cupcakes that Millie and I made this morning especially for him, as a small token of our appreciation.

Dad and I are happily discussing the meaning of life and the existence of anti-matter when the doorbell rings. Dad picks Millie up (who's squealing with delight – as she thinks it's Florence) and goes to the front door.

He returns with a rather anxious look. I hope nothing's happened to Florence. I do worry about her, wandering about that terraced house all by herself. 'It's a young lady with a baby about the same age as Millie – I didn't quite catch her name. She seems a little out of sorts . . .'

I'm intrigued, and make my way to the front door.

'Jane, hi,' says Victoria.

What in the name of Manolo Blahnik is *she* doing here? Victoria's never shown a scrap of interest in visiting us. (And the one time I invited her over, she didn't even make the effort to come.) She has quite a cheek, turning up during our special farewell garden party.

'Can we come in?' she says, pushing her Bugaboo into the hallway before I have a chance to reply.

We squeeze past it back down to the garden. Allegra immediately crawls over to a very excited Millie, who's playing in the muddy quagmire that used to be our lawn (thanks to all the rain this summer) with Pierre (her furry best friend).

'Your phone line's *always* engaged – I had no choice but·to come over in person.' Victoria seems visibly irritated. 'And your emails keep getting returned.'

'Oh, sorry.' I explain about my new hotmail address. (Dad helped me set it up.) 'We've also only got one phone line and Dad's *always* tracking a tornado or tsunami or some such thing in real time.' I shoot a disapproving stare at Dad, who seems to have developed selective deafness.

'Victoria, can I introduce you to my dad, Bert? He's been staying with us this past month – for his sins!' I wink at Dad while saying Victoria's name with *just* enough emphasis so that I can see the penny drop. I'm often bemoaning her and her bloody know-it-all homilies on mothering. Though in some ways, I truly wish I could be more like her. As she seems to be completely content at home. Whenever we're over at her house, she's always up ladders changing curtains, cleaning light fittings, cooking a casserole, mending socks, hosting her educational groups – she may as well put a crèche sign on the front door.

'You haven't been to Bambini Yogalini for weeks,' Victoria reprimands. 'I don't know how you *ever* expect Millie to sleep through the night without it.' The afternoon sun catches tiny beads of sweat spotting her forehead – and when I peer closer I notice she's in a lather of sweat. (Probably just been on her daily three-mile run, knowing her.) 'And what happened to Tumble Tots, Alpha Beta Rocket Reader, Super Signing, Mini Maths and Musical Maestros?' she says in her usual bossy manner.

'I've been busy,' I say vaguely, and smile politely towards Dad as he disappears into the garden shed.

Victoria's clearly unimpressed by my lack of diligence. She takes a sip of the iced water I fetch her, and falters a little, before I hear the most peculiar utterance emerge from her mouth.

'Umm . . . I . . . err . . . need . . . your help.'

I feel like asking her to repeat it, to make sure that I heard her correctly, only she looks as if she's just had to swallow a live mouse. I'm equally tempted to do a small double take and turn round to see if there's someone standing behind me that perchance knows the League Table Results for London Primary Schools, or the Ofsted Reports, by heart.

'Yeees . . .' I say tentatively.

'It's Mary. And the mother-and-baby clinic,' she says gravely.

I frown.

'Have you been there lately?' She again fixes her unnerving gaze on me.

'Umm . . .' Oh, blow it, what's another black mark against my name? 'Not really. No.'

'It's closed down. You'll now have to go across to the next borough – it's not even in our parking zone.'

'But that's crazy . . .' I know I haven't spoken to Mary lately, but even so, she would have come and told me about it. Wouldn't she? It doesn't make sense. At all.

'That's so sneaky of them to do it in the holidays – while no one's around. What's with all the builders down there, then?'

'Aha, well . . . I've done some phoning around,' says Victoria. 'It appears that it's being turned into a state-of-the-art document-storage facility for Health Service medico-legal files. Fully climate-controlled and alarmed, no less! Oh, and with a new kitchen, a lift *and* an office staff of three.'

'You're having me on, aren't you?'

Unfortunately, she's deadly serious and she goes on to tell me that Mary was given notice four weeks ago, too. Heck, I feel awful. I've been so engrossed in my mum shoes world and obsessing over making myself glam for Tim's return that the whole event seems to have passed me by.

Apparently, Mary did not meet any of her new 'patient targets', in particular the 'breast-feeding targets'. Which is, of course, absurd. I doubt there's a maternity-nurse more dedicated than Mary. I, for one, have benefited from the fact that she's always doing home visits above and beyond the call of duty – especially in those early days to help with breast-feeding.

And boy, has she had her work cut out! The past year has seen a phenomenal baby boom around here. What with all the forty-plus career women and their double and triple buggies bulging with gorgeous IVF bubs. Plus we thirty-something mums following closely behind. And not to forget the teen mums who swell Mary's flock.

And then I remember the form that Mary ripped up on my first visit to the new-mothers' group. Oh, no. Her dignity and respect for her patients has been repaid by the bureaucrats giving her the boot. She must be devastated.

Victoria's obviously pretty annoyed by the whole situation too – she's all of a sudden jittery and flushed, and can't seem to sit still. And then she stops in her tracks.

'Can you smell something?' she says, sniffing the air like a rabbit.

'Oh, it's probably a barbecue – the Australians across the back are always at it.'

'No – it smells more like . . .'

And then we see it. BLOODY HELL. A small lick of flame peeks up above the garden-shed windowsill. And Dad runs out. One of his laptops is on fire!

And here I was worrying that he'd blow up the kitchen or bathroom with one of his physics experiments – not burn my garden shed down with a rogue bloody laptop. This is *so* not happening.

Dad frantically darts around the garden, looking for something to dampen the flames, while Victoria and I grab the girls and Pierre and leg it straight inside. In the heart-stopping panic, I have a flash of inspiration. I fetch the fire blanket Tim gave me for Christmas and sprint back out to the shed and throw it on the laptop. It smothers the flames instantly. (Won't Harry and Tim be thrilled!)

A very close call indeed.

My heart is still pounding (about three inches outside my body) when Victoria comes to inspect the ruins, but my attention is caught by her gasp of blatant surprise. And it's not the charred remains of the laptop she's looking at.

'Oh. That's my Cat-a-Pole,' I admit sheepishly, as Victoria glares at the pole in the corner of the shed. I feel obliged to mutter something about how I needed to lose weight (though I don't go into the whole marriage-crisis-makeover thing) and how Dad and I had to be 'resourceful' in finding a cheap alternative to a gym membership.

You see, Millie spied The Cat's DVD, *Cat-a-Pole the Pounds Away: From Mummy to Scrummy in Three Easy Weeks*, on the council dump pile during one of her morning jaunts with Dad, and insisted that she bring it home to me. She recognised the photo of The Cat on its cover. (I think we need to do some more reading of *Peter Rabbit* and a little less of *Hello!*) Dad was highly impressed by Millie's intelligence in identifying The Cat. But not more than me, when Dad assured me that he could rig up a pole in the shed from some old scaffolding that he'd found, and set up our small TV/DVD player so that I could do my exercises up there – in private. And completely for free!

I confess to Victoria that Millie *loves* to watch my Cat-a-Pole routine – as all the moves are done to the primal beats of the Pussycat Dolls (not quite Mozart, I know). And along with my sprints to and from Marco's studio, I think my activity levels have multiplied a hundredfold and my metabolism with it. So my new jeans were necessary not only on the fashion front, but the size front too, as I've managed to lose quite a bit of weight. (Yippee!) I really can't wait to see Tim's reaction when he returns tomorrow.

Victoria pauses thoughtfully and then says matter-of-factly, 'Yes. You do look different. Good for you. Keep it up.'

And at that, she turns and leaves as quickly as she came. But not before getting my new email address and telling me that she will send through her plan to 'save Mary and the mother-and-baby clinic' to me tonight.

I eagerly await my instructions.

Capsule Shoe Wardrobe

A little something to help you build your shoe collection around . . .

Falling-in-love Shoes – classic high-heeled court shoes to show off legs, with a peep-toe and/or toe cleavage to hint of things to come.

Night-on-the-town-with-the-girls Shoes – must be able to dance in these shoes, so go for medium to high heels (depending on your heel endurance) with a T-bar or ankle strap. Patent leather is always good for withstanding busy bar areas. Never wear peep-toes or open toes – you'll get trodden on.

Hot-date Shoes – definitely high-heeled mules – for ease of kicking off in a hurry.

Shopping Shoes – when comfort and flexibility need to take a front seat, opt for a classic loafer or sturdy ballet flat.

Holiday Shoes – should always be sparkly slides for the summer. And low to medium boots for winter sightseeing.

Work Shoes – leave your black stiletto thigh-high boots at home. (Unless you work in a funky ad agency, in which case may I suggest leopardprint dominatrix platforms.) Only do seriously high heels at work if you're extremely confident in them – otherwise senior male colleagues will wipe the floor with you. Best to stick with polished, reliable shoes with a sneak of attitude, like a mid-height heel (demi-wedges work well), slingback or court.

Airport Shoes – must be able to run in these, plus slip them on/off easily and cope with slight swelling after long-haul flights. Flat mules are best or a loose-fitting ballet pump.

Pram Shoes – best to avoid points, heels and anything that can't withstand puddles. To maintain some semblance of pre-baby fashion cred, try an adult version of the Mary Jane for a pretty yet practical solution.

Top Tip

Any shoe with a Velcro fastening should remain the sole preserve of those with milk teeth or ten thumbs. Velcro straps are the clothing equivalent of T-shirts. So please make an effort princesses.

Think about it.

24. Backtracking

From: Tim (Bangalore)
To: Jane (home)
Subject: RE: Millie's Birthday

To My Darling Little Millie

Unfortunately, Daddy has to stay at work one week longer in Bangalore, and won't be able to be with you on your first birthday. But I look forward to giving you the biggest hug ever, very soon.

Your loving Daddy xo

I stare at the email, completely dumbfounded. It's the eve of Tim's *long-planned-for* return home. He *cannot* possibly be serious.

I've been so consumed by my big transformation and having him here for Millie's birthday that I don't know what to think, or how to respond. And not so much as a brief phone call to apologise or explain, either. Yet another Oscar-winning performance in his well-rehearsed role of avoiding-the-hard-questions-from-the-nagging-wife, it seems.

The more I think about it, the more I'm positive that Alex is behind it too. Why else would he be so cowardly?

A wild mix of emotions – anger, sadness, confusion, rejection – whirl within me, eventually coming together in a stabbing migraine. I breathe deeply, trying to remain calm and, dare I say, positive. For when Tim finally does come home next week, I sincerely hope that there is a marriage worth saving. As personally, I'm beginning to think that the emotional baggage under our rug (with the label 'Alex') is getting a little bit too lumpy underfoot to ignore very much longer.

I'm just thankful that Victoria has me working on the save-Mary-and-the-mother-and-baby-clinic crusade all this week (otherwise I'm sure I'd be a gibbering, nervous wreck). And there is no doubt that Victoria is in her element. Churchill's war bunker has nothing on the campaign headquarters in her basement Shaker kitchen – where she, Mary and I are assembled for our first meeting today (tissue box at the ready for Mary).

Poor Mary is bereft. This job has been the essence of her existence for her entire working life. She was literally in shock at being given notice, and had accepted her fate reluctantly and dutifully. And, as it turns out, silently.

That was, until Victoria got wind of it.

Mary's brought along her work diaries from the past few years – in which she's kept a meticulous record of all of the mums and babies that she's seen in the clinic and on her home visits. Unfortunately, she never transferred these to her official time sheets in any consistent manner, preferring to squeeze in a few more visits ahead of sitting in the office ticking boxes – and is why she's in this fix, of course.

Victoria volunteers to trawl diligently through the diaries and pull together some coherent patient data, while Mary and I do house visits to all the mums in the area and get the new-mothers'-pack breast-feeding certificates signed and backdated. We give ourselves two weeks to get it all done.

Millie, meanwhile, is in playgroup heaven. She's upstairs with Allegra being looked after by the neighbourhood mums and nannies, who have all rallied around in support.

From:	Sophie (work)
To:	Jane (home)
Subject:	RE: Save Mary

Hi Jane

Thanks for popping around last night with the breast-feeding form. It was great to catch up with you and Millie too. Seems like years since we've seen each other. After recapping our holiday adventures, have made a mental note never to use the words 'Hugh' and 'holiday' in the same sentence again. (Perhaps it was my nosebleed at the same time as Hugh's projectile vomiting and diarrhoea on the flight home that tipped us over the edge.) And I have to say that you looked amazing! Just goes to show what discipline and hard work can achieve. Trinny would be proud of your new hairstyle – very smart.

Have had a hellish day, already. I'll now clear a £7 profit from my weekly pay if Rhiannon gets her way. She hit me with a pay-rise request this morning – just as I was about to walk out the door – late as usual. Looks like she's been talking to some of the mannies in the park, who, for some bizarre reason, seem to be getting paid loads more than the current going rate. Is it me, or is there a North-west London fad at the moment for male 'affair-proof' nannies? I'm really torn, as up to now I'd have given her my left kidney in order to keep her – and a stable life. But now Hugh's that much older and more independent, I'm thinking of exploring other childcare options. Forgot to tell you that I've just heard (all very hush-hush) that there's a wonderful childminder near us with a vacancy coming up – twins moving to Bath. I'm going to put Hugh's name down. Interested in putting Millie's name down too?

Oh, and of course, no problem at all to eyeball whatever contracts, accounts etc of Mary's that you and Victoria can get your hands on. You go, girls!

S xx

After just four days (and early evenings) of doing house visits with Mary, I'm bowled over by the sheer number of women and babies that she's helped. Far more than one person should be expected to cope with, in my humble opinion. Unsurprisingly, Mary said that she often worked out-of-hours just to make sure everyone was seen to.

I'm also really enjoying meeting all the mums in the area and, in particular, catching up with those from my new-mothers' group (since we drifted apart many months ago). Aside from the obvious thrill of seeing just how much our babies have grown (I'll *never* cease to be amazed by the changes from birth to one), it's been fascinating to hear what everyone's up to – which for the majority is working full- or part-time.

Some mums appear to be juggling the demands of work and home better than others, it has to be said. Definitely those with more flexible employers and/or jobs are the happiest. Like the freelance journalists, hairdressers, bookkeepers and health-care workers. Along with the likes of Sophie, who was senior enough to negotiate good maternity leave and part-time packages, as well as afford high-quality childcare. Oh, and it goes without saying that partners who help out more on the home front make for more satisfied mums too. (But I don't even want to go there right now . . .)

We've also come across a few housedads, plus a handful of couples splitting their working weeks, in varying proportions, between paid work and home parenting. Progress indeed. (It certainly seems that, while I've been at home ranting and raving to Tim, they've quietly got on with it.) I'm now further convinced that I've made the right decision about my trip to Milan – especially if my mum shoes are going to be my ticket back into the world of flexible paid work.

In light of this, I've also decided to take Sophie's lead and put Millie's name down with the childminder (for two days a week). She was delightful and so nurturing and loving towards the kids. And in all honesty, I think Millie would probably enjoy a small break from me – as she's certainly been relishing her time at Victoria's of late. Nothing's confirmed yet. (And isn't likely to be for a couple of months.) But it's a step in the right direction, at least.

And now, the most eagerly awaited and dreaded day of my year is upon me: Friday. Millie's first birthday.

Tim's apparently caught up in meetings (or is it Alex's web?) all day and sends a video e-greeting card to Millie first thing in the morning.

She claps and squeals, 'Da, Da,' with delight, and clearly thinks it's the best thing she's ever seen.

My heart bleeds for her, and yet I smile and clap along too.

To make matters worse, after the disappointment of Tim's bombshell email, and then unexpectedly spending the week doing house visits with Mary, I haven't had the motivation or the time to organise a party for Millie. But, of course, Victoria's had Allegra's big fanfare planned for *months*.

I phone Victoria to let her know that Millie won't need to go over there this morning (while Mary and I do our house visits) as Mum and Dad have come down to spend the day with us. Victoria nearly has kittens when she finds out I haven't got anything planned for Millie, and very kindly proposes that we make Allegra's party this afternoon a joint celebration – seeing as they are almost twins. I gratefully accept her truly generous offer. (And then, of course, feel *dreadful* for every tight-lipped grievance I've ever muttered in her direction.)

Mum, Dad and I head off to Victoria's with Millie, after her nap. And Kate (who's finished work early to pay Millie a surprise visit) bumps into us halfway down the street and comes along too.

It's actually a really lovely crowd Victoria's gathered together for the party, as Mary and all the mums and babies from our new-mothers' group are here – a sort of one-year reunion – along with most of the local nannies and au pairs and babies I know from the park.

We're in the door five minutes when Dad slips rather comfortably back into Pied Piper mode and offers to supervise the animal-petting zoo in the back garden (which is squished around the recently installed timber fortress complete with multiple turrets, swings, slides and a sandpit). Kate's reluctantly roped into assisting Philomena the very un-PC pink fairy in her toxic, scented fairy cave inside the conservatory. (The wet-weather back-up that Victoria decided to go for anyway.) And Mum's having the time of her life down in the kitchen with Victoria – cooking up a storm, whilst comparing brands of hospital-grade cleaning products. (Millie's absolute favourite birthday present was the Twenty-piece Girls Only Cleaning Trolley from Mum and Dad. She insisted on bringing her dustpan and brush with her to the party. Mum's determined to get at least my daughter in a pinny, having failed with me.)

I'm introduced to Victoria's husband for the first time, too. Which feels more than a little strange, seeing as though I've spent so much time in his home this past year. And I must say, he's *very* different to what I'd expected. All he does is wander about sipping red wine and telling us (and in particular, Victoria) what to do or, more annoyingly, what we're doing wrong. And she's so meek and cowering around him, I'm finding it almost impossible to reconcile with the officious Victoria of baby-group infamy. Peculiar indeed.

But most importantly, the party is a huge success. And Allegra and Millie are having a wonderful, albeit mischievous, time together – I caught them just after they'd stealthily climbed up on to the party table and licked the icing off the top of an entire tray of cupcakes. The looks on their faces were priceless: *Who, me?* I found it very hard to keep a straight face myself.

Later in the evening, with everyone gone home and Millie in bed, I'm relieved that the day is over. Even though, thanks to Victoria and my family rallying by our side, it was mercifully a lot better than I'd anticipated.

With Tim's return tomorrow inching ever closer (and my anxiety-levels creeping even higher) I sit down at the computer for my nightly blog-a-thon and of course to obsess over my eBay shoe sales – which are not progressing that spectacularly, I have to say. But Liz keeps telling me to hold my nerve.

I'm immediately intrigued by a website posted on the Shoe Princess noticeboard, which promises to help you create your own baby albums online. Spurred on by how good it looks, and of course by Allegra's baby album, I decide to try my hand at finally getting Millie's done (now that I'm such a techie whizz). For she may have dysfunctional parents but, my goodness, she's going to have the best album of baby memories *ever*.

I spend the next few hours uploading all of her photos on to the website and can't believe that I haven't done this before now. I'm diligently fiddling about, editing, cropping, selecting fancy frames, fonts and backgrounds, and savouring every moment of our journey together this past year. But unfortunately, it really does seem to have been 'our' journey – as Tim is decidedly absent from most of the shots (especially since Alex and Bangalore took over his life). I'm pondering what Millie will make of this when she's older, and if indeed it has harmed her in any way, when the *unthinkable* happens . . .

The computer screen goes *completely blank*.

I lose the photos. In cyberspace. Every. Single. One.

A fretful check of the camera confirms my worst fears – it's empty too.

They're gone. *For ever.*

My mind is spinning and I feel a tight band of tingly sweat round my head. I stare out of the window, frozen in disbelief. A full, heavy moon cowers in the sky, casting its critical glow across the room – illuminating the useless mother that I am.

And I cry.

I cry for Millie. Because I've lost the first year of her life.

But most of all, I just cry.

And once I start, I can't stop.

Running . . . in Spikes

As I always say, the sign of a truly seasoned SP is the ability to run in heels. My sources in Miami tell me that more than 100 SPs, from far and wide, took part in the annual Stiletto Sprint last weekend. An event involving a race down one section of seafront pavement, wearing a minimum stiletto-heel height of around 10 cm.

On behalf of all SPs I offer my warmest congratulations to the winner — aptly a local SP from Miami Beach — who received a $2,000 voucher from an upmarket department store for her stellar effort. (This should keep her in shoes for a little while to come.) I'm also assured that there was not one injury on the day — clearly a class field and not an event for the amateur SP!

Walk the Walk

Barrister SP of Auckland recently had surgery on her bunions, and made sure to take long-service leave and cancel ALL court appearances during her recovery period. As she was certain that the 'other side' would have 'walked all over her' in her monster orthopaedic sandals.

Footnote

Price stickers on the soles of shoes are never a good look.

25. Killer Heels

From: Fi (work)
To: Jane (home)
Subject: HAVE I MADE THE WORST DECISION OF MY
          LIFE?

Hi Jane

Thanks SO much for letting me weep all over your kitchen table on Saturday. (Just like old times . . . Ha!) Poor Millie – seeing her favourite aunt in such a state. I'm glad, at least, that she loved her giant push-along stiletto. (Though I'm still cross with you for not inviting me to her big party.)

At least work's been frantic ever since coming back from hols – have been too busy to obsess over Marco . . . too much. Am on the road now for a few weeks with Jolie Naturelle – so hopefully might have time to clear my head. Or not? Oh, what have I done?!

Ho hum, life goes on . . . even in relationship breaks.

Fi xx

Fi is one thing, if not predictable.

Her visit on Saturday ended, unsurprisingly, in an epic tea-and-tears session in my kitchen. All thanks to her announcing that she and Marco are officially 'on a break'. At her instigation, of course. Because she has 'issues'. 'Issues' being code for Fi-pushing-the-relationship-self-destruct-button so that she can save face, in the extremely unlikely event that she's got it all completely wrong, and Marco was about to dump her anyway.

And so it goes.

She said that she got spooked by the intensity of her month away with Marco (they coincidentally had their first big tiff) and wondered if he was Mr Right after all. Surely she remembers our gap year in Italy – travelling together can test the best of friendships, let alone relationships. And there is no doubt that this is the first 'real' relationship that Fi has ever been confronted with.

As delightfully melodramatic as I found Fi's monologue it *was* a welcome relief to mull over someone else's relationship troubles for a change. Though I'm afraid I probably wasn't quite as congenial a counsellor as I normally am – due mostly to the fact that Tim was due home imminently. I still haven't dared to tell Fi (or anyone else other than Ben, for that matter) about the dark place that Tim and I seem to be in.

But I did tell her that I was planning to go to Milan with Marco and Ben for the day next month – we've been friends too long for me not to. She was plainly a little put out. But this trip is really important to me, and I made it very clear that Marco was taking Ben and me along purely as his students. And in any case, she should be back together with him by then (if she has an *ounce* of sense about her) and can come along too if she really wants.

And to top things off, Fi told me that Alison's just been promoted to team leader at work. (Reminding me that I *still* haven't apologised.) Alison's mum has apparently moved in with her and her husband to help out with the kids. And according to Fi, she's not only getting in to work early these days but she's also making her mark by changing all sorts of policies and procedures (that I must admit have needed shaking up for some time). Simon's apparently seething (tee-hee).

Tim arrived home just as Fi was approaching the bottom of the tissue box. He dropped his luggage in the hall, said that he felt poorly and then went straight to bed.

I've never seen him so unwell – with a raging fever that swung between burning hot and shivering cold, many times over. I was so worried that he might have bird flu or malaria, or some equally exotic illness, that I called in the GP. But she said that it wasn't anything more sinister than a very nasty dose of the flu, and that he should just 'ride it out' with plenty of bed rest and fluids.

So that's exactly what he did . . . for SEVEN comatose days.

I set up camp in the spare room at night. And then during the day left bottles of water and flasks of soup by his bed – as I had to continue my house visits with Mary, while Millie was at Victoria's. (Victoria wouldn't swap jobs for the week, insisting that only she could decipher Mary's diaries. Which seemed a little mean.)

For the most part, Tim barely noticed one day roll into the next, let alone my new makeover. (I was cut to the core.) And in the odd lucid moment that coincided with me being around, he wired himself to his mobile and laptop. And then promptly went back to sleep again.

Though I did manage to tell him about my mum shoes and my trip to Ars Arpel, but he was oddly distant – and what's more, flatly refused to be drawn into any discussions about taking the day off work to look after Millie. Piously claiming that it was a very 'critical' time at work, and that he couldn't take any 'unnecessary' leave – especially after this week off sick. (He hasn't taken *one* day of leave all year, for goodness sake.)

I was livid. Especially after all the support I'd given to him and his career this year. And refusing to babysit really was the *last* straw. In my mind, at least.

On the eighth day he crawled out of bed and went back to Bangalore.

It felt like a dream. A very bad dream at that.

At least Mary and I got our paperwork finished – managing to collate enough signed breast-feeding certificates to keep the bureaucrats more than happy, I should think. And Victoria produced a magnificently professional dossier of patient-number spreadsheets, pie graphs, statistical analyses and cross-referenced research studies. (She's right, I would *never* have been able to do such a great job of it.) Sophie then got one of her work couriers to pick it all up from Victoria's, and she presented it to the relevant government department along with a fearsome legalese cover letter. I shouldn't think that they knew what they were in for!

All fingers and toes remain crossed.

From: Jane (home)
To: Liz (work)
Subject: RE: eBay Congrats

Thanks! Am still a little stunned by it all. There's clearly nothing like a pair of vintage Vivienne Westwoods to bring on a bidding war! (Can see why you're so hooked on eBay – all very exciting.) Definitely have enough money now, after paying Ben back for the flight, to visit the upmarket clothing warehouse near your work. You're absolutely right – can't go to Milan looking anything less than fab.

   Thanks again, Jane xx

There's no denying that my whole prise-my-husband-from-the-claws-of-Alex-with-a-stunning-new-makeover drive was a breathtaking flop. And with the big save-Mary-and-the-mother-and-baby-clinic campaign trail now at an end, and the apparition that I think was my husband back in Alex's arms in Bangalore, Millie and I slip deeper into our old routines of daytime TV, playgroups at Victoria's and spins around the park.

I'm quite frankly counting the sleeps until my trip to Milan in two weeks' time – as outside of Millie's cuddles, Milan's the only thing getting me through my days. OK, and maybe my Cat-a-Pole routine too – I'm completely hooked. Dad's very kindly offered to look after Millie for me so that I can go to Milan – as Mum will be away on a quilting week in Marseilles and not returning until the same night I'm due back.

And with barely any communication from Tim, I increasingly spend my nights in cyberspace – seeking emotional solace from the Shoe Princess and Trash Queenz – with a permanent migraine, which is only mildly relieved by copious doses of painkillers and wearing my sunglasses (all day *and* night – very Cat-like!).

Oh, hell, who am I kidding . . . blow the Jaffa Cakes. Where's the vodka?

TrashQueenz e-lert
Cat Got Your Tongue? The Cat's long-term manager and agent, Big Barry Drake, has broken his silence on the growing media interest in her increasingly erratic behaviour – first highlighted by Trash Queenz, no less. He's appearing on **Brunch with Britain** today to douse those pesky rumours. Don't miss it . . .

Millie, Florence and I are waiting in front of the television with bated breath for the appearance of Big Barry – that's what the tabloids call him. Due in part to the considerable size of his girth but mostly because of his Swiss bank accounts (thanks to all the money he's made from The Cat over the years). He's the eagle-eyed photographer who 'discovered' her outside the changing rooms of Top Shop, Oxford Street, at the tender age of fourteen. And the rest, as they say, is history.

Tamsin seems to be in a rotten mood today. She and Gavin are squabbling over everything, from who reads the weather forecast to who gets what side of the sofa to sit on. And now, to top it off, Big Barry's a last-minute no-show.

Tamsin's less than impressed. (She's a real stickler for professionalism.) Instead, they run with a rushed-together video segment on her 'Cat-aclysmic' decline, and get the resident agony uncle, Dr Pemberton, to give his analysis. I adore the dapper Dr Pemberton and his chestnut Oliver Sweeny brogues and pinstripe suits. I'm also certain that he's got a *massive* crush on Tamsin – the flirting's outrageous.

'So, Doc . . .' Gavin always calls him 'Doc', just to wind him up. 'What do you make of The Cat's Jekyll and Hyde lifestyle?'

She's now out drinking *every* night (always in those oversized dark sunglasses and never talking to anyone other than her bevy of minders). Then spending her days locked behind the walls of her vast West Sussex estate with Happy Sunshine and the latest addition to her litter, Strawberry Blossom (a sweet little Sudanese orphan girl), donating vast sums of money to international aid organisations and tending her organic vegetable patch. Or so we're told!

'I think what we're seeing here is clearly a young woman *struggling*.' Dr Pemberton clasps both hands together and frowns – he's such a drama queen. '*Struggling* with the modern-day pressure to be the perfect "model" mother; *struggling* with the emotional and physical burdens of solo-parenthood; *struggling* to let go of her old career-focused pre-baby life and find a new niche for herself; *struggling* with the body of a woman who has suckled a child; and, of course, *struggling* with unfaithful men who constantly let her down.'

Maybe The Cat and I have more in common than I thought?

'Yes, Gavin and Tamsin, this could well be a very public post-partum adjustment-period for her.'

The camera pans across to Tamsin for the wrap-up, but suddenly jolts and wobbles abruptly back to Gavin, who's already started talking, and seems to have stolen her autocue line.

'. . . team here at *Brunch with Britain* sincerely wish her, Happy Sunshine and Strawberry Blossom well,' he finishes, with a close-up of his furrowed brow and winsome blue eyes.

As the camera pans back out, and just as it cuts across to the news desk for an update, I'm *positive* that I see Tamsin (with a dagger-thin stiletto heel in each hand) lunging towards Gavin's head . . .

Shoe Shopping Is Better Than . . .

Clothes shopping, because:
You don't have to strip down to your bare thighs, bulging tummy and flabby arms to try shoes on.

And they can instantly update your wardrobe at a fraction of the cost of a new outfit (especially if you wear a lot of classic black clothing).

Cosmetics shopping, because:
You don't have a snooty shop assistant peering 3mm from your face and telling you that you have large pores, acne scars and blackheads.

Going to the gym, because:
You can enjoy yourself, burn calories AND look good.

Buying perfume, because:
You can delight in your shoes for ever.
And they won't give you headaches (and goodness knows what else) from all the artificial fragrances and additives.

Kiss My Feet

A respected medical journal reported that stiletto heels placed LESS pressure on the knees than wider (and supposedly more comfortable) high heels. Ha!

26. Stitched Up

THE front pages of the next day's newspapers are all emblazoned with headlines like 'Blue *Brunch* Babe!' above photos of a *very* subdued-looking Tamsin. It's obviously a slow news day, as it's all the nation can talk about. Someone downloaded her 'blue outburst' on to YouTube and it's broken all viewing records.

But of course we saw it unfold live – and it was superb! It happened just after Tamsin's big lunge towards Gavin (which was, luckily for Gavin, heroically intercepted by Dr Pemberton, who jumped at the chance to rugby-tackle Tamsin and hold her in a prolonged embrace on the floor).

Tamsin let loose with a scathing Gordon Ramsay-style tirade, '. . .* off, with this * job, and my * vain as * arse * sidekick and his * halitosis and foot * odour. I have a * First in * English Lit and Political * Science from * Oxford, and was promised I'd be on the * foreign * correspondents' * desk not the * freak * entertainer for every bored as * pensioner and jobless * tracksuit wearing * layabout . . .'

A little harsh, I will concede. But she was clearly having an off day.

She's issued a national apology, on behalf of the network, for what was essentially a 'personal discussion' between her and her production team, during what she thought was a 'segment break'. The network refuses to comment on the conspiracy theory circulating on the Net that Gavin orchestrated the whole slip in order to further his own career.

Anyway, the real masterstroke to this whole affair is that down in the left-hand corner of page three of *every* newspaper today is a teeny, tiny close-up photo of gorgeous little Allegra's face, and a small article about Mary and the closure of the mother-and-baby clinic. Victoria's PR pals pulled some strings and got the article placed. She's one well-connected mamma! Her phone's been running hot ever since.

One week later . . .

From:	Sophie (work)
To:	Jane (home)
Subject:	RE: Save Mary

Jane

You MUST go over to Victoria's with a bottle of bubbly – now!

Am in meetings all afternoon, but wanted to let you know ASAP that have just heard from the other side's legal team in response to our submission. They've ceded on ALL points. We've won! It will be announced formally tomorrow.

Between you and me, the chief exec of the local hospital moving into one of the big houses overlooking Queen's Park (with a wife due to give birth to triplets any day) may have had a teensy bit to do with it. Who says living in a gentrifying area doesn't have its advantages? Not to mention having a PR guru in your mums' group!

Oh, and with all of the work on the stats and the gaping holes in the contracts and finances, Mary will start work again on Monday with the budget for two extra nurses and an admin assistant; and will be keeping the new kitchen and lift that they've already installed (hoorah).

Have a toast for me, won't you! S xx

Unbelievably fantastic, utterly BRILLIANT news!

'Come on, Millie. We've got some visiting to do.'

I've long held the sneaking suspicion that I've fumbled my way through this past year in a sort of haze. And that, one day very soon, the fog will lift and the old me will reappear again – bright, confident and in control.

But absolutely *nothing* could have prepared me for the smokescreen Victoria's been hiding behind. And no matter how hard I try, I just can't shake thoughts of her from my mind. It's 2.30 a.m. and I doubt I've slept a wink all night.

I just keep mulling over and over again my chance meeting with Mary outside Victoria's house yesterday. A lucky coincidence that, in theory, should have led to a cork-popping celebration.

But it wasn't.

It was shocking. And unsettling. And yet, in a weird way, calming too. And I'm not particularly proud of this but, all at once, my rival spectacularly imploded. Victoria was no longer the ultra-perfect-selfless-stay-at-home-mum; but a raw, vulnerable woman just like the rest of us.

If only she'd talked to me – about everything – maybe she wouldn't be where she is today?

You see, Mary was most anxious that we didn't go in and see Victoria, and instead strongly suggested we go for a stroll around the park. I immediately knew by the seriousness of her tone that she was not to be questioned. But at the same time, I was completely flummoxed.

As we walked, Mary slowly told me – in as polite and veiled a way as she possibly could (and in *complete* confidence) – Victoria's story: How she had (unbelievably) been wanting to return to work ever since Allegra was about six months old. But her husband, a devout believer that a woman's place was in the home, refused to let her. Not even for the two days a week Victoria had been offered by the PR company.

All of a sudden, the enigma that was Victoria started to make sense to me. She obviously responded to her predicament by throwing her considerable talents into her new 'mum job'. All the while overcompensating for her lack of control over her own life by being the ultra-bossy know-it-all with us mums and nannies on the park circuit. (I can't tell you how much of a relief it is to understand, at least, her motives.)

But then, Mary said, things started to get a little sticky for Victoria. With each week that she remained at home alone with Allegra (she had no girlfriends with babies; and no extended family in London) she became deeply anxious. About everything – from global warming and pesticide residues in vegetables to parking congestion around Queen's Park and al-Qa'ida attacks on London's water supply. (Which neatly explains why I had to help her lug several hundred bottles of spring water down to her cellar.)

But most of all, she became overwhelmed by the enormous responsibility of being Allegra's sole carer on this earth. (And there was no doubt that she loved Allegra more than life itself.) She *genuinely* feared for who would look after Allegra if she wasn't able to – through illness or, God forbid, death. (Her husband is not hands-on in the slightest.) Victoria's worries magnified to such an extent that she started having anxiety attacks whenever she left the house. (It was around this time, I note now, that we stopped going to Mary's new-mothers' group and she upped the ante on her educational baby groups at home.)

And when I thought about it some more, Clara (one of the mums from our mothers' group) told me that she'd been cutting Victoria's and Allegra's hair at home for the past six months. This did surprise me – but certainly not enough to make anything of it. As Clara's a freelance hairdresser at a number of upmarket Mayfair salons, I'd simply assumed that Victoria had deemed her suitable enough to cut Allegra's precious first locks.

I'd also stopped bumping into Victoria at the park. And at baby clinic – simply putting it down to timing (I'm always late). But of course, she'd stopped going. And then there was her no-show for my afternoon-tea invite. And so it went . . .

The home gym she'd had installed in her loft and the fortress playground in the back garden weren't the vulgar trophy-home adornments we all thought they were. Likewise, her Internet and catalogue home-deliveries. Victoria had, in her inimitable fashion, discreetly and methodically managed to avoid leaving the house. *Ever.*

Except, of course, when she was forced to come over and ask for my help with the save-Mary-and-the-mother-and-baby-clinic campaign. Mary said that this particular visit for Victoria would have been the equivalent of me climbing a skyscraper without ropes or supports. Little wonder she was so agitated.

Poor thing – I had absolutely NO idea.

Mary hadn't thought it appropriate for us to go in and see Victoria because she'd just had a particularly difficult session with her – Victoria was in quite a state. (Mary visits her three times a week – hence, I guess, Victoria's vested interest in keeping her employed.) Apparently, Victoria's husband just can't accept that her desire to 'work' is not about abandoning her responsibilities towards Allegra. But more about a need to use her intellect and skills outside of child- and home-centred tasks; to feel more like an active player in the world and less like a passive observer; and, in a small way, to be less financially dependent on him too. Mary's tried to get Victoria and her husband to seek more appropriate professional counselling – but so far, he's refused.

After doing all these visits with Mary, I also can't help but wonder about the myriad other 'mum secrets' she must be carrying around on her capable shoulders. Confirmation, if ever I needed it, of just how important her job is.

So after our walk, I – very much in shock – took Millie home. And immediately ordered a giant bunch of congratulatory flowers to be delivered to Victoria. It was the least I could do. As the victory was *entirely* hers for the taking.

Dad was waiting for us on the doorstep when we got back – reporting for duty for his Milan babysitting stint the next day. And Tim returned from Bangalore later in the evening – clearly not happy about me going ahead with the trip, but irritatingly still with no particular reason why. He just skulked about the flat, mumbling to himself and glued to his mobile, as usual.

And now, I have to be up at 3.30 a.m. in order to get to Heathrow for my flight (oh, the joys of low-cost air travel). Who needs sleep anyway – I should be used to it by now.

Shoe Are You?

Pristine SP
Immaculately groomed and usually a girlie girl. This princess adores shoes and uses them as the centrepiece of her fully coordinated wardrobe of clothes, handbags, jewellery and nail polish. Flowers, bows, ribbons and beading regularly adorn her shoes, which represent most colours of the rainbow.

Performing SP
Usually the younger shoe princess. She loves to wear platform soles, heelless thigh-high boots or any in-your-face shoes that will gain attention. She often has a great sense of fun and adventure. Most men will abhor her shoes, but she doesn't care. Think 'girl power'.

Pretty Woman SP
This princess is most likely sighted in Harley Street or Stringfellow's wearing 4-inch ankle-tied perspex platforms and a mane of peroxide-blonde hair extensions. Movement of facial muscles is not generally visible and top lip resembles result of first-round fight with Lennox Lewis. Trots along like a fettered deer.

Platinum SP
Money is no object and expensive shoes are amongst the many fine possessions in her life. This princess loves having gazillions of shoes in her colour-coordinated designer wardrobe as a sign of her self-made success and financial independence. She's often quoted as saying that she still has her feet on the ground — but just in more expensive shoes! (Think Oprah.)

. . . keep looking!

27. Footloose and Fancy Free

I DOZILY open my eyes and find myself confronted by Tim's upside-down head.

'I couldn't sleep with all your tossing and turning,' he says gruffly, while contorting his legs and arms into another improbable yoga asana.

The bedroom is shrouded in early-morning darkness and, as I turn on my lamp, a feeling of impending doom envelops me. A quick check of my alarm clock confirms my fears – it's 4.15 a.m. (It looks like I set it for 3.30 a.m., and then forgot to turn it on.) The minicab's due in fifteen minutes.

Damn, damn . . . damn it! I throw my head back on to the pillow in despair. My *one* window of opportunity to visit Ars Arpel and I've *blown* it.

I blearily stare at the beautiful ruby butterfly-sequinned stiletto glistening from the chandelier above the bed. (I kicked it off in gay abandon some years back, and have never seen fit to move it!) It quickly reminds me of my mum shoes and all that I worked so hard for this summer.

Fifteen minutes, huh?

There's clearly no choice to be made.

I jump out of bed and sprint down the hall, swishing past Dad on the way.

'You not ready yet?' he says. 'Tally ho! Quick sticks.'

Near enough to fifteen minutes later, Tim's standing in the hallway, staring at me incredulously as I stoop to put on my black, pointy-toed, stiletto-heeled ankle boots. (Either he's just noticed that I'm distinctly less tubby or he's still in a mood about me going to Milan – whichever way, I don't have the time to care right now.) The boots, from Marco's collection, were my reward for helping out with *A Midsummer Night's Dream*. I've been purposely saving them for today. Macro has a real flair for boots – and not only do they look sensational, but I'm supremely confident they'll be comfortable too.

Tim is visibly startled when I stand up in front of him (aha, so he *has* noticed!) – eight centimetres taller, with a perfectly straight back and shoulders, and perky boobs. Smartly turned out in a fitted black dress and short grey swing coat (courtesy of Liz's great connections). A smidge of make-up, shiny brushed hair and not a ponytail or hair-grip in sight.

I *really* should make an effort to get 'properly dressed' more often – I actually feel half decent!

And with not a second to spare, I peek my head into Millie's bedroom and blow her a giant kiss; give Dad a hug (he knows the drill with Millie and will be more than fine); offer Tim a perfunctory peck on the cheek (while completely ignoring his tight-lipped instructions to go to the kitchen and grab some breakfast); and bolt straight out of the door to Javid and his ever Reliable Minicab.

As Fi always says in situations like these, 'There's not much that a double espresso and three sugars can't fix!'

Before I know it, I'm mid-air and squished into a tiny budget airline seat in between Ben and Marco. And, if the truth be known, a little shaky – coming down from the adrenalin high of the mad dash to the airport and way too much caffeine on an empty stomach, no doubt.

Ben's already got his map out and is excitedly showing me a 'shoe appreciation' tour route that he's devised for our morning in Milan's legendary Golden Quadrilateral – four streets of international-fashion nirvana. (He's been there a number of times before and really knows his way around.)

'Sounds like a morning in heaven!' I say excitedly.

Marco peers up from the notes he's reviewing for our class this afternoon, and counters Ben's offer by insisting that I spend the morning with him – visiting suppliers and sitting in on meetings. He has got a point. If I'm serious about this shoe-making venture I really do need to get to grips with the business side of things. And to tag along with someone as well-connected and experienced as Marco would certainly be invaluable.

But then again, I can't really face all the awkward silences of a morning with him, either. He'll surely want to talk about Fi – who's still got him 'on hold'. And I won't know what to say, other than the obvious: that she's a complete fool for tossing back the best fish she's ever hooked. And that I just hope he doesn't get snapped up by someone in the meantime. (She's playing a very dangerous game indeed.)

An air steward offering refreshments thankfully interrupts us, and it's enough to fob off my reply to Marco for now.

I'm pondering Ben and Marco's kind offers when I suddenly remember a slightly odd telephone conversation I had with Liz last night. After wishing me a wonderful time in Milan, she told me (in *very* hushed tones) to 'be careful', before hastily hanging up. The strange thing is that it wasn't a jolly have-fun-but-beware-of-pickpockets sort of 'be careful'. It was ever so solemn and filled with foreboding.

She couldn't have meant to be careful with Marco and Ben, could she? (Although I guess she *was* the only one at shoe school to witness my little aberration with Marco.) Puh-lease – the pair of them are as harmless as each other. She really is very sweet but, I can confidently vouch, just a tad awash with hormones.

With Marco's attentions back to his notes, I casually flick through his Italian *Vogue* – brushing up on my rusty language skills and falling in lust with the shoes (there really is no better magazine for shoespotting). At least it stops me from looking out of the window too often – overanalysing every *humm* and *whirr* and *dip* of the engines. I can't believe I used to enjoy flying before Millie. I now find it completely unnerving, and valiantly resist the urge to sleep, as if keeping my eyes open somehow wills the plane to stay up in the air.

As I start to relax a little, Marco inadvertently intercepts my gaze. Our eyes lock fleetingly, and I can't deny myself a small excited smile. I really am *very* fortunate to be in his company today.

'Jane . . .' he says tenderly yet firmly. I feel the pulse in his warm palm as he cups it on my shoulder. My heart pounds. And my body jerks a little.

'. . . Please . . . excuse me . . . but we . . .' I sense an urgency in his voice. And all at once, my worst fears are realised: no matter how expertly he thrusts and lunges with his deft sensual touch, there's simply no way he can please me. His enormous foot-last will *never* fit into my dainty satin slipper. *I could weep.*

'Jane . . . we've landed. We have to get off the plane.'
What? . . . Huh? . . . Landed? . . . Plane?

I groggily open my eyes to find Marco with his hand on my shoulder, gently trying to wake me.

OH BOLLOCKS.

I've dreamt about him *again*! (At least it was one of my tamer dreams – though I think Dr Freud might still have something interesting to say about it.)

I immediately close my gaping mouth and fumble to find something to wipe the dribble that's run down my chin. My throat is so dry it takes some minutes of concerted swallowing to regain my composure.

Ben passes me my handbag and gives me one of Marco's London business cards.

'Marco wants us each to have one. In case we get lost,' he winks.

I turn the card over to see Marco's scribbled his local details. I mumble my thanks (still too coy to meet Marco in the eye for fear that he's guessed what I was dreaming about) and we make our way off the plane – the last to leave.

I decide that I'm in love with Milan even before we leave the airport terminal. No doubt the huge Sergio Rossi poster of a magnificent solitary stiletto-heel greeting us at passport control helps a little.

I'm glad that Liz made me make an effort with my clothing too – as the women here are groomed to within an inch of their lives. And they're *all* wearing sunglasses *inside* the airport – in October. Maybe this is where The Cat picked up her penchant for sunglasses. (And to think, if I still had my migraine I'd have fitted right in too.)

And were it not for my stiletto ankle boots I would most certainly feel like I was wandering around the *Jurassic Park* film set – as there are flocks of impossibly tall gazelles milling around. All becomes clear when Marco tells us that the spring/summer fashion shows are on at the moment. Though I shouldn't think I'll run into The Cat here, amongst the 'commoners'. She's probably taxiing down the runway this very minute in Valentino's private jet.

We've struck the morning peak-hour traffic, so I jostle for one of the few remaining seats in the train transferring us from Malpensa Airport to the centre of town. As we pass mile after mile of ugly concrete high-rise apartment blocks, it's hard to imagine that at the end of the line there's a da Vinci and a Duomo I really ought to see. But to be honest, I'm happy with Ben's plan of shoe-ogling in the morning, followed by visiting Ars Arpel with Marco in the afternoon. I just need to tell Marco this . . .

A seat opposite me becomes available and Marco slides in. He's been standing in the aisle, glued to his mobile phone, ever since getting on the train. It seems that an unexpected family drama (so Italian!) has emerged, throwing his morning of meetings and appointments into turmoil. Which of course means that I no longer need to shadow him around. *Phew.* He apologises to me profusely, but promises to meet us at Ars Arpel at 2 p.m.

Seeing Marco with his phone reminds me to get mine. I'm fishing around in the bottomless pit of half-eaten rusks and Wet Wipes in my handbag when I come across a page from his Italian *Vogue.* That's strange – I don't recall ripping anything out. (Something I am prone to doing.)

It's folded in four. I open it up to see that it's a full-page shoe advert, with a handwritten note near the bare flesh of the model's curved ankle – to me. I'm astonished.

The note says that after a morning on Milan's cobblestones in my heels I'm to go to the Ars Arpel Hotel (in the same building as the Ars Arpel Shoe School) at 1 p.m. for a pre-tutorial foot massage. Or whatever I want.

A foot massage!? Or WHATEVER I want?!?!

I furtively compare the handwriting on the note to that of Marco's on the back of his business card. It's identical.

I pinch the skin on the back of my hand. *Yeeeouch!* Yup, and I'm *definitely* awake too.

I dare to glance at Marco, and he fixes me with a glowing smile.

This is SO not happening.

He's supposed to be my **fantasy**, not my bloody **mind-sex partner**!

What on earth could Liz know that I don't?

Red faced, I hastily refold the note and shove it into the side-flap of my handbag. I don't know which way to turn. But I do know I'll be sticking with Ben the WHOLE day.

Kittens

This very popular and wise choice of heel for the SP who's no longer able to do proper high heels but wants a change from flats to smarten up an outfit needs careful handling. For just like their namesake, these adorable, irresistible little creatures can have split loyalties — playful one minute and scratching you on the nose the next.

It's what you wear with the kitten heel that matters:
- skirt just on or just below the knee — prepare for a mauling, especially if one has largish calves.
- long skirt or nearly to the ankles — purrfect
- short skirt (straight) — purrfect
- slimline capri pants or skinny jeans — purrfect

Kindred Spirits

As any SP knows, there's nothing like a fabulous pair of shoes to start up a conversation in the most unlikely places: bus stops, swings at the local park, supermarket queues and lifts. SP of Melbourne travels widely around the globe for her work and always takes her salsa shoes with her. No matter what city she's in, she finds a salsa group and makes instant friends — despite not being able to speak the local language.

28. A Walk On the Wild Side

BLIMEY! I yank my foot up – and regain my composure, yet
again – from one of the hundreds of metal grates (the exact
size of my stiletto heel-tip) that are dotted like landmines across
the pavements here. Between the cobblestones and metal
grates, I'll be astounded if I don't come away from Milan
without a sprained ankle or a slipped disc. At the very least, I'm
going to be lame by the end of the day – having committed the
ultimate Shoe Princess crime of wearing my new boots on a
maiden voyage, without first breaking them in. (The balls of my
feet are already starting to tingle.)

In fact, so perilous is the first half-hour of our walking tour, I
call an immediate coffee break. And within minutes, I unwittingly find myself opening up to Ben (again) about Tim and me.

But I feel distinctly less liberated this time – due mostly to the
fact that my problems have clearly not halved by talking to him,
but seemingly *multiplied*. More than ever, Ben helps me to see
that Tim and I have fallen into an abyss – of nothingness.

And by nothing, I mean exactly that: no blazing rows or
vitriolic exchanges. No deep and meaningful discussions. No

bright and breezy chats. No sex. No laughing. No hugs. No email banter. No daily phone calls. No walks in the park with Millie.

Simply *nothing*.

My heart wrenches just thinking about it.

And yet, as I sit here, with ever more aching feet, I'm reminded of one person who *does* seem to want me . . .

Coffee and rest having revived me somewhat, I slowly wind my way with Ben around the narrow cobblestone streets – spell-bound by how remarkably serene and compact the shopping enclave is. And totally unprepared for how freezing cold it is. A freak Siberian chill has enveloped the city – it's more like January than October. And the fur coats are out in force – the animal-rights movement does not seem to get a look in here. Kate would have an apoplexy.

We've no option but to buy some reinforcements – hats, scarves and gloves – and are spoiled for choice with the array of exquisite shops. Though I guess it's only to be expected when Giorgio Armani is the local chain store. He seems to have a shop on *every* street corner dedicated to one of his different ranges. As well as his superstore, which takes up an *entire* block and has everything from clothes, books, CDs and furniture to make-up. And is the only place you can buy his chocolate – which we feel duty-bound to sample. (Mouth-watering, of course!) I've never considered myself a slave to designers before, but now that I've seen so much outstanding quality and beauty under one roof I'd seriously consider buying toothpicks if they had the Armani logo on them.

With Armani clothing definitely out of my budget, I find myself standing in front of a mirror in a tiny specialist knitwear boutique and trying on various scarves, cloches and berets. Ben, having already made his purchases, is busy discussing with the shop assistants the location of the new interior design store he wants to find.

I fiddle incessantly with a pretty grey crocheted cloche, tilting it this way and that in a vain effort to look more chic and less Miss Marple. All the while mulling over Marco's invite. (To be honest, I've been able to think about little else all morning.)

I study my face in the mirror – peering deep into my eyes. For signs of the old me: Spunk. Passion. Gusto. But all I see is the new me: Tired. Drawn. Dull.

Which begs the question, *What on earth could Marco possibly find so attractive?*

The more I ponder this, the more I'm convinced that what's behind the invite is just his typical thoughtfulness. It'll probably be nothing more than a cup of tea and some friendly shoe banter, with my feet up. And of course, we'll talk about Fi.

As friends do.

What could be so bad about that?

Right.

Unfortunately, the foot situation gets progressively worse. But thankfully, Ben's *really* patient – not moaning in the slightest when I have to stop and rest every ten steps. In fact, he's proved to be quite an enjoyable diversion from my Marco-obsessing (which has been made worse by having to think of him each step by painful step). Ben's been getting me to try on all manner of wild clothes and shoes that I would honestly *never* have the courage to wear these days. (I must admit, I even rather liked the feel of the knee-high gladiator-tied sandal-boots!)

The most fun I've had in ages, though, was trying on the new season's bustiers in Dolce & Gabbana. And despite warnings to the contrary, the shop assistants have been delightfully pleasant and attentive. And not to mention discreet. They did not bat an eyelid when Ben cheekily told them I was his mistress – at which point I *really* had to pull together all my reserves not to burst into fits of laughter. Though I'm sure I didn't do my case any justice when I ended up purchasing said bustier – on Ben's credit card. I had used up my last eBay shoe-sale pennies on my cloche, gloves and scarf, and Ben very kindly *insisted* on giving me a loan until I sold my next lot of mum shoes. (Seeing as though my credit rating's so good!) I definitely would not have been brave enough to buy the bustier without his positive assurances. I guess I truly couldn't believe how good (and dare I say, sexy) I felt in it – I even saw glimpses of the old me.

It's now midday and there's no denying the obvious: I simply can't go on. My feet are in such excruciating agony, I have to take tiny little micro-steps in order not to hobble. (Hobbling's *never* a good look, and probably outlawed in this part of the world anyway.)

Lagging way behind Ben, I manage to hail him down and we slip through the nearest lane to a topiary-lined café in one of the secret magical courtyards dotted throughout the precinct.

As we sit waiting for our order, Ben checks his phone messages and I try valiantly to block thinking about my nearly numb feet. (And, of course, Marco's tempting offer to take them out of their misery.)

During lunch, the pain really does become worrying – I think I'm now starting to lose sensation in some of my toes. *I've never felt anything like this before.* I gratefully accept Ben's offer to get me some paracetamol on his way to the interior design shop he's been talking about.

'Shall I swing back in a cab and get you?' he says rather enthusiastically. 'It's a good fifteen-minute walk to Ars Arpel from here – you'll *never* make it in time.'

'Oh, no. Don't you dare! You've already gone out of your way for me today.'

'Are you sure?'

'Absolutely.' Delightful as Ben is, he can verge on the hyperactive-puppy – some time to myself right now would be nice. 'I'll get a cab – that's no problem at all. Thanks anyway. You go – *enjoy*!'

'See you soon then,' he winks.

I flinch as yet another pulse of sharp pain darts through my foot, and assure him that I *truly* can't wait till we meet again. OH, the pain!

With my throbbing, burning feet resting up on a large ceramic plant pot, I sit in welcome solitude. Watching the very civilised world of Milan go by, my face warmed by a small pocket of sun that's found its way in between the buildings. But of course solitude can be a dangerous thing, and I immediately slip into dizzying circles of do-I-don't-I-Marco-foot-massage-what-ever-I-want scenarios. When really, I know I should be think-ing of Tim. (And Fi.)

As ever, Marco is my drug of choice. My escape. And I indulge some more, dipping my thoughts decadently into his tempting waters again and again.

I'm literally giddy on a cocktail of conflicting emotions when I check my watch and see to my surprise that it's twenty minutes past our rendezvous time. Gosh. I've been sitting here so long I must have been in a trance.

Well, that's it then – decided for me – it's a no-show.

When I see Marco at 2 p.m. I'll just have to act completely vague, as if I never found the note in the first place.

It's probably the best outcome – for everyone.

As I sit staring into space, wondering what Marco's doing and what he's thinking right now, pondering what never was, I spy a flurry of models in the lane, with a photographer and stylists in tow.

They must be suffering from hypothermia. They're in white PVC micro-miniskirts and barely-there bikini tops, with huge sprays of frizzed red hair poking out almost horizontally from motorcycle helmets. (Artistic licence and all that!) And on their stalk-like legs, they're all wearing the same style of knee-high boots (with chunky platform glitter-encrusted heels) but in different colours.

I can't take my eyes off one pair in particular – a sort of crimsony cerisey raspberry colour. The camera flash keeps bouncing off them, glinting at me from every angle. There's something strangely familiar about them, and I can't help but smile.

And to my total surprise, while I'm smiling, I catch the eye of someone next to the photographer, who smiles cheekily back at me . . . Marco!

It can't be?

I slide down in the chair, but it's too late. He's already sauntering over. Though his smile immediately evaporates when he sees my elevated feet and the grimace on my face.

'Oh, I'm *so* sorry, Jane!' he says, sounding genuinely remorseful. 'I'm *so* thankful – to be running into you like this. It's been a *crazy, crazy* day – I had to take my sister to hospital. All is OK now. I'm just running *so* late. Still, it is unforgivable of me. Come . . .' He suddenly leans forward, gathers my handbag and shopping bag, and expertly scoops me up in his capable arms, carrying me out of the courtyard. Calmly and purposefully.

'. . . My car's parked out the front.' His face is so close, I can feel his breath.

Everyone's watching. I barely know which way to look – so wantonly delicious is his smell.

He then gently stands me on the pavement while he opens the car door, and motions me to get in.

'Let's go to Ars Arpel. Pronto. I *insist* on making amends.'

I stand, frozen, at the open door in front of me. Marco's muttering profusely in a sort of broken Italian/English, and all I can pick up is the odd word like 'foot', 'pain', 'heels', 'shameful' as he walks around the back of the car to the driver's seat.

And then, there's the little red devil sitting on my shoulder . . .

'Well . . . he *should* have warned you about the grates and cobblestones and the importance of heel selection *before* today. A little pay-back foot massage wouldn't be *completely* out of order.

Nor would a little TLC.

Plus he *is* on a break from Fi.

And your husband *is* under the hex of an adulteress . . .'

I get into the car.

Bootylicious

I'm pleased that boots are so big of late. I love everything about them – their strength, protection from the elements, sexual energy and hard-wearing loyalty. But with such a variety of styles to choose from, it can be a little mind-boggling. Here's a tip from SP of London that may help you . . .

Think Opposite

Tall SPs: Don't necessarily go for the tight-fitting, long-legged or thigh-high boot. It can make one look like a drainpipe. Try the mid-calf to three-quarter-length boots, with no or low heels – very biker chic.

Short SPs: Likewise, don't think that because you have short legs and wide calves you can't do long boots. Try a long boot with a wide, loose-fitting top and a high, reasonably chunky heel for a surprisingly good look. If you go for the mid-calf or shorter boot with low heel, prepare to whistle while you work *à la* one of Snow White's little dwarfs!

Point to Note

Buy pointed-toe shoes and boots a half to a full size bigger for a much more comfortable fit.

29. Teetering On the Edge

How does it happen, exactly? The distance. The gaping void that wedges itself between two previously intertwined lives. Two lives that created, in love, another life. A little person so complete and perfect that they sat staring at her in awestruck reverence – too scared to breathe loudly, for fear of waking her. United.

How can two such lives drift, in little more than a year? So stealthily. So brutally. So *far* apart.

I'm not sure what one's supposed to think about as you drive to your very first adulterous liaison – sexy lingerie, kinky tricks? But that's what I think about: *How on earth did it come to this?*

In fact, I'm so nervous I haven't spoken a single word to Marco the whole journey. My feet are *killing* me now too. (I actually feel slightly nauseous.)

Marco seems much more relaxed about the whole thing, though. Perhaps Rachel's early misgivings were right, and he's an old hand at it. He's been chatting animatedly about the boots from the photo shoot. Telling me how he made them as a special commission for an up-and-coming fashion designer –

and was desperate to drop by en route to Ars Arpel to see how they looked, not realising how late he was. It's his first major fashion shoot for Italian *Vogue*. He's over the moon.

I decide to satisfy my curiosity.

'What colour would you call those crimsony cerisey raspberry boots?'

'Ah!' His eyes light up as he slides the car into a parking space at the Ars Arpel School and Hotel car park. 'Peony. You're going to be seeing a lot of it next summer.'

Marco gets out of the car and rummages around in the boot.

Peony. Of course! My wedding flowers were peonies . . . I made sure they *perfectly* matched my crimsony cerisey raspberry . . . wedding shoes . . .

I break out in a cold sweat and begin to dig madly in my handbag for the stub of my boarding card.

I note the date.

Oh crap . . . crap . . . crap . . . bloody crap.

It's today. My wedding anniversary's TODAY.

And all at once, everything makes sense. . . .

Like Tim's silent death stares this morning. And saying he couldn't babysit Millie, even though he'd be in town. And when I repeatedly asked him for a concrete reason as to why I couldn't go to Milan on *this particular day*, he just gritted his teeth and looked like a kettle about to come to the boil or made up those stupid work excuses. Indignant, no doubt, and too proud to have to spell it out to me. (That's Tim all over.)

You see, today is the ONE day of the year we vowed (on our wedding night) always to spend together. *No matter what.* I've just been so distracted by my mum shoes and my whole reinvention-winning-Tim-back caper that I *completely* forgot about it.

Maybe this means Alex doesn't have such a strong hold on him, after all.

In any case, I'm in deep, deep trouble. As our anniversary is also the ONE day of the year that Tim prepares a special breakfast for me. He always lays it out on the kitchen table the night before. But of course, I didn't sample it this morning, did I? No. Because I refused even to set foot in the kitchen.

I feel tears welling. And my heart is racing. I'm all of a sudden burning hot, and rip off my cloche and gloves and scarf.

I immediately call an end to my misadventures in Milan and leap from the car.

'Jane! Jane!' I hear a bemused Marco calling after me, as I run out of the car park in a flood of hot, salty tears. And in a desperate bid to rid myself of excruciating pain (and all future evidence of my near-miss with adultery) I unzip the offending ankle boots and hurl them into the nearest rubbish bin, along with the page from *Vogue*.

I can't bear to turn round. I just run and run – oblivious to the incredulous stares of the Milanese (who most likely consider it a certifiable offence to be seen in public without designer shoes). The cobblestones are sharp, lumpy and freezing underfoot, and the wind is biting in my face.

But I don't feel a thing; other than the *urgent* need to be with Tim and Millie.

I don't remember much about getting to the airport.

But I'm here. With newly purchased Benetton trainers (I've always said I wouldn't be seen dead in trendy trainers – ha!) and racoon eyes from crying. Unable to get an early flight back to London, I've had no choice but to sit. And think.

And with every hour that passes I feel even more horrid – about what I contemplated doing with Marco and, of course, the scene that awaits me at home.

The sea of tired travellers in the departures hall abruptly lurches to one side as a gaggle of Eurotrash-meets-Americancruise-liner women merrily barge their way through – resplendent in diamanté-encrusted Versace sunglasses, fur stoles, coiffed hair, red lipstick, metallic-silver trainers and enormous matching silver backpacks. Leaving a wake of gawping mouths behind them.

I openly cringe as they head straight for my departure lounge. And when they stop right next to me, I literally can't believe my eyes.

'Mum! What are *you* doing here?' Of all the times to have her delayed mid-life crisis, she has to choose NOW.

My day's just got a whole lot worse.

She takes off her sunglasses and hugs me.

'Oh sweetheart, I hoped we'd run into you! Look, Betty, it's Jane!'

Betty Malthouse scampers over and greets me. I feel like I've just been air-kissed by a squirrel wearing tartan tights and a twin set. (Betty's one of the few people I know who's shorter than me.)

It turns out that Mum, with one errant click of her Silver Surfers mouse, booked the entire quilting group easyJet e-tickets to Malpensa Airport instead of Marseilles Airport. By all accounts, they've had an absolute hoot of a time in Milan this past week – escorted around by two university students they befriended at their budget hotel. They've done tours of designer factory-outlet malls on the outskirts of town, seen plays, sampled fine cuisine, viewed *The Last Supper* and numerous art galleries, and been down the catacombs of the Duomo. They're buzzing like a swarm of bees high on nectar.

But as soon as Mum asks me how my day's been, and in particular my visit to Ars Arpel, I spontaneously burst into tears. Sobbing and shaking, I blurt out the whole pathetic story of my life this past year, culminating in today's events. She holds me close in the unconditional embrace of mother-love, while Betty and the gang protectively gather round – fetching cups of tea and biscuits, and offering anecdotes from numerous marriages, divorces, affairs, reconciliations and the like.

I feel eerily cosseted in the womb of their life experience. And finally, buoyed by their support, I vow to face Tim when I get home – for better, or for worse.

About an hour later, I spy Marco heading towards our departure gate for the late flight we were all scheduled to return on. I've been *dreading* this happening, almost as much as facing Tim.

If *only* I'd stuck with Ben, I wouldn't be in this mess in the first place.

Mini-Me Survey

I'm sure there's many a SP with a photo tucked away in a 1970s family album, where all female members are dressed in exactly the same outfit. Whether it be sundresses lovingly sewn from Mum's old bedroom curtains; or chocolate-brown ponchos and flares. And, of course, identical flower-trim denim platforms.

The Cat and her adopted three-year-old daughter were recently papped in Sloane Street wearing matching outfits: zebra-print ponyskin boots with tassel fringing, metallic minidresses and oversized sunglasses. Which begs the SP survey question for this month: **In the new millennium, is mini-me dressing neat or naff?** Or just plain scary?

Tittle Tattle

SP shop assistant at an upmarket Milanese department store says that some of her more affluent (and seemingly competitive) SPs regularly buy all four pairs of their size in a high-end designer shoe (usually a new season's signature piece), so that no one else can have it.

Of course, one mustn't be too quick to judge — she could have four wardrobes, each in a different country . . . it does happen!

All in the Mind

Full marks to student SPs of Helsinki, who assure me they only study and sit for exams in high heels. As they can't think straight in flats!

30. Wrong-footed

DESPITE my best efforts at shrinking behind the fur stoles and glitz, Marco spots me and makes his way over, looking rather awkward.

I hold tight to Mum's arm for support and suddenly notice that Marco is holding equally tight the arm of a pretty young blonde model-type. As they approach he pulls her close and kisses her fondly on the cheek. *Has he no shame?* It certainly didn't take him long to find a replacement. I'm *such* a fool.

Marco introduces his youngest sister, Francesca, to us.

Oh.

The sister that he spent the morning ferrying in and out of hospital, with what turned out to be a false case of suspected appendicitis. (Now that I look at her closely, she does seem a little washed-out.) She lives here in Milan with their mum, and is a trainee journalist with a fashion magazine. Her English is impeccable.

Marco sidles up to talk to me, while Francesca captivates Mum and the gang with the promise of gossip from the fashion shows this afternoon. She's quite delightful – and so gregarious and outgoing compared to Marco. Apparently, there's been some high drama. And as much as I'd love to listen in, I've got more than enough of my own dramas to concentrate on right now.

'Are you all right, Jane? I've been concerned for you. I tried calling you on your mobile, but it kept going to your message bank – which is full, by the way.'

Oh, no! I must have forgotten to turn my phone on this morning. No wonder I haven't had any calls. That stupid bloody note really has tainted my whole day. What if something's happened to Millie? Or Tim? Ashamed by my self-absorption, I vow to turn on my phone as soon as I get rid of Marco.

'I'm fine. Really, I am.' Let's just leave it at that. *Please, please, just go away and don't ask any more questions.*

'Here, you left these in my car.' He hands me a bag with my cloche, scarf, gloves and bustier, and then leans in a little closer and says, 'I can't apologise enough. I should *never* have put you in that position.'

Hell, we're both as guilty as each other. Especially with Fi in the loop. I don't know why he's being so noble. But I guess at least he's seen the error of his ways – attempting to seduce a married woman and all. *As if I didn't feel bad enough already.*

Marco's momentarily distracted by an incoming text message.

'Ah. It's Ben.' He smiles into his phone. 'He's staying on in Milan tonight. Wise move.' He gestures to the overcrowded lounge.

'Oh, that reminds me, Ben said to give these to you.' Marco hands me the paracetamol – I could swallow the whole packet! 'Ben was concerned for you too. You missed out on the tutorial this afternoon. We had an embellishments expert – your favourite part of the shoe.'

Oh, dear. It was extremely rude of me to run away like that. And I do really regret not going to the tutorial and seeing the rest of the shoe school.

'Anyway,' Marco continues. 'It's *unforgivable* of me to have made a boot so poorly – and caused you such pain. I will destroy the last for that design and start again – you can be assured. And I will *absolutely* make you a better pair – that you can dance in, pain free. Even on cobblestones!'

I follow his eye down to my trendy trainers.

'Ah!' Marco grimaces. 'And I was going to get you a better-fitting pair of boots. My friend has a shop – very near to Ars Arpel. We had plenty of time before the tutorial and school tour, too.'

'You were *what*?'

'Going to get you another pair of boots – it's the very least I could have done.'

I peer searchingly into his eyes. Is he *really* only talking about boots? And *not* an adulterous-foot-massage liaison?

I think back to the *Vogue* page and the business card with the same handwriting on them. Marco's. That is, unless . . .

'Ben's fiancée must be jealous – missing out on a fun night in Milan,' says Mum jovially from my side. She's been listening in on Marco and me, and can clearly see the cogs turning in my head.

'Fiancée . . . puh!' scoffs Francesca, who's reattached herself to Marco and also butted in to our conversation.

Marco turns an uncomfortable shade of red and clears his throat.

'Jane . . . I . . . err . . . don't know how to tell you this, but . . . Ben is not engaged to be married.'

'But his girlfriend, the vegan. Who works with sick and dying children at the hospital. And in the orphanage. The love of his life.'

'Sorry.' He shakes his head grimly. 'No girlfriend.'

'But what about all the cooking classes and pottery work-shops . . . and French manicures?'

'Well, yes, he did do those. Just like the twenty-five shoe workshops he's done with me.'

My brain's trying to compute what he's saying. This is getting worse by the minute.

'Look, Ben's a great guy. With a lot of creative energy. And very caring too. He's also just a guy who seems to like meeting women of a certain . . . *circumstance*,' says Marco, clearly uneasy with the whole conversation. 'He's, how do I say—'

'Marco, you're *soooo* polite!' says an exasperated Francesca. By now, Mum and the gang are completely agog. 'Ladies, Ben is a good old-fashioned lothario. A red-hot pants-man who likes to *please* (and apparently very well indeed)' – a chortle bubbles through her audience – 'women of the not-so-happily-married kind,' she says with equal measures of disdain and amusement.

Oh no.

It *must* have been Ben, then – that planted the note. What a LOW LIFE!

And what a fool I *truly* am.

I sit down and hold my head in my hands, thinking of all the time I've spent with Ben lately. Which could have been far less, if only I'd taken more notice of Marco (who was clearly trying to protect me from him, knowing all too well how fragile I was). Like when he suggested that I made my mum shoes at home, and not in the studio with Ben over the summer; and of course, strongly suggested I spend the morning with him today and not go on Ben's fateful 'shoe-appreciation' tour.

Little wonder Marco was always so edgy when we girls quizzed Ben about his fiancée too.

My skin crawls when I think of all the intimate details I've confided to Ben. And not to mention trying on all those clothes and shoes today . . . and the bustier . . .

He must have thought I was putty in his hands.

I feel mortified.

An announcement advises us that our plane is ready for immediate boarding.

Great. And now, I have to go home and face that other little ménage à trois – Tim, Alex and me.

Shoe Are You?

Quirky SP

No slave to fashion, this princess has a strong sense of her own style and sticks to it. She would never wear shoes that hurt her or didn't make her feel sexy and empowered. She has lots of Alexander McQueen and eclectic boutique-designer shoes in her collection. And is happy to commission handmade shoes from one of her favourite local artisans, for the right occasion.

Status SP

This princess only ever wears couture shoes by YSL, Roger Vivier, Terry de Havilland, Chanel, Pierre Hardy and the like. She is exceptionally well groomed and confident to mix and match designer pieces to form her own style. She exudes an aura of, 'Don't come near me unless you can handle me.' It takes a very special kind of man to handle this princess – usually a billionaire!

Scary SP

With a penchant for reptilian spikes and dominatrix boots, this princess is in no doubt as to who's the boss!

Sparkelina SP

Adores any shoes with a frosted, bronzed or gilded shimmer. She particularly likes summertime and has a whole wardrobe of coordinated sandals, slides, wedges and spikes with an array of shimmering and shining embellishments.

Pernickety SP

A true fusspot of a princess, she obsesses over the tiniest details in her shoe collection. She often only wears one style of shoe if she thinks it particularly suits her, or completely spurns styles that she abhors (usually cowboy boots and any form of trainers). This princess always stores her shoes in shoebags or original shoeboxes, hangs her clothes on padded coat-hangers, and meticulously lines her drawers with lavender-scented paper (high-altitude French lavender, of course).

Dare I ask if there are any more . . . ?

31. Straight to the Point

WHEN we get back to London I'm limp with physical and mental exhaustion. Though at least I'm not the only one that's had a rotten time in Milan today. The arrivals lounge is littered with evening newspapers, all plastered with the front-page headline, 'Catatonic', above a rather ungainly full-page photo of The Cat (so much for the rail disaster in the north-east), legs akimbo, passed out backstage at one of the big shows today (still with her sunglasses on, mind you).

So far, there's been no comment from Big Barry or the fashion house concerned. But Jolie Naturelle and Mange Tout are said to be 'reviewing their relationship' with her.

Poor Catriona . . . she looks about as good as I feel.

Considering that I rarely use my mobile phone, I'm shocked to see nineteen missed calls when I finally turn it on. And Marco was right, the message bank is full – thankfully with no messages from Dad or Tim. In fact, all are from Liz, Rachel and Fi, telling me the same thing: to log on to Shoe Princess ASAP.

As much as I'd love to sneak away to a corner and lose myself in the computer, I've got a date with destiny that can't wait for anyone, not even the divine Shoe Princess.

When Mum and I tiptoe in a shade after midnight, both Dad and Tim are still up. They're in the front room, glued to some obscure Australian sport on cable TV that appears to be a cross between Gaelic football and a barbarian massacre. After some polite banter about Millie (who's had a lovely day, by all accounts) Mum ushers Dad out of the room to bed.

As I sit down opposite Tim and summon the courage to talk, he suddenly turns off the TV.

'Jane,' he finally says after a pause that feels like an eternity, 'I've got something to tell you.'

I brace myself for the Alex bombshell. My limbs are jelly.

'I've been sacked.'

'What?'

'Well, not sacked *precisely*. "Let go",' he says with bitterness.

'But how? Why? It can't be.' This is the *last* thing I was expecting.

Tim tells me that not only him but also all his team members have been 'let go'. They've known since January that the bank's been haemorrhaging badly from its US sub-prime exposure, and that a number of teams would be sent offshore to Bangalore by the year's end – but not which ones. It's been a closely guarded secret. So everyone's been under *astronomical* stress-levels, while making sure they put in Herculean efforts to try and impress the powers that be – working insanely long hours, travelling ad infinitum, and not taking any leave.

'The team-building conference in the summer was merely a thinly veiled exercise in redundancy planning – IT was always going to be the first to go. I'm on three months' gardening leave. As of Monday.'

'Oh, Tim.' I instinctively move on to the sofa and embrace him. His normally taut frame feels deflated and defeated. 'Why didn't you tell me all this was going on?'

'You've had enough on your plate with Millie and I didn't want to worry you even more.' My eyes well with tears. 'I felt like it was my job – you know, as the provider – to handle it. Myself. I guess I sort of . . . went into lockdown . . . to try and fix it.'

He sighs a deep heavy sigh.

'I've never been out of work before.'

I've never seen him so low.

True to form, I revert to my stock-standard cure for all of life's woes.

'I'll go and put the kettle on.'

I amble down the hall in a daze, trying to digest the gravity of all this, only to find a glass vase of peonies and what appears to be an album on the kitchen bench next to the kettle.

I take a closer look – it's covered in exquisite pink-and-gold sari material, and decorated with fine glass beads. And opening it up, I see that it's full of photos of Millie. From birth to one.

It's truly magnificent. I turn round to see that Tim's followed me in. I can barely see him standing in the doorway through the torrents of tears now streaming down my face. I'm literally speechless as I turn the pages. This really is too much to take in – particularly as I'd already come to terms with having lost the pictures.

'But . . . how?' I whimper.

'Remember the work CD-Rom I had to turn back and get on our way to Oxfordshire? Only it wasn't – I took copies of all the photos on the camera to India with me.'

'But what about these ones?' Tim comes over to look at the photos of Millie and Allegra at their first birthday party.

'Victoria and Kate. They emailed them to me at work. I've been quite busy all those lonely nights in Bangalore, you know.'

I run my fingertips across some gold braiding and then grab hold of Tim's hand, squeezing it tenderly. I'm so *enormously* humbled.

'You can't tell me you did the appliqué and beading too?'

'Ah, yes, there is some limit to my genius.' He smiles. 'Alex kindly helped me with all of that side of things. She's been fantastic, actually.'

Oh. Alex.

My mood completely flattens, and I let go of his hand and fidget about looking for some mugs as I'm snapped back to the reality of our crowded marriage. We can't dance around her a moment longer. For my own sanity, at least.

Sensing my unease, Tim says quietly, 'Jane, Alex's partner is Olivia.'

'Oliver?'

'No, Olivia.'

It takes a few heart-stopping moments for the full impact of this to filter through my overloaded brain. I feel acutely embarrassed.

'Again, why oh why didn't you tell me? You . . . bloody . . . bastard.' I'm overwhelmingly relieved – yet furious too.

'Well, initially, I honestly didn't think it was terribly relevant. If you know what I mean?' I do; and he's right, in a not-batting-an-eyelid sort of way. 'But I guess I was just so offended, after the team-building weekend, that you'd think I'd have an affair – let alone with a work colleague – that I, well, sort of let you sweat it out a bit.'

'Sweat it out a bit!' My pulse races and my temper flares.

'Sweat. It. Out. A. Bit,' I spit again, as I start to pace around the kitchen flailing my arms about in ever-increasing eddies of exasperation. The events of the past year streaming through my head at breakneck speed. 'I THINK I'VE USED EVERY SAUNA IN THE UNITED BLOODY KINGDOM. AND THEN SOME!!!!'

'I'm sorry, Jane. Really. I had meant to tell you, but you just made me so mad. It was never meant to go this far.'

Speaking of mad, I ask him why he didn't comment on my mum shoes or support my plan to set up shoe-making at home.

'I have been a bit *off the planet*, haven't I?' he says contritely. 'I guess I couldn't take it on board. I was just so fixated with trying to hang on to my job – and our mortgage repayments. Plus, I don't remember an awful lot about that week in bed with the fever, I have to say.'

I thump him part playfully, part quite firmly on the chest with my flattened palms. Again and again and again. For all the worry and uncertainty and loneliness he's caused me – and us – this past year. He responds by wrapping both his arms around me and gathering me into his chest. I nuzzle under his chin and inhale his scrumptious smell – I've missed him SO much.

We stand like this, motionless, for some time. Instinctively, our breathing synchronises and we are again one.

And then Tim unfurls me.

'I have to ask . . . What *possessed* you to doubt me?'

I awkwardly explain all the gory details of Gavin and Tamsin's **five deadly Ts of mind sex**, as well as their exposé of the sin city of Bangalore. And of course my mini confidence crisis brought on by dealing with the stresses and strains of first-time motherhood – largely alone, with him in Bangalore so much. And not to mention my general state of obesity and ordinariness compared to Alex the super-sexy executive, and Catriona the supermodel-supermum.

'You know I love you. No matter what your dress size,' says Tim, studying my face closely. 'You do know that, don't you, Jane?' He pulls me close with his hands encircling my waist. 'Though you do look *hot* lately – if I do say so myself!'

I instantly melt on the spot and indeed wonder how I could *ever* have doubted him . . . But I could still KILL him.

'Let's go to bed,' he says, looking completely shattered yet also like a huge weight has been lifted from his shoulders.

'Yes, let's. But hold on a moment . . .' I go and fetch a block of Armani chocolate from my handbag and hand it to him, by way of a peace offering. 'Happy Anniversary – for yesterday! I'm sorry I forgot.' He manages a feeble smile.

Seeing my mobile in my handbag also reminds me of all my messages from the girls. But I decide that the Shoe Princess can wait till the morning. It's now time for the best part of making up: making love.

And boy, do we have some making up to do!

Dress to Impress

Shoe Princesses will hardly find it surprising that four out of five women in a UK survey judged a man by his shoes – ahead of his body and personality! With more than two-thirds citing shoe style, colour and cleanliness as important indicators of what he would be like both in and out of bed. So who are these shoe princes?

Shoe Princes

They may not get as many column inches as we shoe princesses, but they are definitely out there, and they're not all gay! Oh yes, the shoe prince is alive and well . . .

Street Smart SP – the younger SP; quite particular about the brand and style of his shoes – usually a trendy trainer. Confident, but very image-conscious. Can have a larger shoe collection than his partner.

Preppy SP – knitted polo sweater under a suit jacket, teamed with dress trousers and square-toed leather slip-ons. Takes good care of his shoes and appreciates quality. Conservative values when it comes to relationships.

Denim Delight SP – always teams denim jeans with T-shirts/shirts, dark jackets and sports trainers. Not particularly concerned with image or status. High sexual energy.

Bohemian SP – strong sense of individual style. Not afraid to wear pointy-toed snakeskin loafers, trilby hats or scarves. Keen to experiment in the bedroom!

Suit Man SP – single-breasted suit and oxfords are this SP's armour – emotionally fragile beneath it. Often highly ambitious with voracious physical needs.

Sandal Man SP – loyal devotee of upmarket leather sandals. Manages to wear them all summer, from beach to brunch to bar to dinner date. Pleasantly practical, yet with enough style to spurn flip-flops. Easy to please between the sheets.

Boot Man SP – appreciates the utility, comfort and ride of the boot. So do the women!

Vertically Challenged SP – king of the shoe wedge (UK) / shoe lift (North America). He has a cupboard full of 'status shoes and boots' made by a bespoke shoemaker to look exactly like a classically styled oxford or boot, but with a two-inch cork heel-insert – yes, SPs, a concealed high heel! He even wears inserts in his gym shoes. What can I say? Liberty, equality, fraternity!

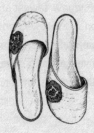

32. Princess Sapphire of Shoelandia

From: The Shoe Princess
To: Jane (home)
Subject: FW: Ogdens

My Darling Princess Sapphire of Shoelandia

Gorgeous hotmail address by the way – you could have at least told me you'd changed it recently!

It looks like the Funky Mammas weren't the only fans of your mum shoes – please see the exciting email below from Ogdens. I wanted to forward it on to you as soon as possible, as the parts of my blog they're most interested in are yours (as much as I would love to take the credit).

Please do let me know how you get on with them – as it sounds like the perfect place for a talented SP like yourself to kick up her heels and have some serious fun!

We really must meet up for champagne and cake, very soon.
SP xo

Dear Ms Shoe Princess

May I take the liberty of introducing myself. I am head of human resources at Ogdens, London's newest premier boutique department store, where we pride ourselves on consistently delivering the ultimate retail experience.

As a company, we actively encourage our staff members to find innovative ways of keeping abreast of our competitors, in order to deliver product ranges of the highest quality, diversity and style. It is in this capacity that your blog has been brought to my attention by our shoe buyers (all of whom assure me that they are loyal shoe princesses and princes).

During the course of the past year, they have noted that sales of certain lines of shoes have increased (fivefold in some instances) in response to your recommendations, for example, Bootylicious, Capsule Shoe Wardrobe, Gain Without Pain, Walk Tall and Toe Tips, to name but a few. Your 'Shoe Are You' SP descriptions have also proved to be an invaluable resource, not only to our shoe buyers, but also to our customer-profiling and marketing teams.

Ogdens is currently planning a major investment programme in our women's shoe department. This is in light of consumer-retail intelligence that reveals that footwear sales for British women 35–44 years-old have leapt by nearly 10% in the past 10 years (the so-called *Sex and the City* effect) with further rises anticipated (especially in boots). We expect that every woman in the country will buy an average of four pairs of shoes this year, reflecting a total cost of more than £625 million or 92 million pairs of shoes. With 2% of women paying £175 or more per pair. Naturally, we'd love as many of these high-end customers as possible to shop at Ogdens.

It would be my pleasure to meet you, at your earliest convenience, to see if there might be a way of working together in this exciting new chapter in women's shoes at Ogdens. (The mum shoes are of particular interest to us, given that one of our shoe buyers purchased a pair and cannot bear to prise them from her feet.)

Our human resources policy is to recruit only the very best personnel. And we have remuneration, incentive and family-friendly packages that match our high sales expectations.

With Very Best Wishes.

Alice Montgomery

Ogdens, London W1

This cannot be real.

Can it?

Who'd have thought that all those hours spent hunched over my home computer blogging on Shoe Princess, coupled with a lifetime of shoe worship, could lead to this: head of product development – shoes, at Ogdens!

I'm still pinching myself.

You see, I met Alice the very next day after replying to her email. We talked for hours – about the plans at Ogdens and the many shoe ideas I've always got swimming about in my head. Incredibly, she loved everything I said, including the prospect of signing up Marco to produce a new range of Ogdens boots, and getting him to help us find some factories in Milan to make my mum shoes on a bigger scale. (Manolo and Jimmy, watch out!) Florence should be happy too, as I seem to have them seriously thinking about a range of stylish shoe queen shoes for the over-seventies – apparently the marketing department loved the idea of tapping into the silver pound.

She offered me the job by the end of my interview. I start in two weeks' time.

It's all happened so quickly that it honestly feels surreal.

Millie's just about to start two days a week with the local childminder (she was lucky enough to get a spot along with

Hugh). And the deal I've struck with Ogdens is that I can work full-time (albeit still with flexible hours and home-working options) during the start-up phase, while Tim's at home. But come the new year – when he (hopefully) finds another job – I'll (hopefully) hire a full-time staff member to join me, and cut my days back to maybe three per week.

That's the plan anyway.

It all depends on what Tim does – he's so indecisive at the moment. One minute he's back in full-on corporate mode, and then the next he wants to put the flat on the market and go and live in Tuscany. Alex wasn't made redundant, as they needed her for her language skills and knowledge of India. But she resigned anyway, as she took the team's loss quite badly. Apparently, she's toying with the idea of setting up her own company, and may get Tim and Charlie and a couple of the others on board. Am *really* hoping that Tim can at least wangle one weekday at home with Millie – otherwise I can feel the wheels falling off our tidy little dual-work arrangement before we've even had a chance to hit the motorway. (Really don't want Millie with the childminder any more than two days a week.)

And then, of course, in amongst this, there's been the fall-out from my Marco–Ben debacle. Soon after getting back from Milan, I met Liz and Rachel for a girlie lunch (while Rachel was in town for a work meeting) and ended up telling them about the events and dramas of this past year, and of course Milan . . .

From: Rachel (work)
To: Jane (home)
Subject: Lunch

Darling
   Wonderful to see you and the blooming Liz – thanks so much for meeting me in Soho (as brief as it was). Pity Fi couldn't make it.

Though probably just as well, as have been musing over our little 'chat' and I think you're being WAY too harsh on yourself:

1. You didn't actually do anything (with Ben or Marco).
2. Ben's a young, hot-blooded hunk who's only interested in flings with desperate housewives. He should be cloned, not castigated!
3. There's nothing to be gained by telling Tim (you were only tempted in the first place because he was off with the pixies; plus, you said yourself that you barely even give Marco a second thought these days).
4. There's also nothing to be gained by telling Fi (again, no harm done; plus, we don't want to spook her – thankful as we are that she's back together with her Mr Right).

And anyway, Ben's magic certainly worked on our little Liz, didn't it! You see, he DID sleep with someone that night at shoe school – only not me. (I'm almost insulted.) Just goes to show, you can never judge a girl by her cream kitten heels. Maybe the odd illicit fling isn't that bad, after all? It certainly gave Liz back her spark – and she and Harry went on to make babies soon after it too. (It's so sweet that you and I are the only people on the planet that know about it . . . and sworn to secrecy!)

Big news is that I'll be back in London in the new year – minus lover. (He's been head-hunted – moving with the family to Switzerland.) Let's do lunch on one of your work days at Ogdens – Carluccio's and quick whizz down New Bond Street sound OK?

Congrats again, you clever shoe princess, you!

R xx

From: Jane (home)
To: Liz (work)
Subject: Honoured

Dearest Liz

Was lovely seeing Rachel, wasn't it? She hasn't changed a bit. (Though don't know why I expected her to have.) Am so very honoured to be asked to be your birth partner. And do think you're right – best kept as 'secret women's business'. Harry would most definitely faint! Can highly recommend the *Gladiator* soundtrack for giving birth – much more warrior-woman strength required than dreamy old Enya (but you'll have to take my word on this one). Thrilled that you loved your bespoke mum shoes, too.

Chat soon, and take care

Jane

xx

From: Jane (home)
To: Fi (work)
Subject: Happy One Year (or thereabouts) Anniversary

Dearest Fi

Hoorah – you made it! Warmest congratulations to you and Marco – a truly deserving couple. Can't wait to hear where he's whisked you off to for your surprise candlelit dinner this evening – he's such a romantic. I wonder if I need to start looking for a hat sometime soon . . .

Just wanted to thank you again for giving me those Salvatore Ferragamo shoes (Kate would never have appreciated them, anyway) for my big interview with Ogdens. They certainly were my lucky charm.

Glad to see you've made friends again with heels and hair dye, too. Though I must admit that the yoga was the best thing to have come out of Tim's time in Bangalore . . . he's even got me doing it now.

Jane

xx

So pleased that you liked the day-dates idea – and that you weren't offended by my suggesting it. A girlfriend of mine put me on to the concept when I went back to work, so thought the least I could do was pass on 'the knowledge'. It really is ingenious though, isn't it – baby-free daytime dates with your husband during the week, when you're both awake AND in a good mood. A sure marriage-saver! (I think the babysitting fees should be 100% tax-deductible.)

Am feeling especially tired these days, of course. Had seriously forgotten how exhausting early pregnancy was. Plus, can't just lie down now and rest when I want to, what with Hugh to run around after etc. Have just negotiated with work to cut back to 3 days per week, after the baby's born. As James got a pay rise, think it's feasible. Plus, I haven't been able to get my chargeable hours up this year on 4 days per week, so thought I may as well downshift – as suspect life's going to be a little busier from now on. (Am emotionally coming to terms with not making partner . . . for time being. Let's just hope I don't end up in the photocopy room by the end of next year.)

At least glad I won't have to juggle double buggy down moss-covered steps to Mary's clinic with bub number two. Popped my head in the clinic door yesterday on my way home from work, and caught Mary setting everything up now that the building works are finished – she was on cloud nine. You do realise that we're going to have to have a gala champagne-opening now!

Best get back to work . . . Huge congrats again on the job.

Sophie x

www.ShoePrincess.com

The awards for the most impressive **SP Shoe Cupboards:**

1. OK let's get the obvious out of the way: any woman who works in an executive position in a fashion house, magazine/media company, or just happens to own a shoe empire. Her bespoke Aladdin's cave of shoes is the envy of all SPs.
2. SP of Amsterdam who keeps her suede shoes in her double oven. Well, shoes are more important than food.
3 SP of Notting Hill who converted her loft into a walk-in shoe cupboard. Complete with a claw foot-bath and chandelier in the middle of the room, and original Andy Warhol shoe art on the walls. My personal idea of heaven!

If the Shoe Fits

SP and nursery teacher of Cardiff agrees with recent studies that suggest our personalities are largely formed by 3 years of age. Naturally, she needed to look no further than the shoes of her pupils for confirmation . . .

Junior Shoe Princesses

Fairy Princess Sparkle – only wears pink, shimmery shoes; often shy; loves to dress up; highly imaginative play.

Funky Girl – trendy boots / trainers in bright colours; high energy levels; adventurous; inquisitive; talkative; can be fiery.

Earth Mother – black / brown boots or trainers; capable; physical; strong sense of duty; little fear.

Hippie Chick – flip-flops and sandals no matter the season; intuitive; caring; prone to going off and doing own thing.

Prefect – Mary Janes with socks/tights and matching sunhat; organiser; facilitator; good at tidying up / breaking up fights.

Junior Shoe Princes

Superhero – socks or no shoes, as more interested in superhero costumes; strong sense of self and world around him.

Clubber – trendy trainers with orange neon laces; quietly confident; artistic; observant.

Euro Prince – classic upmarket imported leather shoes; sophisticated; knowing; calm; articulate.

Sneaker Freak – white trainers; likes to conform and be part of the gang; loves ball games, comics, Lego and wrestling.

Sandal Boy – extremely practical; loves nature and all things outdoors; kind, caring and sensitive.

33. A Clean Pair of Heels

From: Jane (Ogdens)
To: Aunt Margaret (home)
Subject: Merry Christmas

Dear Aunt Margaret

I'm very conscious that tomorrow is the 1st of December, and your family Christmas card will be in the post, without our reply to your email. I do apologise. It has certainly been a hectic year, with much change in the Meadows household.

The most important event for us has obviously been the welcome arrival of our dear little Millie – who is actually 15 months old now. She is an adventurous, curious and happy little girl, and is without doubt the absolute light of our lives. She's just started walking and has almost got the hang of sleeping through the night – thank goodness. (But is prone to the odd 3 a.m. play session in her cot!) Am afraid that she is her mother's daughter, as her first word was 'shoe'.

I've recently taken up a full-time position with a large department store in the West End, and am enjoying it hugely. While

Millie has been particularly lucky to have Tim at home caring for her, as well as doing 2 days a week with a local childminder. Tim is currently assessing his options for work – having been one of many redundancies at the bank this year. It has been quite eye-opening for both of us – experiencing life in the other's shoes!

I'm sure there are more challenges ahead for us in the new year, but we are looking forward to them, surrounded as we are by, and very thankful for, our loving families and friends.

With all our love and warmest wishes to you and your family for a happy and healthy festive season and year ahead

Jane, Tim and Millie

xxx

It certainly has been interesting being in Tim's shoes . . .

And while I'm enjoying working at Ogdens more than words can describe – it really is my dream job of a lifetime – it's quite pressured too. As I've been putting in some seriously long hours to get all my plans (which I sold so well in the interview) up and running. Marco is officially signed up with us, by the way, as our hot new shoe/boot designer; and I'm going to Milan with him soon to look at factories for my mum shoes. There's also talk of work sponsoring me on an Ars Arpel short course – but am putting this on the back burner for now, as I can't get my head round leaving Millie for any longer than a day, just yet. Though I'm sure I'll have to do it at some point. At least I'm being given loads of resources to put my super shoe strategy into action – which is lucky, as the sales targets I received today from the MD are *fearsome*.

On the home front, I've found it incredibly difficult missing Millie's bath and bedtime story of an evening. I cried myself to sleep the first night it happened. But alas, she still cuddled me and jumped all over me in the morning – just as she used to do with Tim. Millie's adapted amazingly well, actually, to the role reversal. But I do find it especially hard at weekends, when she turns to Tim first if she falls over and cries. (Babies, I'm sensing, are incredibly loyal to those that are most loyal to them – in the absolutely purest way.)

But according to Tim, I do have 'control issues' on the home front too. I'm making a concerted effort of late to walk out of the door in the mornings and not leave him with a list of things to do and an instruction manual on how to do them. And of course, Millie's *loving* Tim's more relaxed, adventurous style of parenting – they go swimming and walking together all the time (though the housework mysteriously never seems to get done!).

Tim's doing well with his CV and has been teeing up meetings with companies and contacts on the days that Millie's with her childminder. But so far no firm job options have come up. Hence the pressure of being the sole earner is ever present – and not to be underestimated, either. I'm embarrassed to say that I've suddenly become obsessed with checking VISA purchases online. Plus, I've given Tim a little talking to about spending too much money on coffees and cakes at the local patisserie and the park café – explaining how Millie and I only had the occasional treat, and would mostly take snacks from home.

I do miss our jaunts around the park and of course my pots of tea with Florence and our daily rendezvous with G & T – but I guess I had to rejoin the real world at some point! And as I think back now to how hard some of those early times in the first year were at home with Millie, Mary was right, I don't regret them for a minute. (She was always telling me this.) It's weird and kind of sweet, sitting here at my computer, knowing that she's out there now – pounding the pavements, visiting another shell-shocked new mum and holding her hand through the perplexing minefield of first-time motherhood.

One aspect of work I have found a little unsettling is the slight feeling that some of my younger (child-free) colleagues think I'm a tad scatty. As no matter how hard I try, I seem to be the last in the office each morning – which is irritating. And this week, Millie's been getting her molars and eye teeth at the same time, so we've had a dreadful run of broken nights. (I still get up to her, even though I know I should leave it to Tim.) I actually walked into the office this morning in a pair of my rather well-worn mum shoes – having forgotten to change into my glam work shoes before I walked out the door. Only to realise that I'd also left the draft contract for another new designer I'm signing up on the desk at home. (I've *never* done this before.) I'll now either have to go home and get it before our meeting with the lawyers this afternoon, or simply reschedule.

Yes, I know what you're thinking. . . . Alison. There's clearly one thing I *must* do before the day's end – it's now or never.

But first, to do some work . . .

From:	Jane (Ogdens)
To:	Kate (work)
Subject:	Idea

Kate

Have got an idea to run by you . . . carbon neutral/eco/recycled/ ethical shoes – but stylish, of course! Am thinking that there's a large untapped market, and wanted to put a proposal together for work. Would love to hear your thoughts.

Fancy lunch sometime this week?

Jane x

PS, Am still getting my head around Mum and Dad selling up in Oxfordshire and buying a loft conversion in Clerkenwell. Looks like Mum's delayed mid-life crisis was contagious. J x

From: Jane (Ogdens)
To: Victoria (home)
Subject: RE: Charity Fundraiser

Hi Victoria

Was lovely to bump into you in your front garden on Sunday –
far too long since I've done a spin around Queen's Park. Was my
pleasure to take Millie and Allegra over for a play on the swings – I
think they miss seeing each other these days.

Would be only too happy to help out with your New Year's Eve
charity fundraising idea – I've got the perfect blog to announce it
on. And will see what I can talk Ogdens into doing. Feel free to
drop me a line here at work, any time.

All Best, Jane

TrashQueenz e-lert
Cat's Out of the Bag. Following her collapse at Milan
Fashion Week, and a stint in rehab in Arizona, we can
confirm that it was NOT The Cat, but her **body double**.
Yes, you read it here first. Catriona is at this minute holding a
press conference, orchestrated by *Brunch with Britain*. Find a
TV fast . . .

I immediately bolt down the three floors to the television-and-
stereo department in the basement of Ogdens to watch the
Brunch with Britain telecast (along with a few hundred other
shoppers).

Oh, my. She's beautiful. I'm looking at The Cat (the real
one, Catriona). Freckled – she's not wearing a scrap of make-
up. Full in the face – in a normal sort of way. And still
absolutely, stunningly *beautiful*. She's wearing a demure Peter
Pan-collar tunic dress, Chanel ballet flats and no sunglasses.
Standing next to her is an *almost* identical woman of practically

skeletal proportions. Also with her sunglasses off, but not nearly as glowing.

Oh dear, and Catriona's arm is in a sling. She takes to the podium upon Tamsin's introduction, flanked by her lawyer and Big Barry, and pulls out a prepared statement that she is going to read. You can hear a pin drop. She nervously clears her throat, and then begins.

'It is no secret that I have struggled this past year with the incredible pressure to regain my figure, following the birth of my beloved son, Happy Sunshine. This pressure has been magnified enormously by the vigorous and relentless reporting of my yo-yoing weight battles by the paparazzi.

'It is also no secret that I am a single mother, and my body is my livelihood.'

She takes a deep breath.

'During my Fat Cat relapse in the summer I, under the guidance of my management, hired a body double – Jade.'

The crowd collectively gasps. My eyes can't stop flitting from one woman to the other – I'm flabbergasted at their resemblance. That is, apart from the massive black bags under Jade's eyes. Which are also brown and far too close together, compared to Catriona's hypnotic green feline eyes – aha – the constant need for the sunglasses!

'This was seen as essential to the ongoing bankability of The Cat brand, for all photographic work (mainly the Mange Chat and Jolie Naturelle billboards) and public appearances (like the beach shots in Sardinia, and West End shopping trips) until I returned to my former shape and the catwalk later in the year.

'This practice of hiring body doubles, or "twinning", is becoming increasingly common amongst celebrities – in an effort to try and maintain some modicum of privacy whilst also maintaining that all-important publicity profile.'

Ooh, I wonder who else 'twins'?

'I had planned to do the Milan show myself, but was unable to – due to being a size 10 and the unfortunate break of my arm.' She takes another deep breath. 'I have brittle-bone disease – from spending more than half my life starving myself, coupled with chronic alcoholism. I am prone to breaks at *any* time and had my first break three years ago.'

Blimey.

'Because I was unable to pull out of the shows in Milan, due to contractual commitments, it was decided by my management that Jade would do them. Unfortunately, Jade fell rather heavily for the trappings of the modelling industry and developed an out-of-control methamphetamine and alcohol addiction – leading to her erratic night-time behaviour and eventual collapse in Milan. I have paid for her rehabilitation in Arizona and will continue to support her in whatever way I can in the challenging weeks and months ahead. I cannot tell you how devastated I feel to have put her in this position.'

She pauses briefly for a glass of water, handed to her by Big Barry, before continuing.

'I would also like to take this opportunity to disclose that I did not have a ten-minute water birth with Happy Sunshine, but a planned C-section. I would also like to come clean on my so-called "naturally" perfect body, in the hope that other women and mothers will gain strength from the knowledge that all that glitters is most definitely NOT gold.'

She goes on to describe everything in the lists that I made in the summer and more. Including the fact that she's been having collagen injections since the age of sixteen (under the guidance of, you guessed it, her 'management') and most recently underwent radical (and as yet unapproved) trial medical procedures involving human–growth hormones. And she's had far too much cosmetic surgery for me even to recount.

'I would like to announce that I am retiring from modelling. I'm currently in the process of converting to Buddhism and moving to the South Island of New Zealand, where I intend to live at peace with my children and with nature. I have enrolled to do a degree in Comparative Theology, and hope to adopt more children from Third World countries.

'Thank you, the people of Britain, and especially Tamsin and Gavin, for your continued support.'

The madding crowd of journalists and photographers are yelling questions at her, but she calmly ignores them.

'Oh, and finally, I will be donating the entire seven-figure fee (*including* my agent's commission)' – Barry smiles through gritted teeth for the cameras – 'for my *Lads' Magazine* photo-shoot with Jade to a futures fund for renewable energy sources – on behalf of Happy Sunshine and Strawberry Blossom and all the children of the world.

'Thank you, and good day.'

She pirouettes and disappears back stage.

We are all COMPLETELY gobsmacked.

From:	Alison (work)
To:	Jane (Ogdens)
Subject:	Flowers and Shoe Voucher

Thank you for the magnificent bunch of flowers and shoe voucher – which arrived on my desk after lunch! Your kind words were very thoughtful – but completely unnecessary. I was exactly the same BC (Before Children). Maybe certain female brain-synapses not capable of firing until post-baby?! Who knows – slightly embarrassing, though, isn't it?

Very best with your new job – you'll be great.

Alison

(hugs to Millie xoxo)

From: Jane (Ogdens)
To: Fi (work)
Subject: Partners in Crime . . . again?!

. . . Just got the OK from MD on my budget proposal for a new work colleague – starting next year. Can I tempt you to the gates of shoetopia?

  J xx

TrashQueenz e-lert

Rumble in the Jungle. Love–hate *Brunch with Britain* hosts sign up for the new series of *I'm a Celebrity Get Me Out of Here*. We wonder how many pairs of Manolos Tamsin's smuggling in with her?

All welcome to our very first Trash Queenz get-together: An end-of-year party at the Queen's Park Café, London, NW6 – our unofficial headquarters. Children and dogs welcome. Word on the ground is that you may even spot a shoe princess or two.

Well, I never . . .

The Shoe Princess's Guide to the Galaxy

Continuing with our end-of-year theme, where each of our (many) subgroups of SPs are sharing their collective wisdom with the world (ha!), I'd like to hand you over to the eternally sleep-deprived **Funky Mammas** for their version.

Here goes . . .

- Sleep when the baby sleeps; slow down; and don't apologise for it.
- Accept help, if it's offered; seek it, if it's not.
- Talk, talk, talk to your partner; and listen. Don't drift.
- Routine works. It just does.
- The days (and nights) are very long. But the years are short. Treasure them.
- Learn to trust your instincts — they're normally right.
- Keep physically active and strong. You owe it to yourself.
- One weekday each week, dress as if you're going to work (for housemums) or a smart conference (working mums) — you'll be amazed at how much better you feel and how differently people treat you.
- Never wear tracksuits or pyjamas outside the front door. Ever.
- Laugh lots; and always expect the unexpected.
- You never really know what goes on behind the closed doors of other people's relationships — never be too quick to judge.
- Don't be afraid to sidestep or change careers after having babies — if you ultimately do what you love, and love what you do, there's no end to where the yellow brick road will lead you.
- Top 'n' tail: if budgets (and time) are tight, invest in the best cleanser, tinted moisturiser, mascara, lip gloss, haircut/colour and shoes you can afford for a smart, polished look.
- Nothing ages you more than old-style jeans — update them, if you can, every two years.

- Surround yourself with good people. Always.
- Only wear shoes that make you smile.
- Wearing high heels, like any elite sport, needs training. If you're out of form, don't expect any glory. Downgrade to a style that you feel confident and comfortable in. (Long live the wedge-heel!)
- Throw out all ill-fitting and cheap shoes. They were a mistake then; and they're a mistake now.
- Always seek ways to give; and think of your human-footprint.
- There IS a goddess in ALL of us.

And finally . . .

International Dorothy Day

The Shoe Princess formally decrees that
All loyal subjects in her shoedom shall wear sparkly red shoes
this New Year's Eve.

In exchange for donating money to any charity working hard for mums,
dads, babies, children, grandparents, carers and their families.
(For ideas see links on SP home page –
there are loads out there doing a fabulous job.)

Until next year,
Au revoir, my gorgeous subjects!
SP xx

Acknowledgements

O CEANS of thanks to everyone at Bloomsbury, from the top to the bottom and back again. Especially to Alexandra Pringle for letting my foot in the door. As a first-time novelist, I'm truly staggered by the efforts of so many people in getting a book to print. I shall *never* look at a book in the same way again.

My deep gratitude to the eagle-eyed editors Helen Garnons-Williams, Erica Jarnes and Jenny Parrott for your expertise, enthusiasm and support. Also, to the many readers who have given feedback – all have helped shape what it is today. To my first- and last-drafters, Annabel Morgan (London) and Katrina O'Leary (Melbourne), I'm so very grateful for your generous help and genuine interest. Likewise to the gorgeous Venetia Sarll for your lovely shoe illustrations.

Enormous thanks to Clare Conville for seeing a sassy stiletto in a rather scruffy moccasin, and linking me up with the darling divine Marian McCarthy – editor extraordinaire. To Marian, my humble thanks for your unflinching support of me and this novel from day one to the very end. For your coaching in the craft of writing, attention to detail, and exacting standards I will forever be indebted. For your level-headedness in the face of adversity and especially your hand of friendship in a new town I am truly grateful.

My sincere appreciation to my parents (a constant source of inspiration), family (that's the whole lot of you – in-laws, outlaws etc) and friends, for your unwavering encouragement during what has been a long and seemingly never-ending project.

And last but not least, my heartfelt thanks to my oh-so-patient husband, Kevin. I would not have been able to do this without you by my side – every step of the way! And to our beloved children, Darcey and Max, I strongly suspect that I would not have been able to write this with such passion without you. Thank you for making me a mum and giving me the best job in the world, in so many ways.

A NOTE ON THE TYPE

The text of this book is set in Bembo. This type was first used in 1495 by the Venetian printer Aldus Manutius for Cardinal Bembo's *De Aetna*, and was cut for Manutius by Francesco Griffo. It was one of the types used by Claude Garamond (1480–1561) as a model for his Romain de L'Université, and so it was the forerunner of what became standard European type for the following two centuries. Its modern form follows the original types and was designed for Monotype in 1929.